ZANZIBARI MUSLIM MODERNS

ANNE K. BANG

Zanzibari Muslim Moderns

Islamic Paths to Progress in the Interwar Period

HURST & COMPANY, LONDON

First published in the United Kingdom in 2024 by
C. Hurst & Co. (Publishers) Ltd.,
New Wing, Somerset House, Strand, London, WC2R 1LA

A Cataloguing-in-Publication data record for this book is available from the British Library.

ISBN: 9781911723820

This book is printed using paper from registered sustainable and managed sources.

www.hurstpublishers.com

Printed and bound in Great Britain by Bell & Bain Ltd, Glasgow

CONTENTS

Acknowledgements vii
Note on Transliteration ix
List of Figures and Tables xi

1. In Search of the Zanzibari Muslim Modern: On Modernity, Progress and Development 1
2. Prologue: The Magic and the Modern—Zanzibar, 1904 23
3. The Exemplary Muslim Modern: Burhan Mkelle (1884–1949) in Zanzibar 39
4. The Zanzibar Government Central School and "Modern Teaching Methods" 57
5. Modern Jobs: The Zanzibari Civil Service 85
6. Modern Associations: Ethnic and Faith-Based Associations in Zanzibar 99
7. Modern Islamic Practices: Zanzibar in the Age of Culture Wars 127
8. *Wataniyya?* Towards a Modern Zanzibari Culture 159
9. Conclusions: The Beginnings of a Modern Muslim Zanzibari Culture 177

Notes 185
Sources 215
Bibliography 221
Index 235

ACKNOWLEDGEMENTS

The primary research for this book was conducted in the period 2016–20, followed by almost two years of staying put during the Covid-19 pandemic, pondering whether or not this was an excellent time to write up—or to curse the interruption this virus caused to further research. The outcome was something in between: grumpily writing up some chapters in my home office, while preparing a new project which came into being in 2021 and which led to a renewed impulse to visit the world of the Zanzibari Muslim moderns.

The initial archival research in 2016–17 was funded by the Meltzer foundation at the University of Bergen. From 2018 until the final field trip in February 2020, funding came from the Endangered Archives Programme of the British Library. This project digitized the manuscript and book collection of the late Maalim Muhammad Idris Muhammed Saleh (d. 2012), much of which appear as sources in this book. My gratitude is to Mustafa Sameja, Hassan Abdillah Masoud, Mahaji Muhiddin and Uthman Barwani who worked on the EAP project throughout these years. Their knowledge is a significant part of what I try to present here.

I am grateful for the generosity of Professor Saleh Idris and his wife Moza. Bits and pieces of Maalim's collection that for various reasons could not be digitized were graciously made available to me in their home. My interlocutors in Zanzibar over thirty years are too numerous to name, but each and every one has helped further my understanding of this complex and forever intriguing society. Particular thanks, as always, to Professor Abdul Sheriff for generously sharing his vast knowledge about the Zanzibari past.

ACKNOWLEDGEMENTS

The final pieces of this particular puzzle came together at the beginning of the MPrinT project in 2021–22, funded by the Norwegian Research Council and which is still ongoing. I wish to thank specifically the members of the MPrinT teams in Lamu and Zanzibar for drastically steepening the learning curve; what is presented in this book is a glimpse of a modernity that will eventually be much better documented.

Most of the primary sources in this book are held by the Zanzibar Institute for Archives and Records. I am grateful to both the previous and current directors, Mwalimu Salum Suleiman and Khatib Suleiman Khatib, for their kind assistance in approving my repeated applications for research permits. The staff at ZIAR deserve my everlasting gratitude for their help.

I am indebted to numerous colleagues in the field of Zanzibari, East African, Indian Ocean and Islamic history who over the years have commented on the themes and chapters in this book. In Bergen, the Middle Eastern and Islamic Studies research group at the Department of Archaeology, History, Cultural Studies and Religion provided a reading forum for Arabic translation and for very, very rough drafts. Thank you Eirik Hovden, Knut Vikør, Ariela Marcus-Sells, Kubra Nugay, Mohamed Aidaroos Noor, Raphael Michaeli, Pelle Valentin Olsen and Christian Mauder. Before his death in 2019, I discussed many aspects of this book with my supervisor and friend R. Seán O'Fahey. His always creative comments are sorely missed.

It has been my privilege to discuss the topics and themes of this book with many excellent colleagues, including (in no particular order): Kjersti Larsen, Scott Reese, Iain Walker, Piet Coppens, Annachiara Raia, Franziska Fay, Hassan Mwakimako, Clarissa Vierke, Wilson Jacob, Hassen Muhammed Kawo, Catharina Raudevere, Mohamed Mwenje, Pamila Gupta, Ruqaya Abusharaf, Michele Petrone, Hassan Ndzovou, Nile Green, Jeremy Prestholdt and Hideaki Suzuki.

Last, but not least, I am grateful to the anonymous reviewers of this book, who provided valuable comments that much improved its focus.

And finally, yet again, I thank my family, Per and Nora, for enduring the hardships of Zanzibar and its snow-white beaches.

NOTE ON TRANSLITERATION

In this book I have chosen not to transliterate Arabic names. Instead, names are given in the form they are most commonly known in Swahili, in Latin letters.

I have transliterated Arabic concepts that are not commonly known. In other words, "Sharia" has not been transliterated but "*kafāʾa*" has.

Arabic words and phrases that appear in direct translation from Arabic have been transliterated fully.

For rendering Arabic in Latin script I have used the *International Journal of Middle East Studies* (IJMES) transliteration system.

LIST OF FIGURES AND TABLES

Fig. 1: The Mkelle family in Zanzibar 45

Table 1: Arabic language-related texts in the library of Burhan Mkelle 70

Table 2: Printed editions of Burhan Mkelle, *al-Alfiyya al-wāḍiḥa* 74

Table 3: Sample salaries, Educational and Judicial Departments, 1913 87

Table 4: Sample salaries, Educational and Judicial Departments, 1914 88

Burhan Mkelle, *Modern Inventions*, c. 1940[1]

An age replete with knowledge and gratitude—Brings us wonders for mankind
It brings to us an airplane for travellers—That looks like a jewel in the sky of God
Taking off with its passengers from one city—And flying away to another faraway destination
In this age, the plane has become a boon—For transferring mail, due to its extraordinary speed

Then the telegraph, a wireless device—Whose intricacies amazed the brightest minds
It allowed us, through a magnetic machine—To relish in Parisian and American melodies
Which we could only hear—If someone recited them before us in person
Thereafter came the telephone which allowed—Two people in different houses to communicate in voice
Innovation continued until two people—Feel like they see each other while they talk remotely

Then the phonograph, producing a clear sound—Of various melodies and rhymes
On the one hand, it could play voice—Such as the verses of the Quran
On the other, it could play music—Produced by musicians, accompanied by songs

Electricity brought numerous benefits—There is no place which hasn't seen its wonders
Among them is the bulb whose light—Is a fire unlike any other

And the fans that cool our bodies—From the heat when they whirl

We use electricity to cook our food, and iron—Our clothes with immaculate creases
This is after we have washed them—In the washing machine, that cleanses all dirt and grime
And our printing presses that allow us—To read words with utmost clarity

The steam engine eases travel on land and sea—With great speed the steam ship outpaces the sail.
Where is the camel compared to the train that speeds through the valleys?
And what is a sail to a boiling steam engine when the ocean roars?

In the cinema, images appear that move—Their limbs moving.
Today, they even speak clearly—After being silent for some time
We go to watch its screens (*lāhīn*)—And spend in its halls both time and money
Perhaps even the hungry will spend money to enter its halls with his peers.
If he had some sense, he would buy something to eat with his money
Rather than entering [into the cinema], yawning from hunger, to the images of Shaytan
Even with money obtained by theft or other devious means
Absorbed in the loss of others or himself and will suffer only loss

Behold the car, rolling towards us, through the deserts and the dunes—Speedily covering the longest distance in the shortest time
And the tanks, designed to attack the enemy in the open field—Pouring war-death over them to defeat them

Or the invisible war submarine, hiding at the bottom of the sea like an animal,
attacking an unsuspecting ship and breaking it without warning,
drowning people as if they were overcome by a flood or a typhoon.

We now have the bike, which residents use to get around
Powered by the legs of neighbours, for as long as the legs have power.

X-rays reveal what is hidden inside the bodies and corpses, detecting hidden disease that strikes the misfortunate

The Tirta [typewriter] works with the speed of the human fingertips, its ticking echoing as writing appears

These inventions have astonished man,
who are but mouthpieces to (*lisān*) the power of the Almighty (*al-manān*),
He is the one who created those who invented, like Edison.

Lord protects us always by keeping us from evil, and harmful invention
so that all that is made by my hand is favoured by God and by al-Burhān.

1

IN SEARCH OF THE ZANZIBARI MUSLIM MODERN

ON MODERNITY, PROGRESS AND DEVELOPMENT

This book is a study of how modern Islamic ideals were formulated in the small British-BuSaidi protectorate of Muslim Zanzibar in the period c. 1920–40. It is, in other words, a study of how those who spoke on behalf of religion represented and proposed new ideals that pointed to a future envisioned to somehow be better than the past.

Historically, the narratives of progress have not only been expressed in different languages but have also been rooted in different understandings of what progress is. Moreover, as the cost of particularly colonially imposed progress became evident—the loss of language, practices, modes of interaction and the inevitable sense that things fall apart—many post-colonial writers and poets have pointed out that faith in "progress" approximates to that of religious belief. The nineteenth-century god of progress, as has been shown perhaps most poignantly by Sven Lindqvist, was a jealous god, demanding no less than the physical or cultural extermination of the colonized peoples.[1] While the genocidal element of colonialism had become less prominent by the interwar years, this was the era that laid the foundations for what Achille Mbembe has called an epistemology of difference, a specific "cognitive ordering of extra-European worlds".[2] Referring particularly to colonial developmentalism, the West Indian

Nobel Prize Laureate Derek Walcott (1930–2017) in "The Schooner 'Flight'", lets his protagonist take his scorn further, and reveal the idea of progress itself as obscene, even perverse: "Until I see definite signs/ that mankind change, Vince, I ain't want to hear./ Progress is history's dirty joke."[3]

Modernity, progress, development; all have been accused of being primarily rooted in faith, or more precisely, of wearing a flimsy mask of scientific knowledge to cover the countenance of the real god of profit. Another mask was unveiled by Talal Asad when he stated that the "choice" presented to the colonized peoples on whether to opt for Western "progress" or remain with tradition really was no choice at all, but rather a precondition of collective discipline imposed by colonial power.[4]

Modernity, progress, development; all have also had a long and fraught history of co-existence with actual religion, from pre-industrial Europe, through the enlightenment period and in later numerous encounters beyond Europe, in the lands and territories under European colonial control. The relationship between religion and "progress" has often been violent, with "progress" demanding that existing world views should simply be annihilated—often with a view to creating reliable labour-power to work for progress. Less genocidal paths towards progress were proposed by colonial development programmes in the interwar years, where "old" and "new" were somehow envisioned to reach a utopia of the least common denominator. Lastly, religion itself has adapted to the "progress" narrative, often by shedding the beliefs and practices that most blatantly hinder "progress", as defined by those who speak on behalf of religion.

It is easier at this stage to declare what this book is not. It is not my primary objective to study the adaptations and accommodations made by Muslim scholars on the one hand, and the British colonial administrators in Zanzibar on the other. Nor do I offer a straightforward study of Islamic modernism as it emerged in Zanzibar in the interwar years, condemning one *bidʿa* (innovation) after another to carve out a comprehensive Muslim vision of progress. Rather, this is a history of the emergence of a new ideal, the Muslim modern, from a specific Islamic reformist orientation, in the specific Zanzibari context.

Zanzibari Modernities

What is—or was—modernity? If modernity means connection to global markets, participation in international capital flows, consumerism and the application of certain technologies and information channels to sustain these patterns, Zanzibar was already "modern" by the interwar years.

In economic terms, Zanzibar had been integrated into the global economy since at least the time of Sayyid Said bin Sultan (d. 1856).[5] The trading empire he set up channelled cloves, gum copal, coffee, ivory and dates to consumers in Europe and the USA. For as long as the BuSaidi Sultanate relied on slave labour, Zanzibari domestic products were exported, while cloth and consumer goods flowed back in the exchange known as the *marekani* economy. Cash cropping for export and a cash-based economy was an established mode of production by 1910.

The abolition of slavery in the Zanzibar archipelago—first by the abolition decree of 1897 and subsequently by the 1909 abolition of the legal status of slavery—meant another brick in the building often perceived as "modern": a society where labour is bought and sold, and humans are not. The transition from a slave-based economy, but above all the integration of the ex-slave population into—and alongside—the other communities in Zanzibar and on the East African coast, has been the object of several excellent studies, notably by F. Cooper,[6] P. W. Romero,[7] J. Glassman,[8] L. Fair,[9] J. Prestholdt[10] and E. McMahon.[11] These have all shown the many ways in which social categories were negotiated and disputed following abolition. However, this process was still ongoing during the interwar years, as the bonds broken and re-created during and after slavery were still being litigated in Zanzibar courts during the 1930s and 1940s, as E. Stockreiter has shown.[12]

Consumerism, and its associated habit of expressing ideals and aspirations by buying things from distant places, was also long established in Zanzibar. Jeremy Prestholdt has written insightfully about Zanzibari homes that were already increasingly outfitted with objects signifying cosmopolitanism—and thus an appropriation also of a distinct set of Western-produced consumer modernity—from the mid-

1800s.[13] Mirrors, wall clocks, glasses, vases, chandeliers, tables and chairs, photographs (often of distant royalty or landscapes) were among the objects observed—and commented upon—by Western visitors. State-of-the-art firearms used by the Sultanic army were a further utilitarian and symbolic sign of modernity, as were uniforms and brass bands. The umbrella, seemingly an everyday object that was originally meant to symbolize elite status, but which grew to be used by all, made its appearance in the 1870s and 1880s—utterly confusing British observers who primarily imagined the umbrella in the dainty white hands of the Victorian elite.[14]

In terms of technology, people in Zanzibar were already familiar with many of the "modern inventions" noted in the poem reproduced at the outset of this chapter. Steamships from the British East Africa Line, the Messageries Maritimes, the Norway East Africa Line and others called several times a week at Zanzibar port, *en route* northwards to Aden and onwards to Suez or India, or southwards to Madagascar and Cape Town. Electricity was famously installed in the Bayt al-Ajaib during the reign of Sayyid Barghash (1870–88), based on coal-driven generators. From the 1890s, gaslights appeared in the streets of Zanzibar Town, as house owners were mandated by the government to light up their house fronts.[15]

An Indian postal system had been in operation since 1878 and a Zanzibar Protectorate postal service from 1895. The American-built Bububu train ran the distance between Stone Town and the northern coastal residential area of Bububu from 1905. Cars started appearing before World War I and ambitious road-construction projects were started after the war to improve communications inside the protectorate. The editor of the *Zanzibar Gazette* throughout much of the 1920s, Harold Ingrams, noted that:

> In 1924, there were roads from Zanzibar City to Mkokotoni in the north, to Chwaka on the east coast, to Tunguu a few miles towards the south and to Chukwani on the west coast, and there were no roads in Pemba worth the name. In 1929 when Sir Claude Hollis left, the Protectorate roads ran to nearly every corner of both islands.[16]

The colonial construction of roads, ferry jetties and ports also meant the dispersal of survey agents and engineers to map every corner of the protectorate. By 1920, Zanzibar was also modern in the sense that it was fully mapped, from the urban conglomerate of Stone Town to the remotest corner of the northern island of Pemba.

Information dissemination and processing was also old news in Zanzibar by the 1920s. The island had been part of the global telegraph system since 1872, established by the Eastern and South African Telegraph Company, expanded in 1879 with a cable to Aden.

The printing press, generally viewed as a key agent of modernity,[17] was equally old, having been introduced by Sayyid Barghash in 1879. By the 1910s, it had moved beyond printing Ibadi legal texts and produced Arabic texts authored by Zanzibaris. While it would be an exaggeration to say that Zanzibar had a blossoming media landscape, journals had started to appear that expressed opinions on local developments.[18] The first Arabic-language newspaper, *al-Najah* (Success) appeared in 1910, but ceased publication in 1914. A new Arabic-language weekly *al-Falaq* (The Dawn) appeared in 1929, and printed contributions from Arabic-literate members of the public beyond the Omani-dominated Arab Association, whose mouthpiece it originally was. It also reprinted news items and opinion pieces from other journals in the Arab world, especially *al-Fath al-Aghar*, edited by the Syrian-born Muhibb al-Din al-Khatib (1886–1969). There was also the colonial publication the *Zanzibar Gazette*, which had an Arabic-language section with global and local news. Finally, several new publications appeared in the period 1920–40, some of which will be discussed in the coming chapters.

Public debate was not only shaped by periodicals and newspapers. As earlier studies have shown, printed books too were part and parcel of Islamic intellectual life in Zanzibar by the second decade of the twentieth century.[19] Scholars ordered printed books from Egypt and elsewhere and could own proper libraries of up-to-date Islamic print. Furthermore, and equally importantly, they had their own works printed by publishers such as the al-Hallabi printers in Cairo. They subscribed to journals like *al-Manar* and *al-Hilal*, and—as will be shown in this book—engaged with the editors in the form of questions and news updates. Especially in *al-Manar*, they would read the opinions of Rashid Rida and his colleagues on all the "modern inventions" listed in Burhan Mkelle's poem, from new media to fashion to the legality of toothpaste—as L. Halevi has outlined in his book *Modern Things on Trial*.[20] In the same journal, they could also follow debates and opinions on what constitutes a society, and how community is to be understood among Muslims in a period of rapid change. The notion of a morally guided Islamic society emerged in this period, due in no small part to *al-Manar*, as F. Zemmin has demonstrated.[21]

Clearly, the consumption of Arabic-language print from Cairo, Beirut and Bombay was not for all. In this regard, it is also worth noting that a new medium made its appearance and grew to be an important one towards the end of the interwar years. Radio (wireless broadcasting) was introduced in 1924, and programmes (in Arabic and Swahili) were announced in advance in the *Zanzibar Gazette*. The impact of the radio was noted in the poem by Burhan Mkelle at the outset of this chapter. In a more humorous version, the anticipated role of the "wireless" was hailed on air in 1928—and reproduced in the *Zanzibar Gazette*:

> Oh, Albion! how far away
> From Zanzibar you are
> Yet even as I sing, I may
> Be heard today in Zanzibar
> Since near is far and far is near
> Once Wireless to the ear has sped
> In Zanzibar, perhaps they'll hear
> Quite clear, what in Albion is said
> Whether this Alphabet has gone
> Or hasn't gone, from Albion
> To Zanzibar, well, there you are!
> For all is said, from A to Z
> From Albion to Zanzibar![22]

Cinema, too, was becoming a popular pastime for the upper and middle classes of urban Zanzibari society (Indians being particularly eager cinema-goers), with two theatres operating in the early 1920s.[23] The Royal Cinema Theatre (later Majestic Cinema) which opened in Zanzibar in 1921 was East Africa's first proper building dedicated solely to entertainment.[24] The cinemas screened short European silent films, including Charlie Chaplin movies, and the programmes were advertised weekly in the *Supplement to the Zanzibar Gazette*. By the late 1920s and early 1930s, Zanzibari cinemas were also increasingly screening Bombay productions from the budding Indian movie industry.

Another symbol of modernity that was in place was an emerging medical system, under the administration of the colonial Medical Department. Interestingly, some of the projects set up by the Medical Department were funded by *waqf* (Islamic endowment). Some initiatives were what today we would call "public-private partnerships", such as, for example, the Zanzibar Maternity Association, established as a charity in 1918. The association provided training for midwives and ran a maternity home in Stone Town. Its funding came from the colonial government, *waqf* funds and wealthy donors like Tharia Topan (the younger).[25]

The shifting winds of fashion and trends were not an unknown phenomenon to Zanzibaris. For example, during the first decade of the twentieth century, Sultan Ali (r. 1902–11) had grown closer to the Ottoman court, following a visit in 1907 when he was received by Abd al-Hamid II. Upon his return to Zanzibar, Ali not only expressed frustration with British governance, but also ordered that Ottoman dress code be adopted during official events.[26] The long, black, embroidered Omani overcoat (*bisht*) and dagger (*khanjar*) were exchanged for fez and coat, a "look" that became fashionable in the 1920s. In the late 1930s, as education for girls took off and a new (but still small) cohort of Zanzibari female teachers emerged, new fashion-statements like high-heeled shoes became popular—to the consternation of conservative men.[27]

Social changes were also becoming apparent, as will be further discussed in the coming chapters. Some new habits alarmed especially elite men whose prestige was fading as a consequence of abolition and new colonial categories, notably the love marriage. As has been shown by both E. Stockreiter[28] and E. McMahon,[29] Zanzibari marriages were regulated by the principle of equality in marriage (Ar: *kafāʾa*/Sw: *kufu*), whereby male guardians sought to marry their daughters or sisters to husbands of equal status. As established social categories came up for debate, so did the issue of who should marry whom, and, not least, what were the actual foundations for marriage.

Modernity and the Zanzibari Muslim Modern

The above outline of "modern things" in interwar Zanzibar says much about the openness of its ports to new objects, technologies and pastimes, but little about how these were made sense of. In this book I argue that a specific form of Zanzibari modernity was conceived and propagated during the interwar era. This requires some clarification of the unwieldy concept of modernity.

The following chapters will refer to a dual discourse of modernity. On the one hand, there is the academic understanding of specific forms of personhood that signify modernity. On the other hand, this book will also engage with the ways modernity was formulated in specifically Islamic terms during this era, often formulated by representatives of what has been termed "Islamic reformism".

Modernity as culture and a moral narrative: The choice of life-worlds

To the interwar Zanizbari, modernity was clearly not only the sum of things that became available (although, as Burhan Mkelle's poem showed, it was enough to merit poetic attention), nor the institutions that emerged there. As J. Robbins has stated, "[modernity], in short, is a culture, and it has the kinds of content that other cultures have".[30] As historians, we will normally seek knowledge of cultures past in written artefacts, and this book is no different. It looks for remnants from a culture that existed 80 to 100 years ago. However, it does not look for just any kind of culture, but specifically for a vision of modernity expressed in Islamic, Zanzibari terms, whose aim was—at some point—to make this vision manifest in Zanzibari culture.

Following W. Keane and other theorists of modernity, I view this act of seeking change, of selectively choosing which religious elements to uphold or discard, as in itself modern.[31] The very choices made by the actors in this book, their emphasis on self-cultivation, individual agency, not least their self-awareness, are what first and foremost make them modern.

Moreover, as W. Keane also points out, by making such choices, our actors are part of and producers of a specific narrative of modernity. Modernity, as formulated by them, is not merely a "how to" manual for a better life (say, wealth, better relationships, social harmony). After all, pre-modern societies too had on offer a myriad of such methods, from amulets to incantations to intercessions by authoritative religious leaders. The distinctly modern way of going about this centres on self-mastery and human emancipation—and not least that the individual recognizes his or her own agency. At the core, says Keane, is the transformation of the human subject.[32] This is what makes the narrative of modernity into a moral narrative, which in turn is contrasted with the past and imbued with value-laden ideas such as freedom and individual agency. It is this new vision of a modern person that I present in the following pages.

Implicit in the moral narrative is also a notion of progress—a path that is understood to lead forward to a better way of being a person in the world, and, by extension, a better society. A cultural definition of modernity offered by B. Wittrock[33] and discussed later by J. Robbins, centres on the promise, expressed as a set of "promissory notes".[34] The modern individual is modern precisely because she perceives herself born with a promise, a notion that she may seek self-authenticity in life—an endeavour that may turn out successfully or not, which is beside the point. The crux is that the modern person may seek new and different ways to achieve this, notably through new knowledge systems. This book is concerned with how knowledge systems were adopted, altered and utlilized in the quest for a future that was somehow different from the past.

Local moderns: Speaking modern in interwar Zanzibar

If we define modernity as a moral narrative combined with a distinct future-orientation, it is also clear that modernity can be localized and develop locally in almost unlimited ways without becoming "unmodern". This multitude of parallel—or multiple—modernities emerged as a theoretical framework in the early 2000s, and highlighted processes of localization.[35] They posited a person we may call the *local modern*. While displaying distinct traits associated with modernity—such as a clear awareness of agency—this will be formulated in different ways.

The local moderns in this book lived in a specific place at a specific time. They were Muslims resident in Zanzibar under British rule. In the coming chapters, the reader will be introduced to a wide range of opinions and viewpoints which I interpret as modern. Here, I take my cue from S. Kaviraj, who has posited modernity as a language, which anyone can learn to speak, but which inevitably also will be spoken with different accents (including European accents).[36]

The Zanzibari colonial context is hard to ignore. As we shall see, the colonial state was a constant interlocutor (and in many cases also the employer) of many of our Zanzibari moderns. They lived in a colonial context where a specific type of modernity was imposed upon them by the military, economic and institutional power of the British Empire. However, in this book I do not view our actors as conscripts of modernity, in the sense posited by Talal Asad[37] or David Scott.[38] By no means does that mean that I ignore the totalistic potential of the European developmentalist project, nor the implicit resistance narrative that it sets up (where "triumph" is the desired outcome, but where the struggle itself, as Scott has pointed out, changes the cultural landscape to a specific form of modernity).

Rather, I take my cue from Abdulkader Tayob,[39] who in a 2018 piece emphatically reminded us that the agents of modernity are not objects for analysis but themselves undertaking intellectual labour as producers of self-reflexive and critical discourse on religion. While Tayob's essay refers to discourses in the present, I keep this in mind also for the interwar Zanzibari discourses to be analysed here. What the reader will find is an ongoing conversation between scholars and intellectuals who aimed to produce new religious and political subjects and—crucially—to chart new futures. The actors that populate these pages are, to use Tayob's words, neither "imperfect moderns, hybrids between Islam and the West, nor heretics".[40] Rather, they were developers of, and participants in, an ongoing discourse on religion. In other words, to return to Kaviraj's analogy, this is a study of how a specific Zanzibari generation "spoke modern" and of what accents they used.

Islamic Cultural Programmes for New Moral Communities: From Adab *to* Akhlāq

The purpose of this self-reflexive discourse was to debate, define and implement a common good for a better future. To identify this elusive "common good", I draw on the innovative volume on *adab* and modernity in Egypt edited by Catherine Mayeur-Jaouen.[41] In her introduction, Mayeur-Jaouen does not cast the modernity project in the Middle East as either Western-hegemonic or one-among-several modernities. Rather, she states, emergent Egyptian discourse on modernity was an ongoing series of "cultural exchanges taking place in a modern context".

This framework fits well for Zanzibar too, which—as outlined above—was clearly a "modern context" by the time of the interwar years. The self-reflexive discourse that A. Tayob urges us to look for will here be analysed as "modern-speak", that took place in a language where many accents were already spoken. Hence, the following chapters will revolve around a set of cultural programmes that were formed in a context where a particular form of modernity for at least a generation had been co-produced, not just by colonizer and colonized, Arab and non-Arab, European and non-European, masters, slaves and ex-slaves, but by indigenous peoples and immigrant groups—Sunnis, Ibadis, Shias (Twelver and Bohra/Ismaili), Hindus, Catholics, men and women, urban and rural, wealthy and poor.

Mayeur-Jaouen highlights the passage of the classical Arab-Islamic virtue of *adab* from the realm of etiquette (forms of behaviour) to moral character (forms of being in the world) in the late nineteenth century. This is an observation that I hypothesize is valid also in interwar Zanzibar, and one which posits the ongoing "modern-speak" precisely as moral, as Webb Keane has shown. Mayeur-Jaouen's analysis draws on the writings of Jurji Zaydan (1860–1914) and his adaptation of British concepts into an Islamic vocabulary.[42] Examples are his usage of notions like "educating oneself", being "civilized", and "good upbringing", translated by Zaydan as *al-adab*. Upon these qualities, applied to the individual and to society, hinged nothing less than *progress*, in Zaydan's view. The drive towards improvement—individual and societal, and the relationship between the two—is interpreted by Mayeur-Jaouen as a transformation of the meaning attached to the ideal of *adab* (forms of behaviour) by incorporating the more specific concept of *akhlāq* (moral character/ethics). This conflation, she states, started in the late nineteenth century, culminated in the interwar period and resonates to this day. The former (*adab*: how we behave as moral community), states Mayeur-Jaouen, came to mean the struggle for identity, whereas the latter (*akhlāq*) took on an increasingly puritanical meaning of personal, continuously self-improving Islamic morality.

Identity debates were high on the agenda in interwar Zanzibar, and both *adab* and *akhlāq* were mobilized to construct new communities. The following chapters will show cases of such mobilization on behalf of professional, ethnic, cultural and moral communities, often aspiring to be one and the same.

In Zanzibar: From *ustaarabu* to Muslim moderns

This study also takes much inspiration from the study by E. McMahon where she details the transformed meaning of the concept *heshima* in late nineteenth- and early twentieth-century Pemba, Zanzibar.[43] From being in the nineteenth century a concept that denoted an individual's *honour* through his/her ability to exercise power over others (slaves, women, subordinates), *heshima* in the emancipation period came to denote a configuration of belonging, a socially sanctioned role that was assigned through "proper" behaviour. In other words, *heshima* came to mean *respectability*.

Commanding respectability was dependent on being "civilized", socially manifested in the display of *ustaarabu* (to be or become like an Arab, which during the Omani nineteenth century had replaced earlier *waungwana*/patrician ideals of civility).[44] This was the norm by which a person acquired and maintained respectability—*heshima*. The display of "civility" could be external and material (in clothing choices, consumer patterns, feasts, leisure activities). It could also be socio-legal, by maintaining, invigorating or severing social ties, or having one's identity tried and confirmed in courts typically through probate cases.

I contend that the interwar years were a period when both "civility" and "morality" were subjected to scrutiny by Zanzibari scholars, thinkers and activists. This was an ideal that owed much to the existing *ustaarabu*, but which was rooted in a new morality and new ideas of progress. The aim was no less than the transformation of the human subject, as W. Keane showed in his study of Protestant mission movements in Indonesia.[45]

This was expressed in a highly self-reflexive discourse that revolved—in various ways and in a range of arenas—around aspects of civility and respectability (*ustaarabu* and *heshima*, *adab* and *akhlāq*). Sometimes this was voiced in Islamic terminology (*ḥalāl/ḥaram*, *tawḥīd/shirk*, *sunna/bidʿa*), at other times in cultural terms like poetry praising the Prophet, or the performance of Sufi rituals. Sometimes it was addressed to a specific group (in this study: Comorians), sometimes to Zanzibaris in general, and at other times referred to the Muslims of the world. Sometimes it was voiced in Swahili, sometimes in Arabic.

Thus, this study asks how concepts like "civilization" and "respectability" were used to demarcate new moral (and modern) communities. What were the stated purposes of these communities—and their processes of inclusion and exclusion? Who were their "target populations" in a society where identity was fluid and subject to ongoing negotiation due to long-standing migration and the recent abolition of slavery? In short: What did the ideal Muslim modern look like? Who was he or—as far as sources allow—she?

In Zanzibar, this process was potentially inclusive, but it could just as well be divisive, as Roman Loimeier has pointed out for Islamic reform groups in general. He points to the fact that reformists tend to express "a difference from other groups and signal both a specific programme of inclusion (i.e. only those Muslims who are defined as 'proper Muslims') and exclusion (i.e. all other Muslims)".[46] As we shall see, divisiveness and inclusion was a persistent theme reflected upon by the Zanzibari Muslim moderns. First of all, it was not clear who the potential Muslim moderns were: the various communities in Zanzibar, from the WaPemba and the WaTumbatu, to the WaNyamwezi and ex-slaves increasingly identifying as "Swahili", to the Comorians, the former slave-owning Arabs, the "new Arabs" (Manga)? All Sunni Muslims, or all Muslims, including Shias? All Zanzibaris, as a community or as a nation? Or would the Muslim modern give up all such ties and become first and foremost a member of the *umma*, the global community of other Muslim moderns?

Lastly, this discourse also had the potential to turn political, nationalistic and racial, as J. Glassman has shown in *War of Words, War of Stones*.[47] The latter aspect will not be subject to much attention in this study, except when discussing the inclusivity/exclusivity of the Muslim modern ideal. Unlike Glassman, I do not view the discourse in which the interwar intellectuals engaged as being by definition Arab-elitist, or even racially or linguistically demarcated. However, I do recognize that it could have—and did have, as Glassman has shown—that outcome, as evidenced in intermittent inter-community violence, the *zama za siyasa* (the time of politics) in the 1950s, and, not least, by the 1964 Zanzibar revolution. My contention is rather that the interwar Muslim modern was a potentially unifying ideal, but that there remained throughout the period (in Zanzibar as elsewhere) a persistent ambiguity regarding not only what this ideal contained, but also what it aspired to and for whom. The failure to clarify this ambiguity resulted in what Roman Loimeier termed a "significant deterioration of the political climate in Zanzibar even before the events of January 1964".[48]

Zanzibari Islamic Modern Contexts

If we are to capture the Muslim modern both as a "self-reflexive actor", contributor to cultural programmes and an ideal, some clarification is necessary as to the modern Islamic context in which he/she acted and the ideal was formulated.

Islamic reform, Sufism, and modernity

How is the Islamic reformist orientation connected with the Muslim modern? Why do I, in the coming chapters, view changes such as teaching Arabic, or arguing against "excessive feasting", as indicative of a Muslim modern rather than what at first glance they look like: a turn towards a literalist, puritanist orientation—in short, Salafism? Here, I rely on the conceptual clarifications made by R. Loimeier, in several studies of Islamic reform in Africa.[49] In Zanzibar, the main Sufi orders—the Qadiriyya, Shadhiliyya and Alawiyya—were (and still are, by all accounts) committed to an esoteric episteme, whereby religious authority is based on a chain of earlier shaykhs whose knowledge (esoteric and exoteric) is understood to be passed on to students. This orientation can be clearly observed in Zanzibari works dating from the 1950s and 1960s[50] (and again from the 1980s and 1990s until today) and will also be shown repeatedly in this book. This book takes as a starting point that an esoteric paradigm does not preclude taking part in what Mayeur-Jaouen called "cultural exchanges taking place in a modern context".

The shift in values associated with displays of *adab* to include that of moral character, pietism and puritanism is a shift that is often associated with what we today call Salafism. While I do argue that this shift took place in Zanzibar, I emphatically do not argue that Zanzibar was turning Salafi in the current meaning of the term. Rather, I argue that the Muslim modern emerged from within the Sufi tradition.

As with the social, administrative and technological forms of modernity outlined above, Zanzibar in the interwar years had for a generation been marked by Islamic reformism. This was a global phenomenon. A massive body of literature exists on the emergence of Islamic reformism, both by Muslim thinkers and non-Muslim observers. Debate still continues over the intellectual genealogies of movements like the Muslim Brotherhood, Wahhabism and modern Salafism.[51] Observers have tended to agree that the shift is marked by a rejection of established religious authorities, and an insistence on directly accessing the Revelation (the Quran and Sunna) in order to re-create the original intent of God as conveyed to the Prophet Muhammad. Alongside this went a rejection of (many) Sufi beliefs and practices, which in the light of a re-interpreted Revelation were deemed obsolete or even un-Islamic.

Another element of the Islamic modernist school of thought was a tendency towards historicism, as Monica Ringer has shown and which she argues for as a "missing link" to explain commonalities and variations of modernities in general.[52] Ringer's study shows how nineteenth-century thinkers Syed Ameer Ali (d. 1928) and Jamal al-Din al-Afghani (d. 1897) both operated with an idea of religion as something that develops over time, from the "primitive" to the "advanced" (which the two defined somewhat differently). While I make no attempt in this book to contribute to a debate on the role of historicism in Islamic modernism, Ringer's argument is well taken as it allows for an epistemological framework where Sufism, too, can develop. In line with Ringer's analysis, I contend that Muslim moderns in this book would not necessarily have to "break" from anything; they could simply change traditions to include new values (such as agency, action and morality/*akhlāq*). In line with Keane's project of self-transformation, they could view themselves as becoming more "advanced" as time progressed, measured against a less advanced past. Furthermore, retaining an esoteric paradigm does not mean that a shaykh or a member may not propose a cultural programme that enhances—or in fact leads to—modernization. In other words, a set of beliefs that retains esoteric elements is not by definition anti-modern; it may also be a process of self-expression when chosen deliberately, or, as discussed above, modernly. Thinking otherwise is to ignore the self-reflexiveness of the discourse, the modern context in which these exchanges took place and the localized ways in which new notions of morality emerged. It is also, I may add, ignoring the emic terms of modernity used by the actors themselves, by assuming that modernity may solely exist where reason reigns alone.

Scholars have also argued over what *caused* the Islamic reformist orientation—in the Middle East, in Southeast Asia, in Central Asia and in Africa—citing socio-political historical processes such as the colonial encounter, modern communication, a Weberian "disenchantment", a long-standing sense of grievance towards autocratic rulers, and the rise of Arabic-language print capitalism. In past decades, the rise of Salafism and Jihadism has given rise to an academic discourse in studies of contemporary Islam whereby "tradition" is perceived as analogous to Sufism (local, moderate, non-violent, rooted in oral transmission of authority and expressed through communal rituals) as opposed to "global" Islam (radical, activist, textual and rooted in concepts of change).[53] Recent scholarship has questioned this dichotomy, pointing out patterns of Sufi reformism,[54] Sufi/Salafi ideological crossovers[55] and Sufi leaders as political actors.

In line with the latter scholarship, I view the situation in interwar Zanzibar as one where Sufi leaders had become increasingly oriented towards a reformist stance, while remaining Sufis. The orders (mainly the Qadiriyya, Shadhiliyya and Alawiyya) had recruited broadly since the late 1800s, and by the 1920s they were the main organizers of Islamic religious practice, at least among the Sunni majority population.[56] At the same time, a clear reformist stance made itself felt in the same period, as has been pointed out in several studies.[57] As elsewhere in the Muslim world, Zanzibari Islamic leaders—who were, due to the expansive growth of Sufism, Sufi leaders—voiced criticism against the most extravagant Sufi practices.

The British age of developmentalism in Zanzibar

While Muslim actors were busy producing a discourse on progress and modernity in Zanzibar, another vision of progress was making itself increasingly felt. By the early twentieth century, the new European social sciences had declared that societies not only changed, but could be changed. Change, in this context, meant an unending march towards higher levels of civilization and productivity—or, in short, progress.

With scientific backing from the new social sciences, and as a response to its financial constraints following the war and the subsequent depression, British policy towards its colonies and protectorates changed during the interwar period. From being merely suppliers, the colonies were now to be "developed" in order to sustain themselves—in some cases with a view to future independence. The aftermath of World War I saw a series of committees at work in Britain for the "progress" of the colonies, with the aim of infusing capital into the ailing British economy. The Colonial Development Act was passed in 1929, first and foremost to carry Britain through the depression.[58] It was accompanied by the Colonial Development Fund for loans and grants to further economic productivity in the empire.[59] C. Decker and E. McMahon, in their study of the idea of development in Africa,[60] noted that the interwar period saw the rise of the "development specialist". This was also the period when colonial faith in science completely replaced religion as the main driver of progress.

The Zanzibar Protectorate existed as part of the British Empire for seventy-three years and five months.[61] In economic terms, it was never very important. A small city on a small island, with little in the way of production that could benefit the British industrial machine, Zanzibar was—as Sarah Longair has phrased it—"symbolically significant yet economically inconsequential; part of the East Africa empire, yet viewed as an 'eastern' space".[62] Despite its near-irrelevant production and tiny population, Zanzibar was nevertheless subjected to many of the same developmentalist projects as colonies with much greater economic potential, for example like neighbouring Kenya.

The colonial doctrine of progress viewed the population as a workforce, first and foremost. The role of the workforce was to make the colony profitable. To be profitable it had to be productive, and to be productive it had to be modern. In Zanzibar, as in many other colonies, the modern mode of production was viewed by colonial administrators as a patchwork where each "race" had its designated role, assigned according to its level of "development". The "native" (including the former slave) was assigned the role of future skilled agriculturalist. The role of Arabs and Indians was often less clearly defined, the underlying assumption nonetheless being that they, too, needed to be "uplifted" from their current state. Women, in this context, should also be modern, in the sense that they should offer a stable, nurturing and hygienic home environment to a new generation of workforce. However, as Corrie Decker has pointed out, the colonial government also saw women as an untapped source as direct contributors to the colony's productivity.[63]

It is important to note that in this study I am not primarily looking for patterns of adaptation, rejection or collaboration *vis-à-vis* British colonial policies. Such interactions have been amply demonstrated in previous studies. Notable works here are those by E. Stockreiter,[64] who pointed to the autonomy of the *kadhi* despite British encroachment on the legal system; R. Loimeier,[65] who has described collaboration and resistance to colonial educational policies; and C. Decker,[66] who has shown the same for girls' education. W. C. Bissell[67] has pointed to similar patterns with regard to British efforts to modernize the city itself through a series of "urban renewal" programmes. Finally, J. Glassman[68] and L. Fair[69] have pointed out how British attempts to maintain stable taxonomies of the ethnic groups in Zanzibar—based on notions of race—were met with considerable contestation. Instead, I will view these protracted processes of adaptation, rejection and accommodation precisely as the modern context in which Zanzibari scholars, authors and community organizers could—and would—formulate new notions of civility and morality.

What kind of knowledge is power?

The choice that the modern subject has—one of his/her "promissory notes"—is to seek out new knowledge. During the interwar years, it was becoming increasingly clear that old knowledge—in the sense of classical Shafiʿi Islamic knowledge transmitted in Arabic and upheld by the traditional Arab elite—did not automatically mean power (let alone "progress"), as social order was renegotiated and the above-mentioned reformist ideas grew into maturity. But what should take its place? An imperial British version of Islamic law and society, as formulated in India? The emergent puritanical version of Islam emanating from the new kingdom of Saudi Arabia, as made palatable beyond Najd by the likes of Rashid Rida? The reconfigured version of Sufism, stripped of ecstasy and heavily infused with *fiqh*, that had already been propagated for a generation in Zanzibar? The ideas of Islamic modernism that had been formulated in Egypt and the Levant or as expressed, for example, in Indonesia? Or a reliance on "cultural elements" that were specifically Zanzibari, including the practice of magic, healing, initiation rites and the like? All options were in fact on the table for the Muslim modern. In the following chapters, I trace the emergence of the Muslim modern through arguments for and against all of the above, with different interlocutors and in different discursive arenas.

As for the definition of "knowledge" in this context, I draw on the study by Wilson Jacob on the itinerant Hadrami-Malibari Sufi and would-be Emir of Dhofar, Sayyid Fadl, who was also the main shaykh for the Sufi and chief *qadi* of Zanzibar, Ahmad b. Sumayt (d. 1925). Reflecting on the knowledge that formed the basis of Sayyid Fadl's understanding of sovereignty, Jacob defines this as a type of Islamic knowledge that was "intensely local and of the present, on the one hand, and broadly transregional and historical (and a discursive tradition) on the other".[70] The Zanzibari Islamic knowledge tradition was anchored in Islamic Sufi ideals which had branches way beyond the local. It was also one anchored in ideas of righteousness and—crucially—of enacting this in the world. The properties of the righteous are four, according to Sayyid Fadl: reason (*aql*), knowledge (*ʿilm*), action (*al-amal*) and determination (*al-himma*).[71] As we shall see, the human capacity for action is one much emphasized by the Zanzibari Muslim moderns.

Several parallel knowledge systems were at work in interwar Zanzibar. The British-European rationalist, developmentalist outlook has already been outlined above. However, as the British themselves observed, a wide range of what they termed "superstition" or "witchcraft" was also integral to Zanzibari knowledge, partially integrated with the Sufi-Islamic system and partly outside it. To this day, *uganga* (healing), *uchawi* (sorcery, witchcraft—for lack of a better translation) and spirit possession cults form part of Zanzibari reality.[72]

The clearly opposing Islamic sentiment is evident, for example, in Jurji Zaydan's emphasis on self-education, and the demand for "inner" moral guidance as a prerequisite for progress. That should not lead us to conclude that what we hear is simply an echo of European rationalism. Rather, the picture is somewhat different when viewed from within the Islamic tradition, as Samira Haj has eminently demonstrated.[73] First of all, as was the case in Europe, the reformist drive towards reason as paramount authority risked throwing religion itself out with the rationalist bathwater. While no Islamic reformers—from Ibn Taymiyya onwards—have suggested removing a Supreme Creator from the ontological equation, there certainly has been much debate over the position of geomancy, numerology, *jinn* invocations and related practices in Islamic societies. "Star-worship", *bidʿa*, heresy and transgression are but a few of the labels attached to occult texts, practitioners and practices from Islamic reformists—especially during the nineteenth century, but also long before. Western orientalists added to the chorus by introducing boundaries between "high" and "folk" Islam, the latter representing anything from symptoms of decline to a "native" manifestation of indigenous belief. In either case, the underlying assumption is that magic is practised where rationality does not (yet) reign.

This assumption has led to some misconceptions about the position of occult knowledge within general Islamic teachings. As has been pointed out most explicitly by N. Gardiner, the "occult" in Islamic knowledge systems is neither a separate entity nor one that has been transmitted separately from the "normal" sciences of *tafsir*, *hadith*, *fiqh* or—especially—Sufism.[74] Rather, the occult sciences are intertwined with a Sufi knowledge transmission that is text based, deeply anchored in Prophetic tradition, but favouring knowledge "by other means", including visions, "unveilings" (*kashf*) or mystical insight. Knowing by *aql* (reason), in other words, does not preclude knowing by "knowing"—nor vice versa.

In the interwar years, Zanzibari knowledge agents operated in a setting where magic was a conceivable possibility in human life, and where people conceivably could move across time. During the same period, as R. Loimeier has analysed in depth,[75] Zanzibar itself was becoming fully integrated in global time. School classes and workdays were started on the hour; clocks and calendars regulated official activities. By 1926, the island itself was aligned to GMT (in what came to be known as EAST: East African Standard Time), albeit with the proviso that the clock tower on the House of Wonders would show time according to the sun for people to derive the time for prayer and fast-breaking. This apparent paradox forms the core of this book.

2

PROLOGUE

THE MAGIC AND THE MODERN—ZANZIBAR, 1904

In issue 10/7 of the Egyptian modernist journal *al-Manar*, which reached subscribers throughout the Muslim world in August 1904, there appeared a set of questions from a reader in Zanzibar.[1] The very fact that questions were posed from Zanzibar this early in *al-Manar*'s history is interesting in its own right, and shows the close contact between the Zanzibari intellectual elite and modernist developments in Egypt. However, for my purposes here, it is the questions themselves that we shall turn to—or rather, one of the questions in particular: on the efficacy of Quranic healing.

The questions appeared under the headline "al-Masāʾil al-zinjibāriyya" (The Zanzibari Questions). Rashid Rida, the famous editor of *al-Manar*, started out by quoting the unnamed author, referred to by him only as "one of our distinguished readers in Zanzibar". He also gives column space to the praise heaped on *al-Manar* by the anonymous writer: "Your Islamic *al-Manar* is a boon to the Muslims, clarifying their legacy while stimulating thoughts and exchange of opinions between them [the Muslims]. No issue of *al-Manar* appears which is not of guidance, and it is discussed in clubs who wait impatiently for its arrival." That said, the writer goes on to refer to earlier issues of *al-Manar*, where Rida had denied the Prophet's ability to know the unseen, the Quran's capacity to heal and, finally, the existence of the *Mahdi*.[2] All this, says the Zanzibari reader, was too much for the Zanzibari general public: "Many would reject what you have published and stop reading *al-Manar* until presented with evidence that supports what you published."

The writer, who appears to be in agreement with Rida, now asks the esteemed editor to give a fuller explanation, including references and evidence "in a simple form"—presumably in order to convince the more tradition-bound readership in Zanzibar.

Roman Loimeier has referred to the early emergence of Islamic reformism in Zanzibar as something of a "false start".[3] Here, I will analyse the *al-Manar* questions more as a slow, protracted start towards what can only be defined as an ontological shift. Rashid Rida, in much of his writing, strove to construct an Islamic scientific materialism that would make Islam fully compatible with modern science. He attempted to reform Islam to a point where, to use Webb Keane's words, "Accidents are really accidental, not the workings of spirit agents, for instance."[4] The implication, viewed from Zanzibar, was that Zanzibari Muslims would have to undergo a radical self-transformation in order to live in this brave new world where accidents could not be avoided by placating spirits. This position was far from obvious in Zanzibar, either among the general population, or the *ulama* (the learned community). The clash of world views discussed in this chapter was over no less than Muslim personhood in the cosmos and in the world. It was bound to be protracted.

Reading and Writing to Heal in Zanzibar

The discussion in *al-Manar* centres on whether or not phrases or physical elements of the Quran can have an impact in the world, be that by incantations (*ruqiya*), talismans or amulets (*tamīma*) or spells (*tiwwala*). Various forms of *ruqiya* are—and have been—extremely widespread in Islamic societies. In the African Islamic context—and indeed in the entire Muslim world—uses of the Quran for healing (or for making certain events or outcomes take place) have been thoroughly described in anthropological literature. Debates over the legality (and efficacy) of these practices in the nineteenth century have also been documented, most thoroughly by A. Marcus-Sells on the "sciences of the unseen" (*ʿulūm al-ghaib*) as propagated by the Kunta of West Africa.[5]

Several studies (both past and present) have also taken note of the function of Quranic reading and recitation—i.e. the sound of the Quran—to create "agency", in the sense that it forms communal spaces that in turn aim to produce self-transformation, which may or may not contain an element of healing—especially of mental distress in difficult circumstances.[6] This usage points to the proximity of healing with devotional practices that in one way or another aim to produce an improved state, either of mind, body or the social body.

In present-day Zanzibar, such usage of the Quran has been described in detail by Kjersti Larsen.[7] When faced with distress (be that physical illness, social or economic challenges—or to protect against these things), people may turn to the services of a *mwalimu* who performs a *soma* (a reading). While there exists a general understanding that a *soma* falls within the boundaries of what is permitted by Islam, the term *mwalimu* is often used to differentiate his/her works from that of a *mganga*—a person whose methods could be interpreted as beyond the Islamically permissible. However, the line between "acceptable" use of the Quran and what is transgressive is somewhat blurred.

Soma itself is ritualized (as indicated, for example, by the use of incense and rose water), but still, according to Larsen, it is an event where "the sacred and the scriptural easily conflate with acts and materials incorporated into daily activities, and thus with everyday social, moral and political situations". This, one may argue, also explains its remarkable persistence, despite the fact that the *soma* is and—as will be discussed here—has been contested for more than a century. This understanding of Quranic reading is deeply ingrained with local understandings of the potency of the Quran itself and its role in individual lives. Moreover, the *soma* takes place in a universe populated by spirits (*jinn*, *ruhani*) who may also be part of—or counteract—the healing process, as Larsen has shown.[8] In other words, the well-being of humans is constituted—and acted upon—by forces that are unseen except when called upon through practices often labelled as occult.

It is also evident that *ruqiya*, *tamīma* and *tiwwala* form a core part of the East African Islamic scriptural tradition. Manuscript surveys in Zanzibar show numerous copies of manuals for healing, spells and incantations, as well as "recipes" for recitation for various purposes. The "Zanzibari Library" of the Omani Ministry of Endowments and Religious Affairs contains 177 manuscripts from the Zanzibar Institute for Archives and Records.[9] Of these, twenty-six (14.6 per cent) have some element of healing and/or occult content, including divination, casting spells, writing amulets and the like. The same pattern can be seen in the most up-to-date catalogue of the Zanzibar Institute for Archives and Records (formerly Zanzibar National Archives).[10] For example, the well-known Omani-Ibadi scholarly al-Mundhiri family owned a copy of the grimoire *Shams al-maʿārif al-kubrā*[11] (on which, see more below).

That is not to say that all such texts were produced for the same audience. Some are "recipe-like", probably produced for or by practitioners. They are often written on cheap paper or in notebooks, with little regard for calligraphy or style.[12] Others are extensive scholarly tracts, discussing the occult tradition as derived via Plato, Ibn Arabi and al-Ghazali. One example is a manuscript from the Maalim Idris Collection which is a discussion of the works by the Omani esotericist scholar Muhammad b. ʿAli b. ʿAbd al-Baqi. This 266-page manuscript was copied in 1264/1848 by one Musʿayd b. Suwayʿid b. Masʿud al-Saʿdi, either in Zanzibar or Oman. It contains lettrism, astrology and incantations accompanied by learned discussions on their origins and usage.[13]

A clear indication of how protracted this debate became is that we find this tradition alive and well in the East African corpus into the mid-twentieth century—i.e. long after the "Zanzibar questions" discussed here. *Jinn* incantations and amulet instructions were written and conserved during the 1930s and 1940s.[14] Tracts on medicine and healing (including by amulets) by the Omani-Zanzibari scholar and occultist Nasir b. Jaʿid al-Kharusi (Nasir b. Abi Nabhan; 1778–1847) were copied again and again in the twentieth century.[15] Interestingly, modern copies of occult "recipe-texts" would be provided with an index, for the user to "look up" specific problems and their cure.[16] The tradition was not limited to Zanzibar. Variants of occult/healing texts also show up in the manuscript collection of the Riyadha mosque in Lamu (dating from c. 1880–1940).[17]

The Quran as healer: Thc modernist point of view, and that of Ahmad al-Buni

In 1904, the traditionalist position—which presumably was the position of a majority of the Zanzibari population—was in *al-Manar* only cited indirectly by the anonymous writer. In their view, performing *ruqiya* was simply part of what the Prophet allowed to his companions, although with certain limitations. They point to hadiths to that effect, from the Sahih Bukhari. Rida, on the other hand, cuts straight to the chase in his response, starting out with the well-known statement that for every disease, God has created a cure. Then, without further ado, Rida goes on to say:

> There is no true evidence in practice that the recitation of the Quran or writing of a piece of paper to carry [as amulet] or dissolve it to eat or drink will lead to the cure of diseases or fulfil desires. If that was proven, then many people would have done that—both Muslims and non-Muslims would have practised it as medicine and adopted these as known means for all needs and benefits. This is the argument of reason on the topic (*wa-hadha dalīl ʿaqlī fi-l-mawḍūʿ*).

Furthermore, says Rida, the purpose of the revelation of the Quran was above all guidance, as is repeatedly stated in the book itself. He asks rhetorically: If the purpose was healing by talismanic usage, would that not also have been mentioned?

That said, Rida acknowledges that there are hadiths to the effect that the Prophet permitted usage of Quranic phrases for healing. He starts out by stating that the initial position of the Messenger was clear: spells, incantations and charms were practices of the *Jahiliyya* (the pre-Islamic age of ignorance), pure and simple. In other words, he is setting a starting point whereby these were to be left behind as superstitions of the past. However, accidents and injuries befell the companions, and two important exceptions were narrated in several hadiths: incantations are acceptable in the case of stings from scorpions, snakes and the like[18]—and to combat the Evil Eye. Rida is careful to include hadiths that allow *ruqiya* for other purposes too, including to still bleeding and to heal "the self" (*al-nafs*). However, he says, none of this changes the overall argument that *ruqiya* is fundamentally a practice of the *Jahiliyya* and that what the Prophet did was to "narrow down" (*fa-ḍīqa ʿalayhim dāʾira al-ruqiyya*) the cases in which such practice is permissible: "He did not allow [*ruqiya*] for any other issues. Nor the amulets used for protection of children, nor to prevent disease, nor against *jinn*, nor writing of Quranic phrases or other [practices] like that." What is the problem with Quranic healing, in Rida's view? Why would the Prophet make such tight restrictions on the practice? The main problem, according to Rida, is that reliance on incantations, talismans and spells contradicts the fundamental principle of *tawakkul*—trust and reliance on God and God alone. Eroding this erodes the very principle of *tawhid*—the unity of God and the foundational principle of Islam.

In his response to the Zanzibari reader, Rida also points out that trust in God only extends to the point where you knowingly expose yourself to harm. The Prophet did not prescribe that his companions should go out in the cold without a warm cloak, for example. Another better-known hadith to the same effect, which Rida does not quote, is: "Trust in God, but tie your camel."

Ruqiya is simply not compatible with *tawakkul*, says Rida. It has become part of tradition only because charlatans (*dajālīn*) have taken advantage of vulnerable souls who are led to believe that such incantations are glorifying the Quran—when in fact they are not. Instead, he says "the perfect believer (*al-muʾmin al-kāmil*) is obliged to be distanced from such illusions in order to enlighten his mind and strengthen his certainty (*yaqīn*)."

This argument was not new in Rida's time, nor is it unknown today. Ibn Khaldun (d. 1406) and Ibn Taymiyya (d. 1328), to mention two prominent critics, both relegated any instrumental usage of the Quran to the realm of pure unbelief on the basis of its infringement on *tawhid*.[19] This criticism was repeated in the modernist mode by Muhammad ʿAbduh in the late nineteenth century, whose views on miracles very much influenced Rashid Rida.[20]

However, no amount of modernist criticism could stop the emerging printing and publishing houses from running off copies of the most widely known (and condemned) occultist grimoire, the *Shams al-maʿārif al-kubrā*. This is a collection of incantations, numerology and other magic attributed to the thirteenth-century scholar Ahmad al-Buni.[21] For the purposes here, it is sufficient to rely on the description of the *Shams* by Noah Gardiner, whose study of this text is the most seminal to date:

> *Shams al-maʿārif al-kubrā* is a lengthy, talisman-laden, quasi-encyclopedic work on the occult sciences that is replete with texts on alchemy, astrology, geomancy, the science of letters, and other topics that could be gathered under the broad heading of "occult sciences". It is in fact an amalgamation of bits and pieces of some of al-Būnī's authentic works with texts by other authors.[22]

By the nineteenth century, lithograph copies of the *Shams* seem to have been produced as soon as the technology was available.[23] One of the earliest prints was produced by the Cairo-based printer Maktabat ʿAbd al-Rahman Muhammad in 1864.[24] Another batch was printed in Bombay from 1887.[25] Yet another widely circulated set of copies were printed by the Matbaʿa al-Husayniyah al-Misriyya in 1905. Not to be outdone, the ever-productive Babi al-Hallabi label in Cairo printed a new and improved version in 1926, using the preface to explain its decision:[26]

> Due to the great demand, the book *Shams al-maʿarif* was printed repeatedly [in Egypt and India]. The Egyptian printing presses took care to correct it, but it was not without errors and distortions due to the lack of correct copies. This time the text was printed [based] on the copies of Egypt and India and other copies in the handwriting of Haji Mirza Hussain with accuracy in correction with the knowledge of a committee of the best scholars of Egypt. It was re-corrected by the great scholar, Sheikh Abd al-Rahman al-Jazīrī. It is [now] the best printed version.

This is perhaps the version the British colonial officer Harold Ingrams mentioned as circulating widely in Zanzibar during the 1920s.[27] Whichever printed version reached Zanzibar, it almost certainly supplemented the occultist manuscript corpus described above.

What Happens when the Quran Heals? The Islamic Modernist Understanding of the Self

The background for the "Zanzibar questions" was a series published by Rida in *al-Manar* under the title "al-Karamāt wa-l-khawāriq" (Miracles and the Supernatural).[28] Tackling the subject head on, Rida here bases his argument on many scholars, but above all on Muhammad ʿAbduh's work *Risālat al-Tawḥīd* (The Theology of Unity). Rida discusses the nature of miracles and supernatural events, and postulates the concept of *Sunnat Allāh*; the manner in which God permits miracles to happen—or, conversely, the manner in which God lets the natural order of things run its course. According to Rida, God had allowed miracles to the early prophets (Abraham, Moses and Jesus), because that was what was needed at the time. By the time of Muhammad, the Quran was the only miracle necessary to make people turn to the straight path. Now, in 1904, the time for prophethood is over, hence the time for miracles is over. It is worth pointing out the historicism in Rida's argument here, as was outlined by Monica Ringer and previously discussed in Chapter 1. Religion can—and will—develop over time, says Rashid Rida.

Moreover, Rida discusses the possibility that the miracles of Moses and Jesus were not miracles at all, but rather had rational explanations. He entertains the possibility that the parting of the Red Sea was simply a very low tide. The girl raised from the dead by Jesus was in fact in a deep sleep. Lazarus may have been in a coma, says Rida, as "it has been known that people can sleep for several weeks and months, then wake up with or without reason".

Most relevant to our discussion here is Rida's suggestion that the conception of Jesus occurred because Mary's encounter with Gabriel affected her so strongly that it produced a child within her womb. In other words, Mary's own mind caused the foetus into being, as an emotional reaction to meeting the archangel.

Returning to the Zanzibari questions, Rida suggests the same is at play with Quranic healing. Having matter-of-factly refuted the idea that Quranic text can heal by being recited, Rida then turns to a discussion of the efficacy of Quranic healing. He says that the Prophet's permission to perform *ruqiya* in certain cases (like scorpion bites) was motivated by compassion for fellow humans in need. He also acknowledges that humans may be affected by illnesses and states for which there is no clear cause, where both the reason for and the nature of the illness is unseen—or illusory. Here, he mentions specifically ailments that people attribute to the Evil Eye, and points out that these are often the result of delusions, i.e. psychosomatic, or simply mental illnesses. It may even be, says Rida, that they are in fact caused by the Evil Eye, but to him this is beside the point. He offers the following example:

> I know a scholar of the cream of the *ʿulamā* with *yaqīn* [certainty in belief], who distances himself from the illusionary. There came to him a woman with a neurological disorder (*marḍ aṣabī*) which the doctors could not treat, and the woman displayed confusion (*al-waswās*). This disease is delusional imagination (*wahm*), and so is its cause, but there was no other way than to accept a *ruqiya* for her, *as long as she believed it worked* [my emphasis].

The latter part of the sentence introduces an argument which, among scientists in Rida's time, was known as placebo—or the fact that a patient may subjectively and objectively experience healing due to his or her faith in the remedy and/or healer. The term placebo itself simply means "I shall please", as in pleasing a patient with a remedy that is soothing or comforting. This was common practice in earlier European "bedside medicine" before the emergence of standardized hospital procedures. In fact, medical historians have claimed that "the history of medicine is the history of placebo".[29] By the late nineteenth- and certainly in twentieth-century Europe, there had emerged an understanding that while such remedies lacked actual efficacy, they could still produce an effect, based on the patient's trust in either the physician or the remedy, or both. Whatever healing occurred by traditional, faith-based or spiritual healing practices—ranging from mesmerizing to bloodletting to Christian healing—was increasingly understood as the result of placebo. However, only during the 1920s did the term *placebo effect* come to denote the effects of a completely inert substance, mainly used as a methodological tool in controlled trials.

So, how does Rida's argument about the patient's belief in *ruqiya* align with the scientific understanding of placebo? Firstly, he concludes that this reasoning follows from the Prophet's view on diseases caused by the Evil Eye. The pre-Islamic Arabs, says Rida, believed in the effect of *ruqiya*, so they may have been healed by it simply for that reason. Consequently, the Prophet allowed it for certain ailments, simply because it worked due to people's belief. In other words, the Prophet recognized the placebo effect (while not naming it as such) and allowed certain—and very limited—healing practices for compassionate reasons. He makes a similar argument for Quranic recitation as a cure against "sadness" and sorrow or grief:

> It is no surprise that *ruqiya* removes this emotion from him [a patient]. What this is, is simply something that the person [the one *ruqiya* is performed upon] believes in, and it is *wahm* [delusional, imaginary] like the emotions [are illusory, not physical], where the strongest outweighs the weakest. The sting of emotion may have real effects on the body, but this is in most cases weak and the person may heal for no particular reason.

Is this Rashid Rida condoning Quranic healing (with the limitations set by the Prophet) simply on the basis that it may lead to alleviation of suffering due to its placebo effect? In other words, is his reasoning based in modern science more than Islamic arguments?

Here, I turn to the particular brand of scientific materialism expounded by Rashid Rida in *al-Manar*. In an excellent article on the emergence of scientific materialism (rendered in Arabic as *dahiriyya* or *māddiyya*) in the Middle East, D. A. Stolz has pointed out that pure materialism (coupled with socialism) first came to the attention of Arabic readers through Jamal al-Din al-Afghani.[30] That said, by the dawn of the twentieth century, this impulse to refute "pure" materialism was coupled with a view of "correct" Islam as fully in harmony with modern sciences. In short, what emerged was a debate that centred on the nature of materialism itself, and its theological implications in the modern world. The argument, then, was that materialism was acceptable in so far as it did not deny God, but limited itself to pointing out the absence of physical evidence for His existence.[31] In a typical argument recounted by Stoltz, Rida defends the possibility that God may choose to break the laws of nature (i.e. allow miracles to occur), while immediately adding that most such "miracles" are simply "'superficial' and 'artificial' phenomena, performed by the skill of humans, and credited as miracles due to the ignorance of the 'masses' (*ʿawwām*)".[32] In other words, while scientific materialism may be a threat to faith, the superstition of the masses is a greater threat to the Islamic community overall.

I argue that something similar is going on in Rida's response to the Zanzibaris on the efficacy of Quranic healing. In Rida's argument, pure materialism is refuted while "correct" Islam is being presented as fully in harmony with modern science. It may, in fact, be that God chooses to break the laws of nature and nullify the effect of scorpion venom (say) in a patient. However, the greatest proof of God is the *Sunnat Allāh*, the ordinary workings of nature (including potential death by scorpion venom). Any attempt to interfere with this is a breaking of *tawakkul*, because God's decision to allow miracles is His alone.

That said, the masses may feel that Quranic healing helps because, Rida adds, more or less implicitly, they do not know better. If placebo can give some relief, it is *Sunna* to give them that within the prescribed limits—at least until the masses are sufficiently educated. In such cases, according to Rida, the transformative power of the Quran is in the mind, and in the mind alone.

In Zanzibar: Quranic healing and the rise of the Muslim modern

By the interwar years, the Muslim modern in Zanzibar often found himself partnering with the British colonial authorities in promoting reform—above all educational reform. However, as C. Bolton has pointed out, the two were less aligned than their shared rationalist outlook might indicate. British educational goals were "qualities that were conducive to economic productivity, including thrift, discipline and hygiene".[33] The Manarists, on the other hand, emphasized moral qualities (*akhlāq*) and an understanding of Islam that would extinguish exactly such habits as *ruqiya* healing and the use of talismans. Behind the two reformist drives were fundamentally diverging notions of what constituted progress in the Zanzibari context; commercially viable agriculture post-slavery and skilled industry on the one hand, and a science-compatible Islamic modernity on the other.

What they shared was the objective of reform: the Quranic school education that emphasized learning-by-heart, healers and soothsayers, ritual practices such as prolonged funeral rites—in short anything that was unconducive to industry (viewed from the British side) or un-Islamic, and thus unconducive to the rise of the Islamic *umma* (viewed from the Muslim modern side). Their goal, echoing both Muhammad ʿAbduh and Rashid Rida, was a Muslim community educated to *understand* their religion and make the right choices based on *rational knowledge*.[34] This world view left little room for esoteric knowledge reached by illumination—let alone for the occult.

Unfortunately, we do not know how Rida's response was received in Zanzibar. Some years prior to the *al-Manar* exchange, the influential Sufi scholar Ahmad b. Sumayt (d. 1925) had published his own views on miracles in his work *Manhal al-Wurrād*.[35] Here, Ibn Sumayt clearly viewed miracles as a gift which God may choose to bestow upon his most dedicated servants (especially the *awliyāʾ*, the saints), and lists several examples ranging from Mary miraculously receiving sustenance from God, to the moving of Queen Bilqis' throne from Yemen to the court of Solomon by Asif ibn Barkhiyya. The influence of a scholar like Ahmad b. Sumayt to influence learned opinion in Zanzibar should not be underestimated.

Furthermore, judging by the circulation of healing texts (manuscript and printed) throughout the twentieth century (not to mention observations of current practices), the "anti-healing" stance had only limited impact. A strong reliance on "cultural elements" that were both generally Islamic and specifically Zanzibari, including the practice of magic, healing and the use of amulets, continued both as a scriptural and performed tradition. In fact, when discussing Rida's *fatwa* with informants in Zanzibar today, two madrasa teachers branded it as simply "Wahhabi" and "quarrelsome".[36]

In other words, the efficacy of Quranic healing at some point became politicized in a struggle over world views and what constitutes progress. Magic (here taken to include healing practices) is often mentioned at the top of the list of cultural practices deemed irreconcilable with progress, be that in the transition to capitalism in Europe or on the pages of *al-Manar*.[37] By placing healing power in the mind, Rida in effect gives an ontological statement on the nature of reality. The natural order of things does not allow for miraculous healing, but the mind itself has the power to provide an experience of healing or improved well-being when stimulated by remedies believed to work. In other words, Rida is here proposing a concept of the self that is compatible with scientific rationalism and modernity. The mind has no extra "dimension" for esoteric or magical experiences. When such experiences occur, it is illusionary, induced by belief. The mind has one singular capacity, according to Rida: *activism*, within the bounds of the natural laws. Thus, Islam provides mankind with the incentive to better itself, to strive, to work. It is hard not to read W. Keane's definition of the modern into the notion of self that Rashid Rida proposes here.

Modern Minds, Modern Societies

"The new Muslim self is a doing self", noted Francis Robinson in his article about nineteenth- and twentieth-century Muslim reformists in India.[38] There he argued for four distinct shifts in the formation of individual identity resulting from the reformist turn in India: self-instrumentality (the "doing self"), self-affirmation (individual autonomy, the "choosing" of religion), the affirmation of "ordinary life" (the elevation of the "good person", the Prophet being the prime example) and, finally, self-consciousness. While some of these aspects may be hard—if not impossible—to subject to historical research, the emphasis on self-instrumentality is well taken after reading Rashid Rida's response to the magic-prone Zanzibaris. When the world is no longer shaped by invisible forces, but by mankind alone, the responsibility is on each believer to act accordingly by eschewing magical thinking and moulding him/herself into an agent for good, within the boundaries set by religion. As historians, we may see this impulse in the emphasis on education, in the way the Prophet is portrayed in *mawlid* texts, and of course in the curricula and reading materials of the period. This is not to say that interest in the self, in shaping and sculpting one's personhood, has not been present in the Islamic tradition before modern times. The autobiographical tradition is a testament to an enduring interest in introspection, often from within Sufi circles, as D. F. Reynolds has shown.[39] However, by the nineteenth and especially the twentieth century, this became fused with an emphasis on science and self-improvement. As O. El Shakry has pointed out, scientific interest in "the self" was also rising in Egypt during the interwar period, where works by Sigmund Freud, Carl Jung and Alfred Adler were increasingly referenced in Arabic. By 1938, the journal *al-Hilal* (also widely read in Zanzibar) noted that Freudian ideas were popular among younger Egyptian readers.[40]

If people changed, society would change with them. This vision mirrors that analysed by S. Federici in her 2004 book, *Caliban and the Witch*. She stresses that a world view (knowledge system) where reality is consistently drawn into question has historically been at odds with capitalist modernity, where the regularity and productivity of work is the measure of progress.[41] In Federici's analysis of the witch-hunts in Europe, pre-capitalist knowledge was destroyed in a process of purging pre-capitalist beliefs and practices. The literal destruction of the female body (during the witch-hunts) and the female body of knowledge (in the centuries that followed, up to the present), paved the way for capitalist rationality. For the purpose of understanding the Zanzibari questions in *al-Manar*, her argument that magic stands in the way of "progress" is useful for deciphering the many paths to progress charted in the period.

When the cosmos is understood as a living organism populated by unseen forces, how can power be exercised, work be regulated? Magic, as Francis Bacon noted, kills industry, and cannot co-exist with ideals of timely, organized production—or, as Rida formulated it: Islamic progress and modernity.

Federici uses the example of a widely held belief in pre-capitalist Europe, which is also well known in Sufism and Islamic occultism, that a body—under specific circumstances induced by incantations, etc.—can be in two places at the same time, change shape or be invisible. From the point of view of productivity (and thus progress), the person needs to be fixed in time and space to ensure the regularity of work. What took place, again according to Federici, was the emergence in Europe of reason as the central judge, inquisitor, manager and administrator, as voiced by Descartes and Bacon. Self-mastery and self-control become ideals for the "enlightened", while for commoners, there was law, and more law to regulate social conduct.[42] The goal was plainly evident, says Federici, to "rationalize human nature, whose powers had to be rechanneled and subordinated to the development and formation of labour-power".[43]

It is very tempting here to read Rida's response to the Zanzibari question as precisely an attempt to promote reason as the main judge, while leaving the "commoners" with, if not law, then at least the placebo effect. Rida's positioning of the mind as the transformative agent (rather than God or occult powers) promotes exactly this: a self-transformation towards a new subject characterized by rationality. The start of this shift was indeed a slow one in Zanizbar and one that lasted beyond the interwar years—and one that many will say is still ongoing. However, as we shall see, this conception of reason as core to the Muslim self formed a foundation for the Muslim moderns of the interwar years.

3

THE EXEMPLARY MUSLIM MODERN

BURHAN MKELLE (1884–1949) IN ZANZIBAR

This book investigates an ideal, a mode of being Muslim in a certain place (Zanzibar) at a certain time (c. 1918–40). However, ideals are discursively constituted, and rarely lived up to in the real world of everyday life. As stated at the outset, the aim here is to examine a broad cultural programme, voiced by teachers, community leaders, scholars and members of the general public. To do this, I have relied on the writings of contemporary Zanzibari scholars, and in particular on those by one person, Burhan b. Muhammad Mkelle (1884–1949). During his lifetime, Burhan Mkelle was active in all the arenas where such programmes were formulated. As will be shown in Chapter 4, he taught two thirds of the youngsters in the colonial Government Central School. In Chapter 5 we will encounter him as part of a new generation of "salary men". Chapter 6 will show that he spent much of his life active in the new host of *jamʿiyāt* (associations) that emerged in Zanzibar. He was also involved in several of the ongoing, global Islamic discussions regarding education, ritual practice and text circulation, as will be discussed in Chapter 7. A persistent problem in researching Islamic reform in the Zanzibari context is the differentiation between reform and the formation of new identities—communal, national or global. Mkelle argued on all these levels, as will be discussed in Chapter 8, which raises the question of whether the

Muslim modern was in fact the new Zanzibari national. Given his activism in so many social arenas, and the nature of his network and his writings, I have tended in this work to view Burhan Mkelle as the "exemplary" Muslim modern, in the sense that he was explicitly working to "improve" or "develop" his community. As will be evident in the following chapters, he was not alone, nor did he fall into any neat category like "European-oriented", "modernist" (Islamic or otherwise), "Sufi", "Salafi"—or even reformist.

In retrospect, Burhan Mkelle is best remembered in Zanzibar as a poet in the Arabic language. Among his contemporaries, he was known as "the Sibawayh of Zanzibar",[1] referring to the leading Persian grammarian and Arabic linguist Abu Bishr Amr b. Uthman Sibawayh (d. 796 in Basra). Burhan's *Diwan* (collected poetry), which exists in several versions, consists of at least sixty poems of various lengths,[2] some of a religious nature, others composed on various occasions in Zanzibari history, others in turn composed on occasions in his own life. In my interpretations, I have worked on the assumption that poetry is composed to express—in writing or through recitation—not only individual emotion or the beauty of the language itself—but a form of opinion. Who is being praised (and who is not)? What occasions merit a poem and which do not? What exactly is being taught in the didactic poems, like those outlining the life of the Prophet Muhammad? What ideals are being instilled in *mawlid* texts and salutatory recitals in the schools? And, not least and by far the most complicated question to answer: Who are the addressees? In short, what is the Muslim ideal projected in this particular *Diwan*?

A Modern Life

To show the complexity of the Muslim modern identity, Burhan's background warrants some attention. He was the heir to a rich legacy of Zanzibari Islamic scholarship and a long-term colonial employee; a Comorian-Zanzibari under French protection under British rule; a Sufi shaykh and a reformer; an Arabist and a Swahili speaker; a member of an urban elite and an intellectual of his time. His was a life that cannot be easily confined to neat categories, neither the contemporary ones defined by the British government, nor those constructed retrospectively to narrate Islamic intellectual history. In the long list of annual events in Zanzibar, Burhan does not feature among the "great *ulama*" who are honoured with *hawliyya*s on their date of death, like, for example, the leading Sufi shaykhs, legal scholars and *qadis*, father and son Ahmad (1861–1925) and Umar b. Sumayt (1886–1976).[3] Rather, he is remembered as a poet "between *din* and *dunya*", i.e. between the religious and the worldly.[4] To map these complexities, a biographical sketch is as good a place to start as any.

In their neatly handwritten biographical introduction to their father's *Diwan*, Burhan's sons Ahmad and Muhammad note, not just once but repeatedly, that their father rarely left Zanzibar. He never studied abroad, they write, but was "brought up here in Unguja".[5] Moreover, he explicitly "never visited Kenya, Tanganyika or Mozambique",[6] but, his sons state, "he did visit Pemba" (a tour that inspired him to write a poem about the vistas of the "Green Island"). For relaxation, he—like many urban Zanzibaris of some means—would go to his *shamba* (farm), of which he had two. The only exception to this—by Zanzibari standards—sedentary life was his journey to the Haramayn for *hajj* in 1935.[7] On this trip, he stopped by Mombasa to stay with his friend Shaykh al-Amin al-Mazrui[8]—which somewhat contradicts the statement that he never visited Kenya, but which says much about the Zanzibari perception of Mombasa, both in Burhan Mkelle's time and at the time of his sons' writing.

Finally, as if to drive home the point of a locally born-and-bred scholar, the sons state that Burhan Mkelle was born and died in the same house in the *mtaa* (quarter) of Malindi-Jongeani where he lived his entire life.

The intimate portrait of Burhan drawn by his two sons also contains glimpses of a lived life—beyond the public roles that generate food for archives. As is often the case with filial biographies, positive traits are very much emphasized, and some statements are clearly addressing the times in which they were written (late 1990s/early 2000s) rather than Burhan's own era. Nonetheless, the man Burhan Mkelle can still be gleaned from the sons' memories.

In the Malindi quarter, Burhan was first and foremost known for his Ramadan teaching sessions in the local Jongeani mosque, today known as the Tawba mosque. Every afternoon, every Ramadan, for more than sixteen years, he would teach the "Jalalayn"[9] to an assembly of about fifty students. According to the biography by Burhan's sons, the final sessions were held every year on the 27th of Ramadan.[10] On these occasions, the chief *qadi* of Zanzibar, Umar b. Sumayt, would be present, as would the later chief *qadi* of Zanzibar, then Kenya, Abdallah Saleh al-Farsy (1912–1982)—above all, a testimony to the network of which Burhan was a part and which will be revisited in the following chapters.

Throughout his life, Burhan was a devout follower of the Prophet Muhammad. As we shall see, he composed numerous *mawlid* and praise texts in the Prophet's honour, for use on a variety of public occasions. On the very local level, he was a core person in organizing a *mawlid* recitation in the square in front of the Jongeani mosque, while on the public level, he was a regular on the committee that organized the official *mawlid* event in Mnazi Mmoja.

During Eid days, he received visitors in his house. Among those who frequented his house was his best friend, Abu Bakr BaKathir (d. 1943), the son of Abd Allah BaKathir (d. 1925), who founded the influential Madrasa BaKathir in the Ukutani quarter of Stone Town. Another frequent visitor was the aforementioned Abdallah Saleh al-Farsy. To al-Farsy, Burhan was first a guardian and mentor then a friend and colleague in the Zanzibar school system.

Eid al-Fitr celebrations were marked by another ritual; both the Qadiriyya and the Shadhiliyya orders of Zanzibar would come to Burhan's house and perform their *dhikr* in front of his door. The relationship between Burhan and the Shadhiliyya and Qadiriyya was close and cordial throughout most of his life, but—as the following chapters will show—that did not preclude Burhan from being involved in reformist activities leaning more towards the Salafi line or suggesting Saudi Arabia as the new bastion of Islamic education.

While in his Malindi house, Burhan—again according to his sons—liked to read, and his books were all in Arabic. The sons even stress that Burhan did not own a single book in English, nor did "he ever utter a word of *kizungu* in his life".[11] Why they would want to make this point, and what it may mean in the contested field of Zanzibari education, will be further explored in the following chapters. Perhaps Burhan's most lasting legacy is as a poet, and his sons state that he did most of his writing at home, after work.[12]

Burhan was, according to his sons, "one of the select ulama who was invited to attend the weekly Thursday *mawlid* readings in the home of Sayyid Khalifa b. Harub".[13] Here, we may assume that Burhan's supreme command of Arabic, and long-standing interest in *mawlid* composition and recitation, were what gained him entry to the private readings of the Sultan.

As a busy teacher, civil society activist, scholar and poet—and decided non-traveller—Burhan nonetheless "loved a change of air". He preferred his *shambas* to foreign destinations, and to visit the villages. This made him well known to the people in the countryside where, according to his sons, he was "better known to the locals than any other scholar"[14] and earned the nickname "Sheikh wa Mashamba".[15] According to his sons, "farmers and fishermen would come, and they would invite him to their homes, and have a book read by him there". Some would even pass one of their young sons into Burhan's care, to be brought up by him. Burhan's sons, in retrospect, see this practice as an example of their father's *birr* (Ar: righteousness, charitable disposition). According to them, Burhan made sure that his elderly and infirm relatives and neighbours were supplied with food, sent from his own dinner table with his children as delivery-boys. "We realized that this was a way of teaching us the practice of *birr*", they write.[16] On Eid al-Hajj, he would slaughter a goat and divide it into seven portions—one for his own household, with the remainder again being distributed by the young Mkelle children to elderly and poor relatives.

While on his *shamba*, Burhan did not read, as was his habit while in town. Instead, he prayed, and travelled around the villages on foot to view the landscape and to greet people. He was, his sons say, "calm and careful in character, paying close attention to order and details in his life". Burhan also seems to have achieved a reasonable work-life balance: "He divided his time between reading in solitude, teaching, relaxing and physical exercise, such as swimming in the sea (*ahata kuogelea baharini*)."[17]

The following chapters will show Burhan as part of what may be termed several Zanzibar intelligentsias—from the teachers in the government schools to reformist-oriented Muslim groups, to the traditional Sufi orders and the Comorian community in Zanzibar. His sons, however, show another side to the person that most of all demonstrates how Islamic knowledge and scholarship in Zanzibar could serve as entry to palaces, schools, civil society positions and the humble village home.

The Mkelle family in Zanzibar

The Mkelle family hailed from Ikoni in Grande Comore and were thus among the many residents in Zanzibar Town who were of Comorian origin.[18] Contemporary observers in nineteenth- and early twentieth-century Zanzibar noted the presence of a Comorian community. An influx of Comorians—the majority from Grande Comore, but also from the other islands—took place in the BuSaidi period, and their role in the state apparatus as ministers, soldiers, interpreters and legal scholars was considerable. However, their numbers have always been estimates, and wildly varying at that. Iain Walker sums up the contemporary observations in his 2014 study, where the numbers range from 2,000, to 4,000 (Sunley, British consul in Ndzuani), to "dhows full of Comorians" (French consul, Zanzibar, 1882).[19] To add more confusion to the numbers, Burhan Mkelle himself states that the number of Comorians in Zanzibar at the time of writing (mid-1920s) was 5,000, "most of them living in town (*al-balada*) and a few of them in the countryside".[20] A decade later, Burhan's fellow Comorian-Zanzibari, Ibuni Saleh, stated that "approximately 2700 Comorians of both sexes" were resident in Zanzibar, "nearly two fifths of whom are local born and the majority of the rest are permanently domiciled in the Protectorate".[21] A more sober assessment was made by Mohamed Ahmed Saleh in 1998, stating that the Comorian-Zanzibaris probably made up no more than 2 per cent of the total Zanzibari population at any given time, during and after the colonial era.[22]

The lack of reliable figures can, of course, be explained by the fact that censuses from the period are unreliable. However, more relevant to the discussions in this book is the fact that Zanzibari (and Zanzibari Comorian) self-ascribed identities—both on an individual and collective level—have tended to vary over time and across situations. As I. Walker has pointed out, identity among the Zanzibari Comorians in the first half of the twentieth century was very much linked to

Fig. 1: The Mkelle family in Zanzibar

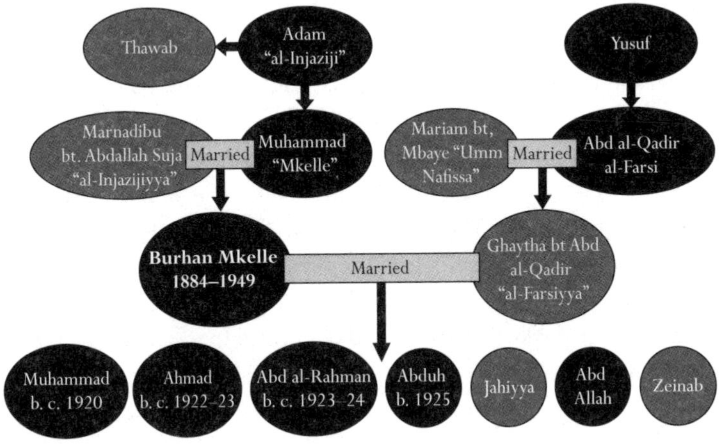

French subject status and the categorizations applied by the British protectorate authorities in Zanzibar.[23] At the same time, what it meant to be Comorian in Zanzibar was shifting in the first decades of the twentieth century, in ways that were beyond the grasp of the simple "racial categories" assigned by the colonial government.

Muhammad "Mkelle" b. Adam (1855–1925)

No full biography exists of Burhan's father, beyond what Mkelle Burhan himself wrote about him in passing and what we can piece together from a few, rather random, sources.[24] His full name was Muhammad (Mkelle) b. Adam b. Nuh al-Shirazi, and he was born in Zanzibar in Rabiʿ I 1272/November 1855. His father, in turn, was a Comorian trader who moved between Zanzibar, Moroni and Mukalla in Hadramawt. Muhammad (Mkelle) was born just as his father was about to depart for Mukalla in Hadramawt; hence the son got the Swahilisized version "Mkelle" as a lifelong nickname. Later in life, Burhan integrated a biographical sketch of his father in his narrative about the Comorians of Zanzibar, saying that:

> When he was six years old, his father [i.e. Adam, Burhan's grandfather] sent him [i.e. Mkelle, Burhan's father] to the *ʿālim* ʿĀmur

> al-Matūjī to learn the Holy Quran, which he did. Then he continued to the late Muḥammad Mlomrī to study religion (*amūr dīniyya*), and he learnt it from him. After that, his father wished for him to study a craft, and the making of jokhos [*al-jawākh*, embroidered robes used by the Omanis in Zanzibar] was becoming a foremost craft in Zanzibar. His father sent him to an Indian who was a great master (*ustādhan kabīran*) of that craft. He [Mkelle] learnt and he mastered the art to perfection. Then, the master craftsman travelled to India, but a few days (*bi-ayām*) before his departure he sent my father to al-Ḥājj Makkī al-Baḥranī to work for a salary with him. After some years al-Ḥājj Makkī died and my father decided to start a sewing shop for himself where many of the young people of Zanzibar came to learn. When Sayyid Barghash heard about his skills and that of his pupils, he gave him a place to establish his workshop in Hurumzi, by the grave of Binti Khān ʿAlī, near the family house of the Sultan. He ran this shop until the death of Sayyid Barghash and the accession to the throne of Zanzibar by his brother Sayyid Khalīfa b. Saʿīd.
>
> My father remained in his place and with his service and found a house in Malindi Jongeani. This house had no roof, so he placed a roof on it, and he refurbished it and lived in it.[25]

We know that Mkelle b. Adam was twenty-nine years old when his son Burhan was born. We know that Mkelle stayed put in his house in Malindi and that he was still there in 1915, when he received a notice from the Zanzibar Sanitary Inspector. The letter, issued with reference to the Public Health Decree of 1909 (for curbing larvae of malaria-carrying mosquitos) instructed Muhammad to ensure that "barrels, drums and other vessels containing water are thoroughly cleaned out at least twice each week, and then properly covered".[26] Samples had shown that mosquito larvae had been found on the property, malaria control being one of many public health concerns that the still relatively new colonial government grappled with.

This was the same house in which Burhan was born, lived and died. The year of the order—1915—indicates that the Mkelle household was a typical Zanzibari multi-family household, where several generations lived under one roof. The fact that it is addressed to the then sixty-year-old "Sheikh Muhammad b. Adam", and not Burhan (who was thirty-one at the time), shows that the elder Mkelle was still the head of the household.

Finally, we know that Mkelle b. Adam died on 5 May 1925, at sixty-nine years of age. We know this because Burhan included his father in the elegy he composed for his teacher and master Ahmad b. Sumayt, who died two days later:

> I am grieving doubly today, as one loss came after another
> I lost him [Ibn Sumayt] after having lost my father;
> Only two days separated their deaths[27]

Marnadibu bt. Abdallah Suja "al-Ingazijiyya"

The only glimpse we get of Burhan's mother is from his account book, where he noted his financial transactions. According to the *nisba* (family name) assigned to her by Burhan, we may assume that she, too, was of Comorian origin. The role of Comorian women as important family nodes and keepers of land in the Comoro Islands has been much discussed by anthropologists of the archipelago, and the matrilineal division of property in combination with Islamic law has intrigued Islamic scholars. However, the social organization among Comorians resident in Zanzibar in the late nineteenth century is less known, but we may assume that Marnadibu, as a Comorian wife married to a Comorian man, operated considerable networks of her own. The role of Comorian women as madrasa teachers will also be discussed below, and it is not unlikely that Marnadibu had such a role for her children.

We do get an impression of the close relationship between Burhan and his mother from the elegy he composed in her memory. The year of her death is not given in the poem, but based on other notes by Burhan, she probably died some time in, or shortly after, 1931. Losing his mother and grandmother in rapid succession, Burhan composed laments to them both:[28]

> In the month of Safar, with the passing of my grandmother, to the mercy of her Lord
> And in Rabīʿ II, I lost my mother, may God forgive her, who was confined to bed

Only a month and a few days separated their deaths.

I had neither endurance nor perseverance as I entered
Into the sea of sorrow (*maʿāṣī*) from which there is no rescue

Malindi life

The *mtaa* (quarter) of Malindi was—and still is—one of the most densely built and populated areas of Zanzibar Stone Town. Like the rest of the city, Malindi was subject to all the flawed efforts to create colonial order, followed by flawed socialist attempts at modernization—and finally, in the 1990s and 2000s, the equally flawed attempts at crafting a "heritagized" version of Zanzibar Town, a particularly troublesome prospect in the urban agglomeration that is the Malindi quarter.[29]

The colonial efforts to "renew" Stone Town were begun in 1893 by the Department of Public Works. In the decades that followed, the colonial government made several attempts at organizing the city into bounded homogeneous quarters, each inhabited by the various "races" they perceived to be living in Zanzibar.[30] W. C. Bissell has pointed out how the urban renewal projects in Zanzibar wittingly or unwittingly drew on colonial categories of race and of particular groups' "traditional" custodianship over the various parts of Stone Town. The surveys in effect charted "the imprint of race on space", not necessarily with reference to historical ownership, but rather to notions of architectural style.[31]

Burhan's lifetime corresponded not with the conquest or struggle for dominion over the islands—that was concluded during his infant years—but with the increasing colonial mastery of Zanzibari urban space. The maze-like streets and the intermingling of residential, official, military, agricultural, commercial and religious activities (including the main execution site and several graveyards) bewildered consecutive British observers, who tended to view the city primarily as a place of "chaos and confusion" in need of "cleaning up". As a Zanzibari born-and-bred, Burhan undoubtedly saw neither chaos nor confusion, but knew the city's streets and alleys by heart. He was, in other words, a typical resident of a typical pre-modern city; a person who moved about in the unplanned, organically evolved urban environment without the need for a map, street signs or the GPS apps that modern-day tourists in Zanzibar resort to when they venture beyond the "safe zone" of Shangani, Forodhani or Mnazi Mmoja.

Burhan Mkelle witnessed the colonial remaking of the Stone Town urban space not only in his capacity as an employee of the newly established Department of Education, but quite literally on his way to and from work at the Government Central School. This was not a mere matter of new buildings and bridges, as W. C. Bissell has pointed out, but a drive to "refashion cultural landscapes", thus altering behaviour and, as an ultimate ambition, Zanzibari culture.[32]

From 1914, Burhan would walk to work passing by stone houses in his neighbourhood in Malindi that were fitted with numbers on the doors, in a colonial attempt to carry out disease control—and get a grip on the city by the same token. Some of the main pathways were even given names—some of which were actually adopted by the public, the remainder existing mainly as figments of colonial imagination—again in an attempt to standardize references to places. At least some of the city streets were cleaned and lit by courtesy of public funds.

From August 1921, he would have to negotiate the construction work for the extension of Zanzibar harbour, which built a new wharf and a controlled dhow harbour next to it. The project demanded the demolition of parts of Malindi, and in effect separated the Jongeani *mtaa* (quarter) from the rest of Malindi.[33] However, endless budget quarrels and the subsequent firing of project leaders and redrawing of plans meant that the harbour works continued for much of the 1920s.

From 1924, when the school moved to Mnazi Mmoja, Burhan Mkelle would have his workplace next door to the building site of the Peace Memorial Museum, the famous dome-adorned construction that was one of two main monumental buildings realized during the colonial period.[34] On his way to work, Burhan Mkelle would also be able to follow the gradual filling of the creek, the lagoon that separated the Stone Town from the "other side", the Ng'ambo. The gradual land reclamation of the creek started in the late 1920s, to create a tidal canal and basin.[35] However, Burhan did not live to see the creek become entirely reclaimed land; this happened only in the 1950s.

The neighbourhood of the Mkelle family was one of intellectual learning and one with a distinct "Arab" flavour to it. The influential

Farsy family were immediate neighbours in Jongeani. One of the Farsys who lived next door was Burhan's near contemporary, Shaykh Saleh b. Abdallah al-Farsy (1886–1958), later to become better known as the father of Abdallah Saleh al-Farsy.[36] Shaykh Saleh was himself a scholar, and was known as one of the first Zanzibaris who mastered English. He was also one of many members of the Farsy family who took up positions in the colonial administration.

This was also a neighbourhood where women—and particularly Comorian women—ran small *vyoo* (Quranic schools) in their homes. Abdallah Saleh al-Farsy received his first Islamic education in the home of just such a woman in Malindi-Jongeani, Bibi Zawadi Fatma.[37] The Malindi quarter was also the home of the Sumayt family, the chief *qadi* and Burhan's main teacher, Ahmad b. Sumayt, as well as his son and Burhan's friend and companion, Umar b. Sumayt.

Malindi-Jongeani was also home to several Sufi orders, and public *mawlid* recitals were held very year on the Prophet's birthday in open squares and in front of mosques. One such location was the square in front of the Jongeani mosque where Burhan was teaching. This particular open space was also the scene of a special reconciliation event that is highlighted by Burhan's sons. As was indicated above, the Comorian community in Zanzibar was plagued by discord, as their social organization was structured according to place of origin in the Comoros. The affiliation that an individual had to the maternal village (*miji*) was what provided support for migrants, forming what were known as "counties". These hierarchical organizations also accumulated funds for the *grande mariage* (*harusi ya aada*) and elaborate funerals through a "taxation system", and held the power to denounce and exclude members. The redistributive economy of the "village groups" meant that rivalry between them was rife, and the groups could at times be at odds with each other to the point of violence.[38] A particularly hostile situation developed in the 1930s between two factions known as the "*Yaminis*" (right) and "*Shimalis*" (left/north). This conflict escalated to nothing short of a "war" (Sw: *vita*), according to Burhan's sons, "where sticks and spears and hammers were used" and "people were burying their dead night after night".[39] In this situation, Burhan took on the role of community leader, in what became a public meeting in Malindi to resolve:

> [...] the discord that had fallen between the Shadhilis of Zanzibar and Burhan b. Muhammad Mkelle settled a peace (*ṣulḥ*) between them. Without him, the Shadhiliyya of Zanzibar would have been two opposing parties [...] When the shaykh [Burhan] heard news of this divide, he offered them a reconciliation. He gathered them in a place, an open yard by his [Burhan's] house. Muhammad Khayr's party was on the one side, and Muallim Harun on the other. Many people were present to witness the peace accords, most of them people from Malindi, to see how these two factions reconciled. When the meeting was over, Shaykh Burhan Mkelle came to the place of treaty, and met Muhammad Khayr and Muallim Harun. In his hand he had a paper and written upon it was a poem on the treaty. The poem was recited on the occasion of the *ṣulḥ*.[40]

While the intercession of Burhan Mkelle may have created unity within the Shadhiliyya (of which Comorians in Zanzibar made up no small part), factionalism was an undercurrent in the Comorian community throughout the interwar years, as will be discussed further in Chapter 6.

Staying put in a mobile world

Travel is Zanzibari, as the saying goes; one journey elicits another. This is part of Zanzibari self-perception to this day and has been apposite to academic studies of almost any aspect of Zanzibari life. From the present-day "watu wa June–July" (Omanis of Zanzibari background who spend the hot months in the cooler climate of Zanzibar) to the early migrants settling from South Arabia and Persia, movement is the predominant trope of a culture shaped by migration. Uncles live in London, Paris or Stockholm; grandmothers go to Dubai to see grandchildren; travelling salesmen (and women!) make their way to China and students go wherever scholarships may take them. By Ramadan, or by the European or Gulf school holidays, they return to visit, to get married, to renew the Zanzibari culture of travel yet again. On the darker side of this trope we find the involuntary travellers, as the pre-1890 land transaction files in the Zanzibar Archives show, the phrase "that which is upon it [the land]" obscuring the thousands of men and women brought to the archipelago as slaves. Others came simply to work, like the Comorians and Bravanese who joined the BuSaidi state to take up jobs as policemen, clerks, court officials and *qadis*.

Women travelled too. Some were sent to relatives in Zanzibar for marriage, from the Comoro Islands, from Oman and Hadramawt. Others went on regular tours, like Bibi Raya bt. Hemed b. Rashid al-Barwaniyya. When she died in 1938, at the age of seventy-nine, *al-Falaq* highlighted her travels in her obituary,[41] noting that this "venerable Arab lady" had visited Hijaz, Syria, several times, Palestine, Turkey, India, Tabora and other places in Tanganyika, Kenya and Grande Comore. Above all, Bibi Raya travelled to Egypt, where her grandchildren—including her granddaughters—were schooling. "All these places she visited alone", the note says, implying an independent and modern female traveller.

Burhan's life may at first glance seem "small" compared to that of his contemporary and friend Nasir b. Sulayman al-Lamki (d. c. 1932/33), for example, the head of the Arab Association in Zanzibar who had travelled to Egypt in 1900–1, and who later twice travelled to Europe (on both occasions welcomed home by Burhan's poetry). Burhan's life seems very much homebound, also in comparison to that of his teacher and Sufi master, Ahmad b. Sumayt (d. 1925), who spent extended periods of study in Cairo, Istanbul and Hadramawt and who published his books in Mecca.[42] Finally, the most high-ranking of Burhan's associates, the Sultan himself, was also a traveller. When he left for England in May 1929, Burhan gave him a poetic send-off.[43]

In sum, Burhan was a close disciple or teacher, close friend or colleague of Zanzibaris who travelled almost routinely to far-flung places. They were scholars who wrote (and surely also spoke) at length about their journeys in their travelogues (*riḥlas*). One such author, another exemplary Muslim modern and close friend of Burhan Mkelle, was Muhammad b. Ali al-Barwani, known as Abu Harith (1878–1953). In 1914–15, Abu Harith went on a tour of Egypt, Palestine and Syria, experiencing at first-hand the wonders of modern technology and the pace of urban life in Cairo, Beirut, Damascus and Jerusalem.[44] His views on modernity will be discussed later in this book (Chapter 7).

On the departure and return of his roaming companions, Burhan would be there, in the welcoming committee at Zanzibar port, ready to receive the returnee and host receptions in his (travellers were men, with few exceptions) honour.

The flavour of such a "welcoming reception" can be gained from the narrative by Burhan's close friend Umar b. Sumayt. Umar was Burhan's fellow student in their younger days and the two were close also in their later years. While Umar spent time in the Comoros, lived as a trader in Madagascar and undertook two long periods of study in Hadramawt, Burhan stayed at home and prepared welcoming poetry for his friend. While on his way home from his second sojourn in Hadramawt in 1913, Umar was unexpectedly delayed in Mombasa—or rather, he missed the ship's departure after indulging in an overly long round of religious and scholarly visits. Telegrams were hurriedly sent to Zanzibar, the welcoming gathering rescheduled, receptions rearranged and arrival poems given some extra time for polishing. After a 24-hour delay, Umar finally set foot on the Zanzibar landing pier:

> The pier was full of friends to receive us, and other sons of the homeland and its shaykhs, among them my father. Upon seeing his face, all the troubles of the journey faded away. We spent the entire day there, greeting those who welcomed us. On the morning of the third day, the seekers of knowledge and others of our friends held a celebration in the madrasa of our shaykh Abd Allah BaKathir, attended by my father and most of the students. After reading some of the texts of the Salaf, there was a reading of the poem by Ali b. Muhammad al-Hibshi, which starts [two *abyat* quoted]. After that, poems were read by Abu al-Hasan Jamal al-Layl and Ustadh Burhan Mkelle al-Qumri, […] and by Salim b. Abd Allah Waduʿān.[45]

Burhan also extended a long series of similar welcome greetings to *ulama* and *tariqa* representatives from elsewhere, and many of them will be encountered in the following chapters. In time, he saw them depart to teach or proselytize in new locations, again often accompanied with a verse from Burhan for safe journey and success.

Lastly, Burhan's own students left Zanzibar to become Islamic or Arabic teachers as far away as Tabora. In other words, in a world where intellectual life was marked by frequent departures and arrivals to and from the Hadramawt, the Middle East or Europe—so often portrayed as the very definition of the Zanzibari way of life—Burhan seems to have been a "constant", the stay-at-home exception to the rule. When his travelling friends and colleagues returned, he wrote poems in their honour, which he recited in welcome receptions to hail the "wisdom" and "light" they brought with them from afar.

Through the six decades that saw the start of colonial rule, the formation of colonial institutions, several rounds of urban development, the rise and fall of policies and ideologies, and the beginning of the end of colonialism—he was there, in the house in Malindi where his father had lived and died, where he himself also lived and died.

The death of Burhan Mkelle

Burhan Mkelle died on 27 Rabiʿ I 1368/26 January 1949, at sixty-five years of age. His passing was recorded in all the major newspapers in Zanzibar and his family received notes of condolence from the colonial administration, which particularly highlighted his role as an educator. The Director of Education sent a special note, which emphasized the central role Burhan had played during the interwar years, when education was particularly hotly debated in Zanzibar. The department remembered his "incalculable service to the education of the boys and girls of the Protectorate at its most difficult stage".[46]

For his funeral, Burhan's body was carried from his house the short distance to Jongeani mosque, where he had been teaching for decades. His bier was draped with the flag of the Shadhiliyya order, to which he belonged his entire adult life. From the mosque, Burhan's bier was carried to the graveyard in the neighbourhood known as Raha Leo,[47] in what was then a residential part of the Ng'ambo area. Burhan's son Ahmad has given a more detailed account in Arabic, where the role of the Shadhiliyya is highlighted:

> They [the Shadhilis] went with his bier until they reached the burial place. They buried him with their hands (*bi-aydīhim*) and instructed his departed soul (*talqīn al-mayyit*).[48] Then they gathered around the grave and recited the *waẓīfa* of the Shadhiliyya, which is the Mashīshi-

yya prayer, named after its author, the ʿ*ārif bi-llāh*, the Sufi master, bearer of secrets, the ʿ*ālim* Shaykh ʿAbd al-Salām ibn Mashīsh.[49]

The Shadhili honours bestowed on Burhan were, according to Ahmad Mkelle, offered in gratitude for the peace which he had negotiated between them several years earlier. The recital of the *al-Ṣalāt al-Mashīshiyya* was—and is—the practice of the Shadhili order upon the death of a devotee. The prayer conveys a sense of the Sufi outlook on life and death, the position of man in the universe, and the vision of the Islamic faith as an "ocean of *tawḥīd*" (unity). As will be evident in what follows, this outlook on life may seem at odds with parts of Burhan's long life as a "Muslim modern". For this reason, it is worth quoting the prayer at some length here:[50]

Glorified be your sustainer, the Lord for Glory and Mercy
Beyond all which they attribute
And Peace be upon the Messenger and Praise be to Allah,
The Lord of all the worlds
Thousandfold Peace, Thousandfold Peace
Thousandfold Peace in our hearts

[…]

Oh, First, Oh Last, Oh Manifest, Oh Hidden
Hear my plea as you heard the plea of your servant Zakkariyā
Carried surrounded by your Victory
And strike through me at the false, that I may destroy it
And plunge me in the Seas of Oneness
And remove me from the quicksands of unicity (*tawhid*)
And drown me in the Source of the Ocean of Unity (*tawhid*)
Until I do not see, do not hear, do not find and do not sense, except by It

Oh, Allah, truly he is Your All-Encompassing Secret who leads to you
And Your Supreme Veil raised before you between Your Hands
Oh, Allah, join me to his descendants and ascertain me by his account
And [let] me know his [with] the knowledge that saves me from the
wells of ignorance

That I might drink to repletion from the wells of graciousness
And carry me on his path to Your Presence

[…]

In the name of Allah, the merciful, the compassionate
Oh Allah, blessings upon the one from where the secrets are opened
And stream forth the lights
And in him rose up the realities
And in him descended the sciences of Adam [by which] all creatures
  are made powerless
And in front of whom all understanding diminishes.

4

THE ZANZIBAR GOVERNMENT CENTRAL SCHOOL AND "MODERN TEACHING METHODS"

Burhan Mkelle was a teacher, first and foremost. He taught at the colonial Government Central School in Zanzibar Stone Town for more than thirty years, from 1908 until his retirement in 1939. When he set out as a twenty-four-year-old Arabic teacher, the school was still new, having been founded in 1905 to teach a handful of boys from leading Arab families. This was the institution where Burhan Mkelle came to make use of his combined Arabic skills and pedagogical abilities. He developed teaching material for the young sons of the same "leading Arabs" who—as Burhan also noted—knew precious little Arabic themselves. He composed songs and supplications that were recited at assembly, instilling in students the "right attitude" to schooling. The Government Central School was an institution where a new generation of relatively young Zanzibari scholars could find a voice and a vision for a Zanzibari future. This was a rapidly expanding group. When he started out in 1908, Burhan was one of four teachers; when he retired in 1939 the colonial school system counted no less than 110 teachers.[1]

In this chapter, I argue that the government school was an arena where religious discourse was produced in a modern context. A recurring theme was the purpose of education. What aspects of religion were to be taught to young Zanzibaris, and how? This led to further questions, such as: How to teach religion? How to teach the language of the Islamic religion, Arabic? What teaching material is most efficient? Was the school system to aim for "functioning adults" in the sense of "respectable adults"? Or was the intention—and perhaps also the expectation from parents—that education should shape moral character and thus also the character of the nation?

Colonial and Islamic Education in Zanzibar

The history of the colonial education system in Zanzibar has been outlined in detail by Roman Loimeier and others,[2] and will not be repeated here. That said, a background to the colonial educational system in Zanzibar, and in the Islamic and African context, is needed in order to fully grasp the role of Burhan and his contemporaries. R. Loimeier outlines three distinct periods in the history of colonial education in Zanzibar, the first being the early years, 1905–21, when the colonial view of traditional Islamic knowledge was negative—if not outright hostile. The second period from 1921–40 was marked by several attempts at integration—between religious and secular education, from Arabic to Swahili, and debates over which subjects were "suitable" for which population groups. The final period, which does not concern us here, saw the partial incorporation of the Quranic schools into the colonial education system.

In an overview essay, R. Loimeier further concludes that the two first periods, i.e. from 1905 until c. 1940, were essentially "a series of crises" where the Department of Education (and the many schools established in Zanzibar rural areas) "failed to make an impact on education in Zanzibar".[3] Parents boycotted the new schools, refused to enrol their children, or—if they did—withdrew them in favour of the traditional madrasa.

Loimeier points to three main reasons for this failure. First of all, the colonial government introduced Latin script for Swahili, which was perceived by many religious leaders as outright unbelief. Furthermore, the very aim of the colonial project to be the one and only, all-encompassing educational system, alienated and threatened the teachers in the existing religious schools. Finally, and most relevant to the topic of this book, the government failed to introduce programmes and syllabi for religious instruction that could convince parents that their children would receive acceptable religious—and thus social—skills. Despite several efforts (especially during the 1920s),[4] parents withheld children from government schooling. In other words, parents feared that their children would not become adults who could command *heshima* (which, as noted in Chapter 1, had increasingly come to mean respectability rather than honour). They would, the parents feared, become lacking in *adab* (forms of behaviour), if we are to follow C. Mayeur-Jaouen's terms. The question to be raised, then, is what parents, and not least teachers, meant by *adab* in these debates. Was the school system to aim for "functioning adults" in the sense of "respectable adults"? Or was the intention—and perhaps also the expectation from parents—that education should shape moral character and thus also the character of the nation?

Burhan Mkelle's career fell within this "period of failure". He was, again to quote Loimeier, one of the pioneers of colonial government education, among those who "tried to find a place in the new system of education and to translate British concepts of education into Zanzibari contexts".[5] This raises the question of how Burhan, as an "organically grown" teacher, viewed his own workplace and education in general. With reference to the first reason for failure, we may ask how he, as an Arabic-language teacher, viewed the language issues that were so predominant and controversial in the implementation of colonial education. We have already seen that his sons stated that Burhan never spoke "a word of *kizungu* in his life", nor owned a European-language book, which may or may not be true and which may or may not have been opportune to write in the late 1990s. Moreover, with regard to the religious education debate, we may ask how Burhan and others contributed to syllabus development, and what such syllabi may say about changing views on the purpose of education.

These were questions which Muslim scholars and teachers, be they in the madrasas, Islamic higher education institutions, colonial schools and universities, or in any hybrid in between, grappled with for much of the colonial period. What is useful education? Is Islamic education—from the early *chuo* to long-standing institutions like al-Azhar—proving useful knowledge for the next generation? How can teaching be adapted? What should curricula contain, and who should decide this? What language should be prioritized? Arabic? The vernacular—Swahili? What script should in that case be used?

On a more fundamental level, these questions stand in for an underlying inquiry, for the twentieth-century scholar who pondered them, and for the historian who endeavours to trace their views. How is *modernity* to be understood? And how is education to prepare for it and be part of it? What constitutes a "break"—and from what? "Tradition"? What, if such a thing ever existed—let alone had clear demarcation lines—is "tradition"? As outlined in Chapter 1, this book is based neither in a "bewixt and between" argument of colonial ambition on one side and Islamic reformism on the other, nor is it a straightforward story of Islamic reform. Rather, what I will show is a new ideal being proposed, a new Zanzibari who was equipped to meet future demands due to his (and, by the 1930s, her) moral qualities, combined with secular education.

In the educational field, this may play out in many ways. On the one hand, we have what Robert Launay has called the "very self-consciously modern" ideas of schooling—particularly so in Africa where people (at least quite large parts of the population) were "stigmatized as primitive and consequently backwards".[6] As in much of the British Empire, the "development argument" is omnipresent when you read the files of the Department of Education in Zanzibar, as is the absolute faith in Western education—albeit racialized to fit British ideas of the "suitability" of the different communities to specific vocations.

The "development argument" was also very much present in debates that took place beyond the colonial structure, typically among scholars and intellectuals who were following the same debate in Egypt, the Levant, India or Indonesia, and who at times have been retrospectively labelled "Islamic modernists" or "proto-Salafists".[7] Notions of "development" or "progress" through education were also voiced by groups and actors that may—on a superficial examination, at least—be termed "traditional", in the sense that religious beliefs, practices and teaching were still rooted in an episteme where saints have power and spirits may heal.

As R. Launay also has stressed, the entire "traditional/modern" dichotomy is very limited if we confine ourselves only to the divide grounded in colonial ideology, whereby "tradition" denotes stagnation and superstition, as opposed to colonial progress.[8] As outlined in Chapter 1, I find that educational debates in Zanzibar are better approached as what C. Mayeur-Jaouen called cultural exchanges taking place in a modern context. These exchanges took place on the inter-Islamic epistemic level, where a line may be drawn between esoteric versus exoteric or rationalistic knowledge (*aql*), while at the same time noting that the two may easily co-exist (and indeed traditionally always have done) within the same educational system.[9] However, it is also clear that by mere chronological logic, the fully rationalist episteme reserves the right to label any esoteric element as outdated, counter-productive to "progress" or simply *bidʿa* (a wrongful innovation).

To a concerned citizen like Burhan Mkelle, ideas on the ultimate goals of education, as well as its means and methods, were formed through an ongoing navigation exercise between all of the above—voiced in different modalities and settings depending on the subject at hand and the audience.

The Government Central School in Zanzibar in the Interwar Years

The Government Central School (or GCS, for short) was the one of the early "flagships" of British colonial Zanzibar. When it opened in 1905 it was located in the Nyumba ya Moto in Forodhani (today Forodhani Secondary School), right next to the Sultan's palace. Its inauguration even made it to the "News from the Muslim world" column in *al-Manar*, where the editor, Rashid Rida, praised Sayyid Ali for the initiative. Rida heaped more praise on Sayyid Ali for being a man not bound by tradition: "He [Sayyid Ali] is virtuous, inclined to follow the path of the Salaf (*manhaj al-salaf*), contemplate the Quran, while questioning and researching its commentaries."[10]

However, Rida added cautiously, very much foreshadowing debates within the GCS, it remained to be seen just how modern this school would turn out to be: "We were very pleased with this great news, but [at this time] we do not know the school foundation charter (*qanūn al-madrasa*) nor its education programme (*barnāmij al-taʿlīm*)."[11] The language question that was to become so hotly debated in the following decades was also foreshadowed in an *al-Manar* news clip:

> The latest report, which may be correct, stated: There are concerns whether languages will include French and English and lastly Arabic, because its supervision is in hands of the Europeans (*al-Afranj*). [The report said:] This has not been verified, so hopefully some readers will provide us with verified news, then we will express our opinion on it.[12]

In the early years, the GCS primarily catered to boys from Arab families within or near the Sultan's immediate circle.[13] In the first year, a small cohort of seventeen boys attended. Student attendance grew, if not quickly, then at least steadily, in the following years.

The Government Central School relocated in 1924, this time to a brand-new building at Mnazi Mmoja, on the Stone Town edge of the creek that divided it from the N'gambo.[14] The building itself was constructed in the period 1923–25 and was designed according to colonial ideas of how a modern school should be: two spacious wings containing classrooms, and a central hall in the middle for assemblies and social functions. The architect, Mr P. C. Harris, was praised in a later note by the Director of Education, William Hendry, for creating a structure that led to the "immense improvement in physique of the Arab and African youth of the town".[15] One must also assume that the new building meant improved working conditions for the teachers.

By 1924, the population of Zanzibar Town was estimated at 39,000[16] and the student population was growing. In the coming years, the new Central School structure housed the Teacher Training School, a commercial school, as well as the elementary school for boys.

From 1926, a novelty was introduced to the colonial school system, in the form of education for girls.[17] The first iteration was called the Arab Girls' School, and taught Swahili and Arabic reading and writing, arithmetic, religion, geography and physical education. However, as Corrie Decker has pointed out, the school also heavily emphasized *adab* in the classical sense of etiquette, such as proper salutations and Arab traditions.[18] The school was open to Arab girls, but after some negotiation, Comorian girls were also allowed entry from 1928. From 1930, the school was known as the Zanzibar Government Girls' School, and in principle open to girls of all backgrounds who were envisioned by the government as "agents of development". During the 1930s, three more primary schools for girls were opened, in Chake Chake, Wete and Chwaka.[19] By the late 1930s, a small cohort of girls were trained as teachers, but—as C. Decker has shown—there was considerable "wastage" as girls dropped out of the profession upon marriage.[20]

It is important to note here that the male teachers in the GCS were generally very much in favour of education for girls. In the late 1920s and early 1930s, several articles appeared in the journal *Mazungumzo ya Walimu* that encouraged more and better education for girls.[21] Corrie Decker has perceptively underlined the ambiguous nature of the push for girls' education. Viewed from the male (Arab) side, it was a way to bring their daughters (often the offspring of African women) more into line with Arab, Islamic culture, while at the same time putting their Islamic modernist ideals into practice. Viewed from the female (African) side, it was a loss of authority over their daughters and granddaughters, which no amount of Arab respectability could compensate for.

Even more so than the schools for boys (who had, after all, also been educated before the British period, at least the upper-class boys), the educational facilities for girls reflected the colonial faith in literacy and secular knowledge as part and parcel of development—as well as their urgent need to increase the productive and reproductive power of the workforce. At the same time, irrespective of colonial ambition, education for Muslim girls was also becoming more widely acceptable in the Muslim heartlands, with notable female graduates in Egypt and Syria making their mark as educators themselves.

By the mid-1930s, the Government Central School was no longer the elite all-Arab boys' school it had been in 1905. Its funding was secured by the colonial government, although intermittent reports from various events and jubilees in Zanzibar show that donations were also made to the school by prominent residents. In 1936, for example, on the occasion of his Silver Jubilee (twenty-five years on the throne), Sultan Khalifa b. Harub donated 300 shillings to the school. Interestingly, the report in *Samchar* says that the school decided to spend the money immediately, taking all students and staff on a picnic to the grand home of Isa b. Ali al-Barwani in Bububu.[22] On the same occasion, the family behind the trading company Messrs Karimjee Jivanjee & Co. set up a scholarship fund to enable youngsters to further their education after government school. The report continued with an appeal to similarly "liberal-minded persons" to augment this fund "which has an extremely laudable object behind it". The stated purpose of the scholarship very much emphasizes the usefulness of education for the young person fortunate enough to obtain such a grant: "[it will] enable the aspiring, ambitious and deserving youths to fortify themselves with further education in order to fight the battle of life that awaits them in this bleak world!".[23]

Colleagues, friends—and Zanzibar moderns?

Colonialism in Zanzibar, like elsewhere, maintained, undermined or created new elites. As will be discussed in Chapter 5, the colonial structure was an employer that recruited a wide range of staff, from the Stone Town High Court *qadis* to the street sweepers and the labourers who worked on the many colonial construction projects. In the upper half of this range, we find the government-employed teachers, who were in fact an entirely new category of people when the Government Central School opened in 1905. The government teachers as a group have received comparatively little attention in Zanzibar history. A notable exception is J. Glassman, who analyses the schoolteachers pre-World War II as a liberal, unity-oriented intelligentsia.[24] However, Glassman views the teachers and civil servants as an elite whose rhetoric of unity was underpinned by a view of urban, Arab-influenced civilization that excluded large parts of the Zanzibari population and ultimately led to the "war of stones" (*vita vya mawe*) and the Zanzibar revolution of 1964. Here, the efforts of the new colonially employed teachers will be positioned not on the "Arab/non-Arab, urban/rural" divide, but as part of a broader discourse on the role and purpose of education in Muslim societies.

Thus, the purpose is less to investigate the recruitment and education of government-employed teachers in Zanzibar and their relationships to the colonial government, but rather to introduce the teachers as a group of individuals who in total made up what Glassman called "an inordinately influential circle of intellectuals".[25] I view this circle as a group whose relationship may have been forged by a shared workplace, and a shared experience of working within a colonial system, but—as will be discussed further below—whose outlook was formed equally by their involvement in other Zanzibari Muslim groups and organizations, and in a broad and far from clear-cut array of current Islamic religious and political thought.

The Egyptian Arabic teacher: Shaykh Abd al-Bari al-ʿAjizi (1878–1946)

Like several other Egyptians in Zanzibar, al-Ajizi was recruited during the reign of Sayyid Ali (1902–11), who was influenced by Ottoman and Egyptian ideas. Shaykh Abd al-Bari started his career in the Zanzibar Government Central School upon its opening in 1905.[26] He continued his work there until he departed for a leave of absence in 1928, never to return, due to failing health.[27]

From intermittent reports in the *Supplement to the Zanzibar Gazette*, it appears that Shaykh Abd al-Bari was generally well received by the Arab elite in Zanzibar, upon whose invitation he came in the first place. When he departed to Egypt on his first leave in 1908, a *hafla* (party) was held in his honour that gathered no less than 300 people, including teachers and pupils. Also present—and giving speeches—were leading members of the Arab community, like Muhammad b. Hilal and Ali b. Muhammad BaQashmar.[28] For more than two decades to come, Shaykh Abd al-Bari was the main Arabic teacher in the GCS, except for his periods of leave in Egypt. His recurrent departures for leave were marked by receptions hosted by the Arab Association, with poetry of praise and prayers for his speedy return. His impact as a teacher was noted also by his students, including the later scholar, politician and exile Ali Muhsin al-Barwani (1919–2006). Having been a young student in the GCS in the mid-1920s, Ali Muhsin's memoirs credit Shaykh Abd al-Bari with introducing proper Quranic recitation to the Zanzibar schools, along with Arabic calligraphy. While appreciative of this, Ali Muhsin noted that "we were taught by him only in the eleventh hour when his vigour and vitality had gone".[29]

We know little about Shaykh Abd al-Bari's religious and political outlook. Some authors have labelled him as a politically motivated teacher, claiming that he "propagated Pan-Islamism and Islamic Modernism against British imperialism" in his classrooms.[30] His educational background was from al-Azhar, but the details of his time there are not known. However, it is not unlikely that he was influenced by the educational views that were current in Egypt during the late 1800s.

These new Egyptian educational ideals were quite familiar to Zanzibari scholars who, as was shown in Chapter 1, subscribed to their journals, including *al-Manar*. The Egyptian intellectual Rifaʿa al-Tahtawi (1801–1873), for one, was adamant that education (of men and women) should be the core organizing principle of society as a whole. Not least, as will be further highlighted below, the impact of the Dar al-Ulum (est. 1872, fully functional from 1874) in Egypt, and its emphasis on teaching Arabic according to modern methods, became part of the argument, also in Swahili-speaking Zanzibar.

During his years in Zanzibar, Shaykh Abd al-Bari became not only an influential teacher of Arabic to an unknown number of Zanzibari boys, but also—as we shall see—an "assimilated Zanzibari" who was elected to commissions for various events, such as the Eid celebrations. His final departure was marked with several receptions and speeches of gratitude. The Arab Association[31] hosted one farewell gathering, while another was hosted by the Government Central School.[32]

Burhan Mkelle, as the second Arabic teacher in the GCS, clearly had a cordial relationship with Shaykh Abd al-Bari. He composed poems in his praise on several occasions when the Egyptian *ustadh* returned to Zanzibar from leave. "Your words are like rain that moistens and enriches the soil", wrote Burhan about his colleague.[33] We may also detect a tone of "developmentalism" in lines such as: "You returned to illuminate our school, and perfect our knowledge."

For Shaykh Abd al-Bari's final farewell reception, Burhan recited a poem composed for the occasion in which he praised his colleague for his knowledge and long service.[34] The poem itself centres on the complexities of the Arabic language and was composed in the *al-wāfir* metre. Burhan was thus showing off both his own skills and honouring his colleague by reserving this advanced praise for his appreciation:

> [...]
>
> So, today I say farewell to my friend, my dear brother
> The teacher who came to my country to build it based on the highest example

[…]

Oh, son of the Nile, you were like the Nile to us, we survived on your bounty
Even if our bodies are separated, we will keep you always in our hearts
So travel in the safety of God, back to Egypt, land of glorious achievements

Abu ʾl-Hasan Jamal al-Layl[35]

Unlike Burhan and Shaykh Abd al-Bari, Abu ʾl-Hasan Jamal al-Layl was primarily a religious studies instructor at the GCS. He was employed from 1916 to 1927,[36] which is exactly the period when the colonial government endeavoured to produce a "minimum curriculum" for religious instruction in the schools. We shall return to Abu ʾl-Hasan Jamal al-Layl in Chapters 6 and 7 when we discuss the formation of new religious associations and new rituals. For now, suffice it to say that Abu ʾl-Hasan was part of the Hadrami-Alawi religious network, and—like Burhan—a respected poet in Arabic. Having been born in Madagascar, he was also close to the "Comorian network".

Abd al-Rahman b. Muhammad al-Kindi

Abd al-Rahman al-Kindi was an arrival from Oman who took up work in the GCS during World War I. He was an accomplished poet in Arabic,[37] but according to Ali Muhsin, Abd al-Rahman al-Kindi had only "patchy" knowledge of Swahili, preferring throughout his tenure to speak Arabic to staff and students.[38]

Abdallah Muhammad al-Hadrami

Al-Hadrami was clearly among the most politically driven teachers at the GCS. iIn his memoir, Ali Muhsin al-Barwani paints al-Hadrami as a teacher whose political views were explicit in class, telling stories about the nationalist movements in India, Turkey, Syria, Egypt and elsewhere.[39] Abdallah al-Hadrami became headmaster of the Government Central School in the early 1930s. In Glassman's assessment, al-Hadrami was "perhaps the pre-eminent figure on the editorial board of the *Mazungumzo ya Walimu*, and certainly one of the most erudite".[40]

Language in the Zanzibari Colonial Education System: Teaching "Modern Arabic"

As outlined above, the hotly contested nature of language instruction has been viewed as one of the reasons why the colonial schools failed to attract students. However, from the very beginning, the colonial administration realized that Arabic had to be part of the curriculum, if only to placate the Arab elite whose sons were the first cohorts.

Burhan Mkelle was hired to the Government Central School as a "Native Arabic teacher", assigned with the task of teaching young students to be fully literate in the language that—in many cases—was spoken only by their fathers or grandfathers. His teaching load is difficult to assess from the sources, but most likely he was a full-time teacher, every day from morning to afternoon. The 1921 Special Report on Education[41] states that students were expected to have six hours of Arabic each week, throughout primary school. Even if we assume that Shaykh Abd al-Bari and Burhan shared this task, the teaching load amounts to many hours in the classroom every week, every year, as the student numbers grew. By 1925, Burhan had worked in the Central School for seventeen years. He was then one of seventeen teachers, and was charged with the Arabic-language education of almost 200 boys.[42]

The 1921 report had noted the need to introduce "sounder principles for teaching" of Arabic, in order to "achieve better standard than at present".[43] The question of how to teach Arabic to non-Arabic speakers was an issue very close to Burhan's heart, and one that he pondered in his pedagogical writings and in his poetry. However, in the corridors of colonial leadership, Arabic was rapidly falling in popularity, the preference clearly being Swahili—one language for all, and especially for all the East African colonies. The Director of Education, William Hendry, was crystal clear in his assessment in the 1925 report: "These youngsters need proper Swahili if they are to become productive citizens, not more Arabic."[44] The language debate that followed was long and polarized, and has been studied in detail by—among others—A. Ghazal and R. Loimeier. Arab elite families insisted on the leading role of Arabic in Zanzibar, whereas the colonial administrators saw only a Swahili-literate future, developing within the framework of Britain's East Africa empire. In essence, this was a struggle over the very nature of Zanzibari society: an Arab Sultanate or a Swahili-speaking part of the British East African empire? Opinions were still being voiced as late as 1939, as shown in the "Letters to the editor" section of *al-Falaq*. A typical argument was voiced by one unknown author, who stated that Arabs simply will not give up their sense of Zanzibar as an "Arab" country, and argued for the strong need to teach Arabic with the fact that this is "essentially an Arab country and ruled by an Arab Sultan".[45] The letter was a response to accusations in *Zanzibar Voice* and *Samchar* that African children (boys and girls) were in fact given inferior education.

Here, I will show how Arabic was taught in the Zanzibar Government Central School, on the basis of teaching materials and ideas around language acquisition. Since sources do not allow any insight into the results (i.e. how well students knew Arabic, how well they liked or how strongly they disliked the classes), this section focuses solely on pedagogical changes.

"Modern Arabic Teaching Methods": Arabic Language Instruction in the Age of Colonial Ambition and Islamic Modernity

How did the "Sibawayh" of Zanzibar, the Arabist whose level his sons considered "unmatched" by 2001, propose to teach Arabic? Burhan's own library is perhaps the best testimony to his own educational background as an Arabist. While he did own books on *fiqh* and Sufism—and not least a collection of modern Egyptian writers—the bulk of his (known) library is concerned with Arabic grammar, language and composition. Table 1 shows the books concerned with Arabic language in the Maalim Idris Collection that are known to have belonged to Burhan. The collection shows a library that contained both "classics" as well as "updated" literature, such as works by Jurji Zaydan.[46]

Having himself mastered the "standard" works of the classical tradition, this did not necessarily mean that Burhan considered them the ideal teaching tools for Arabic in modern Zanzibar. In an autobio-

Table 1: Arabic language-related texts in the library of Burhan Mkelle

EAP Ref No.	*Title*	*Title Translit.*	*Author*	*Topic/Content*	*Ownership Note*	*Publication Date*	*Publisher*
MIC-006	شرح عقود الجمان في علم المعاني والبيان	Sharḥ ʿuqūd al-jumān fi ʿilm al-maʿānā wa-l-bayān	Jalāluddin ʿAbd al-Raḥman al-Suyūṭī	Balagha/ rhetoric	Notes in the volume in Mkelle's hand	ND	Dār Iḥyā al-Kutub al-ʿArabiyya, ʿĪsā al-Bābī al-Ḥallabī, Cairo
	In the margin: حلية اللب المصون بشرح الجوهر المكنون	In the margin: Commentary on the poem Jawhar al-Maknūn by ʿAbd al-Raḥman al-Akhḍarī (d. 1546),[47]	In the margin: Aḥmad al-Damanhūri (d. 1778)	In the margin: Rhetoric/ eloquence			
MIC-043	حاشية شيخ الرفاعي على شرح العلامة بحرق اليمني على لامية	Ḥashiyyat shaykh al-Rifāʿī ʿalā sharḥ al-ʿalāma bi-ḥaraq al-yamanī ʿalā lāmiyya	Aḥmad al-Rifāʿī [d. 1182. Founder of the Rifaʿiyya]	Morphology	Burhan Mkelle Jumada II 1322H/ Aug.–Sept. 1904 Idris Mohammad Saleh 1976	1318H/1900CE	Muṣṭafā al-Bābī al-Halabī, Cairo

EAP Ref No.	*Title*	*Title Translit.*	*Author*	*Topic/Content*	*Ownership Note*	*Publication Date*	*Publisher*
MIC-045	مختارات جرجي زيدان	Mukhtārāt Jurjī Zaydān	Jurjī Zaydān (1861–1914)	Selected, edited essays by Jurjī Zaydān on Arabic language	Burhan Mkelle, ND Idris Mohammad Saleh 1978	1919CE	Maṭbaʿa al-Hilāl
MIC-048	حاشية الدمنهوري على متن الكافي	Ḥāshiyyat al-Damanhūrī ʿalā matn al-kāfī	Sayyid Muḥammad al-Damanhūrı [d. 1288 H/1871 al-Azhar, Egypt]	Urūdh, Arabic language	Burhan Mkelle 1321/1903 (??) Idris Mohammad Saleh 1981	1316H/ 1898CE	Muṣṭafā al-Bābī al-Halabī. Cairo
MIC-051	شرح شواهد ابن عقيل	Sharḥ shawāhid ibn ʿAqīl	ʿAbd al-Munʿim al -Jarjāwī Ibn ʿAqīl	Grammar, Ibn Aqil's commentary on Ibn Malik's Alfiyya	Burhan Mkelle, ND	1301H/1883CE	al-Maṭbaʿa al-Amīra al-Sharqiyya

EAP Ref No.	*Title*	*Title Translit.*	*Author*	*Topic/Content*	*Ownership Note*	*Publication Date*	*Publisher*
MIC-053	كتاب نيل الارب في مثلثات العرب	Kitāb nayl al-Arab fi muthallathāt al-ʿArab	Hasan b. Quwaydir al-Khalīlī (d. 1846, Cairo)	Morphology, the art of poetry	Burhan Mkelle, ND	1319H/1902CE	Maṭbaʿa Hindiyya, Cairo
MIC-074	المقامات الحريري	Al-muqāmāt al-Ḥarīrī	Abū Muḥam-mad Qāsim b. ʿAli al-Ḥarīrī[48]	Arabic language	Burhan Mkelle, 1321H/1903CE	ND	NP
MIC-096	كتاب درة الغواص في اوهام الخواص	Kitāb durrat al-ghawāṣ fi awhām al-khawāṣ	Abū Muḥam-mad al-Qāsim b. ʿAlī al-Ḥarīrī (Al-Hariri of Basra, d. 1122) Aḥmad Shihāb al-Dīn al-Khafājī	Grammar in verse form	Burhan Mkelle, ND	1299H/1881CE	Maṭbaʿa al-Jawāʾib, Istanbul
MIC-103	كتاب همع الهوامع شرح جمع الجوامع	Kitāb hamaʿa al-hawāmiʿ sharḥ jamʿ al-jawāmiʿ	Ḥāfiẓ Jalāl al-Dīn ʿAbd al-Raḥmān b.Abū Bakr al-Suyūṭī	Arabic language/ Grammar	Burhan Mkelle	1327H 1909CE	Maṭbaʿat Sādat bi-jawār muhāfadat, Miṣr

graphical fragment, Burhan Mkelle recalled the time he spent in Mecca in 1935 together with Shaykh al-Amin al-Mazrui (see below, Chapter 7), and a conversation about Arabic language instruction with the state *ulama* of Saudi Arabia. Here, he made a confession which may serve as a clue to his later efforts to make Arabic accessible to non-native speakers. It is a hard language to master (as anyone who has tried would know), and harder still when aided by outdated pedagogical material:

> The following night we were invited to a lecture-room in the government school (*al-madrasa al-ḥukmiyya*) to attend a lecture held by one of the professors there on the subjects of *ʿilm* and particularly on the teaching of the Arabic language. In this lecture we met many of the most prominent sons of Najd and Hijaz. After the lecture, our conversation continued on various subjects until we reached the topic of the futility of teaching grammar and morphology by the old methods and of the benefits of modern books.
>
> I told them that I had myself found it difficult to learn these two subjects (*naḥw* and *ṣarf*) and that [at that time] I told myself to strive to learn the sciences in the old system, until I would be able myself to write a manual of grammar and morphology, and the meaning of the letters, and to strive to make them clear until they are easy and no longer require a long explanation, including examples from Quranic verses to enable progress. [I also told them] that, when I reached this level of knowledge, by the grace of God, I was able to compose an *ajrūz*[49] of 1,000 stanzas on the subjects of *naḥw* and *ṣarf* and the meaning of the letters. One of those present asked me to read a few lines from the *Alfiyya*, and so I did. They said to me: "If the rest of the lines are like the ones you just read, you have truly succeeded in your endeavour." After this exchange we called on the lecturer, thanked him and went home.[50]

Here, Burhan says first and foremost that the "prominent sons of Najd and Hijaz" are authorities in the Arabic language—not unexpectedly, insofar as they are Arabic native speakers and geographically and dialectally near the origin of the language. More surprising is the consensus between Burhan and his counterparts that Arabic is difficult to learn, and futile to teach from the classical works. Furthermore, Burhan freely admits to having struggled greatly as a student, and points to the teaching material as the main cause of his difficulty. The overall message is clearly the need for a new pedagogy and curricula for teaching Arabic—a modernizing that would suit students and teachers alike.

Arabic by verse: *al-Alfiyya al-wāḍiḥa*

The outcome that Burhan refers to in his memoir is the work *al-Alfiyya al-wāḍiḥa al-mulaqqaba bi'l-jawāhir al-munaẓẓama*. This is a poem of 1,000 *abyat* (verse lines), modelled upon—but simplifying and making accessible—the *Alfiyya* by Ibn Malik.

The *Alfiyya* by Burhan was printed at least three times in the twentieth century. This was by far Burhan's most widely known work, being circulated and known also beyond Zanzibar. According to Burhan's son Ahmad, it was read by scholars at al-Azhar and other teaching institutions in the Arab world.[51] Two printed versions, as well as a manuscript copy, can be found in the Maalim Idris Collection (see Table 2).

Table 2: Printed editions of Burhan Mkelle, *al-Alfiyya al-wāḍiḥa*

EAP1114-MIC-072[52]	EAP1114-MIC-041[53]	EAP1114-MIC-116[54]
Al-Alfiyya al-wāḍiḥa Probably the first edition. No place, no date. 136 pages with index.	*Al-Alfiyya al-wāḍiḥa* 3rd edition, printed by Isa al-Babi al-Hallabi, Egypt. No date. 36 printed pages with index. Includes a photo of Burhan Mkelle.	*Al-Alfiyya al-wāḍiḥa* Manuscript version. Manuscript in lined notebook. No date. Possibly 1920s, by visual appearance only.

The purpose of this text is clearly not so much to change the sequence of Arabic language acquisition as the idiom in which it was taught. The actual vocabulary used for examples is more quotidian, relevant to students in the 1920s. However, it may be argued that this "modern" *Alfiyya* still shares one trait with its famous predecessor: it relies primarily on the listening mode of the student. The rhymed form appeals to the traditional, audiocentric mode of instruction rather than treating grammar mainly as words on paper.

Arabic by Modern Primers: Murshid al-Fityān *and* al-Tamrīn

In addition to his actual role in the classroom, Burhan Mkelle's main concern was to produce suitable teaching material for Arabic-language instruction. His first printed instruction booklet appeared in 1917, produced by the Zanzibar Government Print, and was meant for use in the higher grades. This was entitled *Murshid al-fityān ilāʿulūm al-bayān* and was meant for students who already had a firm grasp of Arabic. Here, the student was introduced to the style, grammar and metres of poetry, as well as to the verbal expression (recitation) of the Arabic *qasida*. Here, Burhan explains step by step the grammatical forms used as well as certain elements of its content. The *Murshid al-fityān* was printed in several editions by the Zanzibar Government Print, and later (after Burhan's death) by the Hallabī press in Cairo.[55]

More so than the *Murshid al-fityān*, Burhan's most widely used and known educational work was *al-Tamrīn*, a primer of Arabic grammar which placed emphasis on the speaking (pronunciation) of Arabic. The booklet was meant to suit students who knew about 1,500 words of Arabic. It was printed by the Zanzibar Government Print in 1918, explicitly for use in the government schools.[56]

In the preface, Burhan Mkelle (together with his co-author Saleh bin Ali) stated his reasons for producing such a book:[57]

> The non-existence in Zanzibar of books on Grammar written in simple language has made it difficult for Arab children who speak Swahili from their infancy to learn Arabic Grammar easily. Such books as are available here emanate from Egypt or Syria. They are invariably written in grandiose and abbreviated language and therefore serviceable only for purely Arabic-speaking pupils, while for non-Arabic-speaking children they are of little service. For this reason, we have endeavoured to furnish the children of Zanzibar with a book from which they can learn their first lessons of Arabic more efficiently than they hitherto have been able to do from the Egyptian or Syrian books. This is the object with which this book is written.

> We have copied from the English grammar books the simple method of explaining different grammatical terms, and of setting sentences as examples for the exercise of the pupil, but apart from that we have followed the ordinary course of Arab compilation and composition.[58]

The Arabic-language introduction has a somewhat different wording:

> The non-existence in Zanzibar of a book of grammar and easy pronunciation has caused great difficulties for Arab children. Since they speak Swahili during their childhood (*mundhu saghrihim*), they are not able to fully understand their grammar lessons. Egyptian or Syrian grammar books of various sorts have been present in Zanzibar but have not been put to beneficial use except with the children who speak Arabic and they are few. When it comes to the children who do not speak Arabic, they are in the majority and they have very great difficulties.

Here, the first thing worth noting is that, according to Burhan, "few" children in Zanzibar spoke Arabic from childhood. This, of course, is an indication of the ways in which successive generations of Arab (Omani and Hadrami) migrants would become Swahili-speaking in the course of a generation, but also of the relative diversity of the boys actually attending government school in 1918.

More importantly, it is worth observing that Burhan points to "grammar primers from Syria and Egypt" that had proved of little or no use for the Swahili-speaking children of Zanzibar. It is not clear what type of text Burhan refers to here, nor exactly what is meant by their "grandiose" language. He may have meant classical Arabic teaching material such as the *ʿAjrūmiyya* by Ibn Ajurrum (d. 1323), or the *Alfiyya* by Ibn Malik (d. 1274) with its commentary by Ibn ʿAqil (d. 1367), all of which were widely known and circulated in East Africa in the nineteenth century, and which—as we have seen—formed the basis for Burhan's own education.

In Egypt and Syria, these had partly been replaced by modern primers, produced by the Egyptian Dar al-Ulum from c. 1900. These works were mostly a product of the self-conscious drive to produce a "modern Arabic for modern times". Author, publisher and linguist/

historian Jurji Zaydan, one of the foremost representatives of the Arabic language reform, had much praise to offer for new dictionaries and grammars that appeared in the late nineteenth century. According to him:

> We still need many books of this kind, including philosophical approaches that are pleasing to the intellect and easily remembered, such as Good Thoughts by Jabr Effendi Dumit, professor of Arabic language at the Syrian Protestant College which we have referred to in al-Hilal more than once. We do not deny that many Egyptian and Syrian men of letters have been active in writing in this style, but we ask them to do more, and may God increase their reward.[59]

As the above table of Burhan Mkelle's library shows (Table 1), the works of Jurji Zaydan featured on his bookshelves, and there is every reason to believe they were well known and circulated in Zanzibar before Zaydan's death in 1914. One of the most widely used Arabic primers in Egypt—and among those explicitly referred to by Zaydan—was *al-Durūs al-naḥwiyya li-talāmidh al-madāris al-ibtidāʾiyya* (Syntax Lessons for Primary School Students). In the Maalim Idris Collection we find a 1913 edition of the *Kitāb al-Durūs al-naḥwiyya*, published by the Amiriyya Press in Cairo—evidence that these texts were known and circulating in Zanzibar in the early years of the Government Central School.[60]

This primer was authored by four scholars from the Dar al-Ulum in Cairo and was introduced into Egyptian schools as early as 1887 and revised in 1911.[61] The book was authorized by the Shaykh al-Azhar Muhammad Al-Inbabi, whose authorization is also printed on the front page of the book. By the 1920s, it had replaced the *Alfiyya* in many teaching institutions in the Islamic world, including the government schools in the Hijaz.[62]

Along with similar publications, *al-Durūs al-naḥwiyya* differed fundamentally from more traditional teaching tools like the *ʿAjrūmiyya* and the *Alfiyya*. Unlike the classical texts, it starts with examples and then goes on to define the parts of speech contained in the sentence. It also provides the students with sample sentences to analyse, expressed in standard Arabic. However, the new textbooks maintained the terminology of classical Arabic and introduced the students to the discipline of *iʿrāb* (case endings). However, perhaps the most major shift was that from "learning by ear" (aural learning) to "learning by reading" (visual learning). Hilary Kalmbach has pointed to this shift in Egypt from what she terms "audiocentric" to "ocularcentric", resulting in an entirely new pedagogy.[63] She concludes that what was condensed into one line in the aurally based *Alfiyya*, in the new ocularcentric primers became "multiple pages of explanation, review, and exercises".[64]

However, as Kalmbach also has shown, the new textbooks did not change Arabic-language instruction in the sense that the language itself underwent reforms. K. Versteegh, in his study of Arabic-language instruction in the non-Arab Islamic world, has also noted that the changes were more a matter of presentation than content, and he has concluded that the results were not impressive: "As before, Arabic grammar remained one of the most unpopular and feared topics in the curriculum."[65]

This sentiment may very well have been Burhan's experience in the Zanzibar Government Central School. As a primer for what Burhan Mkelle called "Arab-but-not-Arabic-speaking" children, *al-Tamrīn* was clearly more akin to the Egyptian Dar al-Ulum publications, in the sense that it was structured very differently from classical Arabic grammars. However, as is stated in the English-language introduction, the basic layout is copied from modern English grammar books, where grammatical terms are explained by their function and sentences given for exercise. *Al-Tamrīn* was thus a true modern hybrid, between modern English grammar and the modern grammars produced in Egypt—meant for children who did not speak Arabic in their daily life. It is also an example of generational transition: whereas Burhan himself learnt Arabic by Ibn Malik's *Alfiyya*, his students learnt from pedagogical primers.

Inducing Moral Character: Songs and Recitals in the Government Central School

Burhan Mkelle's life was very much that of a teacher, and his views on education were marked by his outlook on the role and function of the Arabic language as both access to the Revelation and a marker of *heshima* in the Zanzibari context. However, these views are also evident in the many poems and recitals he composed for use in the GCS and (as we shall see in Chapter 6) the Comorian School. Many were *mawlid* texts, to be recited by the students on religious occasions, as will be discussed below in Chapter 7, where debates over religious practice will be analysed.

However, many also clearly indicate his overall views on what education is meant to produce, i.e. what type of moral foundation the students are expected to build during their years in school. One example is the following school anthem, which contains advice (*naṣāʾiḥ*) for the pupils of the GCS:[66]

> If you search a little knowledge, you will benefit greatly
> By that, you will rise from low to the highest level
> Those who benefit from knowledge will rise
>
> [...]
>
> When you achieve knowledge, you will act with knowledge
> So stay with religion, perform the fasting and prayers
>
> [...]
>
> So seek what is good and rewarding from those who are high
> Be a brother to every Muslim, accept him and greet him
> Help him when he is in need, and you will be granted a greater reward

This verse links knowledge—i.e. the knowledge acquired in the Government Central School—with being a good Muslim. The element of action is also present; obtaining knowledge enables the student to act with knowledge, and as long as they remain steadfast in religion, they will "rise".

Among the songs used in the GCS, we also find this one, which more clearly draws a line between not only the individual benefits of knowledge, but also the societal:[67]

> The position of knowledge is an elevated one,
> to the highest ranks of *ʿilm* and *ḥukm*
> The flower of our world is the knowledge of our nation (*qawmnā*),
> yearn for it, and to be of service!

From an educator's point of view: Becoming Zanzibari Muslim moderns

This chapter has shown the efforts in the Government Central School to strengthen Arabic, and the debates over how best to do this. I view the educators we have met, Burhan Mkelle among them, as modern in the sense that they sought change, and that their ultimate aim was the self-mastery of the students. To achieve this, they had to know Arabic in the full, rational sense; not formulaically or as a function of rote learning. The teachers engaged in pedagogical arguments that we may view as part of a moral narrative; the students were to become exactly the Muslims Rashid Rida envisioned in the previous chapter. Knowledge is the key, and the self is the transformative agent, both for the individual and for society.

The interwar years were the period when Islamic knowledge was embedded into the Zanzibari modernizing project. This process was a fraught one, frustrating the British colonial administrators, the parents of the potential pupils—and the teachers themselves. This enduring frustration was never fully resolved. In many ways, the efforts of the Zanzibari teachers are best viewed as responses to the very same frustrations that Muhammad ʿAbduh voiced as early as 1897 in the preface to his *Risālat al-Tawḥīd*. Here, he recalled his period of teaching in Beirut, and his failure to convey to the students the nuances of theology:

> I became convinced that the lectures on this theme fell short of their objective and failed to benefit the students. The major works were beyond their comprehension and the intermediate textbooks were in the idiom of another time. I came to the conclusion that it would be more appropriate to present things to them in closer relation to their capacities [...].[68]

Epilogue: The Impact of a Teacher

Like many who spend a long period as a primary school teacher in a community, Burhan became a public figure, and—through his young protégés—an influential one. In his account of the emergence of secular education in Zanzibar, S. al-Mughayri states that no less than nearly two thirds of the youth of Zanzibar Town were taught by Burhan Mkelle.[69] The memoirs of Juma Aley offer another glimpse of Burhan the teacher, when Aley recalls his days in the Government Central School: "Even as a little boy in Standard IV in 1926 when he taught us 'Tamrin-Atfal' I could see with what deep respect Mr. W. Hendry, the Director of Education, treated him."[70]

Among the students who spent their early years in the GCS, three in particular must be singled out, as they were to become influential teachers in their own right, and also soon to be colleagues of Burhan Mkelle.

Juma Aley was born in 1915, in the same neighbourhood as Burhan. He grew up in Stone Town and studied with Burhan in the GCS in the 1920s. He then continued to the Teacher Training College (TTC) and to Makerere College. Later, he was selected to study at SOAS in London, where he spent the years 1944–46.[71] In the 1930s, he was an active contributor to the *Mazungumzo ya Walimu* and made his mark as a public intellectual.

Abdallah Saleh al-Farsy has already been mentioned. He came to the Government Central School in 1925, aged thirteen, and studied Arabic with Burhan Mkelle. Upon graduation, he proceeded to the Teacher Training College and became a teacher himself in 1933.[72]

Another young student who was to make a lasting impact on Zanzibar was Sayyid Omar Abdallah (1919–1988), later known as Mwenye Baraka.[73] Another Zanzibari of Comorian origin, he joined the Government Central School in 1928, and after graduation proceeded to the new secondary school and onwards to Makerere College. Later, he graduated from Oxford University and remained a public intellectual throughout his long life.

Also a student at the Government Central School during Burhan's tenure was Ali Muhsin al-Barwani (1919–2006). He went on to study at Makerere College, and later became the editor of the influential journal *Mwongozi*. His political career in the Zanzibar National Party ended with exile following the Zanzibar revolution. In his later years, he was best known for his translation of the Quran into Swahili.

On the occasion of Burhan Mkelle's retirement in 1939 from the Zanzibar government service, no less than two farewell parties were held. The first was hosted by the Government Rural Schools on 10 December 1938, to honour his role in building up the school system in the Zanzibar countryside. The main celebration was hosted by the staff of the Government Central School, where Burhan had spent the bulk of his career. As *al-Falaq* reported, "a large number of people attended" including the Director of Education, Mr W. Hendry, the long-term secondary school principal, L. W. C. Hollingsworth, and all the teachers of the central government schools. Abdallah al-Hadrami, who by then was headmaster of the GCS, gave a long speech in Arabic, and the English translation was reported in full by *al-Falaq*. In addition to expressing grief at Burhan's departure, al-Hadrami highlighted precisely the role of the teacher as a model for "good citizenship", and the usefulness of knowledge for the future—as well as the importance of Arabic in attaining this:

> [...] To us, you are one of the torch-bearers of knowledge, a model of good conduct, and an example of diligence and hard work. Throughout your long career you have unremittingly instilled into your pupils useful knowledge, you have inculcated virtue in all its commendable endowments and have taught good citizenship which is a necessary sequel to obedience to authority and the observance of the laws of the country. Above all, you have got them to love and appreciate all that is useful to themselves as well as to others. When we, therefore, stand before you to enumerate your noble qualities, we are only giving vent to what has always impressed us in your sociability, good bearing and your unassuming behaviour despite your scholastic attainments on the one hand and your high position as the Head of the Comorian Community on the other.
>
> Your contributions to the Arabic Language are inestimable. It would be enough to mention your monumental work in composing one thousand verses in the art of grammar—an achievement which was hitherto supposed to be the monopoly of Imam Ibn Malik—the greatest Arab grammarian that ever lived. In this achievement, you have enviably placed yourself on an equal pedestal with this immortal oriental scholar of Arab fame.
>
> In this connection, it is pleasing to mention your literary accomplishments in poetry, many of which have become national songs, and your sonnets in praise of the Holy Prophet, have become so popular that they are chanted by your countrymen of all ages and both sexes.[74]

The speech was followed by Abdallah Saleh al-Farsy, who recited a poem he had composed for the occasion. Burhan was then presented with the entire speech and the poem in a silver casket, with images of the school buildings embossed on the outside. There were light refreshments, of course, and the obligatory group photograph.

At the end, Burhan thanked the Department of Education for the thirty years he had spent in government service, and for the "handsome casket" that he was given as a present and which he would "cherish as a memento of a happy life spent among his colleagues and leave as an heirloom to his descendants". He also offered a prayer for the continued success of the school.

Burhan's influence as a teacher was also noted by Sultan Khalifa b. Harub, who, as we saw in Chapter 3, also included Burhan Mkelle as one of the readers for his Thursday *mawlid* events. As only one of two teachers (the other being Shaykh Abd al-Bari al-Ajizi, the Egyptian teacher), he was awarded the medal "The Brilliant Star of Zanzibar" in 1936 for his long service.[75] He was also granted the less prestigious Sultan's Jubilee Medal in 1937, alongside several other teachers.

As an intellectual and a religious scholar, praise in the form of medals was, predictably, of little importance to Burhan, if we are to believe the biography written by his sons as a preface to his *Diwan*: "The Sheikh [i.e. Burhan] wore these orders during these [awarding] occasions, but later only at official events and for events welcoming official foreign representatives (*za makaribisho ya wageni wa kiserekali walotokea nje ya nchi*)."[76] The fact that they mention the medals at all is perhaps best read as an indication that they were indeed tokens of pride, carried proudly (if rarely) by a long-term servant of the British-BuSaidi state.

5

MODERN JOBS

THE ZANZIBARI CIVIL SERVICE

The previous chapter outlined the Zanzibari educational system as a workplace that recruited a new type of scholar, the *mwalimu*, whose authority did not lie in his (somewhat later, her) religious authority, but in the hierarchy established by the colonial government.

The teachers were "salary men", and as such they represented a new form of authority. They were not the only ones: *qadis*, too, became salary men in this period—as did other actors in what I view in this book as participants in a self-reflexive discourse on religion. Several scholars have noted how the participants in the modernist Islamic discourse (or the moral narrative of modernity, to return to W. Keane's terms) were "middle-class", and how they aimed to shape Islam to their particular needs and preferences. D. Commins has shown this process for early twentieth-century Syria, emphasizing the role of the "middle rank *ulama*" as the main agents of Islamic reform.[1] While Commins' analysis is aimed at identifying the social roots of Salafism, his description of the typical reformist is recognizable in Zanzibar too.[2] He (at this time, the actors were almost exclusively male) was typically of middle status in the religious hierarchy, and of middle wealth. Most importantly, he was employed, often the first of his family to be so. His employment was typically mid-rank. He was influential in his circles, be they demarcated socially, ethnically, or in terms of family or class.

This description fits Burhan Mkelle and his colleagues in the GCS well. Burhan spent almost his entire adult life as a civil servant in the employ of the colonial state that was established upon the declaration of the Zanzibar Protectorate in 1890. This was a state that between 1900 and 1930 was finding its permanent form, as a highly hierarchical structure where European employees held the top positions, top salaries and the most lucrative benefits, such as paid leave and pension rights.

In this chapter, I give an overview of the employment situation our Muslim moderns found themselves in. Their employment, which will be discussed below (Chapter 6), reflected the emerging view of professional, social and cultural identities as something that could—and should—be *organized*. Another underlying assumption here, following Commins' argument above, is that employment in itself gave for a specific Islamic outlook that later in this book (Chapter 7) we will see as debates over ritual and magic practices in Zanzibar. Finally, the Zanzibari civil service brought members of many origins together under one common employer, which in turn may be viewed as a seed for a shared Zanizbari identity.

The "Non-European" Civil Servant in Zanzibar, 1910–1920

In the period between 1910 and 1930, the colonial state became the main employer of educated Zanzibaris. They were hired as anything from *qadis* to clerks, teachers and administrators in local bureaucracy. Under British-BuSaidi rule, the state administration was not only growing more complex, but also more ethnically diverse. In true colonial fashion, a complicated salary scheme was drawn up that regulated the employment, leave and pension of "European" and "non-European" staff, and the rights and responsibilities of civil servants. By the early 1920s, a system was in place that regulated the entire public sector as a workplace and which by then incorporated men (and a few women) from many ethnic groups in Zanzibar: Swahili, Goanese, Indian, Arab and Comorian, alongside recruits from other countries, notably India and Egypt.

Before the outbreak of World War I, the Staff and Salary ledgers of the Zanzibar government show that "native" staff consistently earned approximately one third of the salary of their European colleagues, who in general were placed in leading positions, such as "Director" or "Headmaster" in the Department of Education, or "Chief Judge" or "Town Magistrate" in the Judicial Department. Salaries for Europeans were increased incrementally according to seniority and additional education. Salaries for "non-Europeans" were increased too, but with smaller increments, as they were placed in so-called "subordinate" categories (Tables 3 and 4).

Table 3: Sample salaries, Educational and Judicial Departments, 1913[3]

Name	*Title*	*Annual Salary (RS)*	*Monthly Salary (RS)*	*Department*
S. Rivers-Smith	Director of Education	9,015	750	Education
Abd al-Bari al-Ajizi	"Egyptian teacher"	2,340	195	Education
Ali Ba Qashmar	"Native teacher"	744	62	Education
Abdul Rahman Mahomed	"Native teacher"	444	37	Education
Haythorne Reed	Town Magistrate	9,620	Uneven, due to leave	Judicial
Burhan al-Amawi	Qadi	4,200	450	Judicial
Ahmad b. Sumayt	Qadi	3,000	250	Judicial
Ali b. Muhammad al-Mundhiri	Qadi	2,760	230	Judicial

Table 4: Sample salaries, Educational and Judicial Departments, 1914[4]

Name	*Title*	*Annual Salary (RS)*	*Monthly Salary (RS)*	*Department*
S. Rivers-Smith	Director of Education	9,375	775	Education
Abd al-Bari al-Ajizi	"Egyptian teacher"	2,400	200	Education
Burhan Darwish	Arab Clerk	480	40	Education
Ali Ba Qashmar	Native teacher	780	65	Education
Abdullah Suliman	Native teacher	480	40	Education
Haythorne Reed	Town Magistrate	9,920	825	Judicial
Burhan al-Amawi	Qadi	4,200	450	Judicial
Ahmad b. Sumayt	Qadi	3,000	250	Judicial
Ali b. Muhammad al-Mundhiri	Qadi	2,760	230	Judicial

By far the highest non-European "earner" was the Sultan himself, Sayyid Khalifa, whose allowance featured in the salary ledgers like that of every other employee. His monthly allowance was a generous RS 10,000, which more or less equalled the *annual* salary of the Director of Education. Among other non-European "high-earners", we find various members of the Sultanic family who received "allowances", figuring in the salary ledgers under professions such as "uncle", "aunt", and even "children of great-uncle". The salary for being a (more or less distant) relative of the Sultan ranged between RS 2,000 and 4,000 per year, which was up to ten times the annual salary of a locally hired teacher.

Among "non-European" staff who actually worked, the *qadis* employed by the Judicial Department were clearly the biggest earners, reaching salaries of up to RS 4,200 per year. It is worth noting that this was almost double the salary of the "Egyptian teacher" Shaykh Abd al-Bari who was portrayed in Chapter 4. *Qadis* were clearly much harder to replace than teachers, a point that the colonial government was to lament on a number of occasions right up until 1963. Even so, the *qadi* still earned only about half that of the Director of Education, S. Rivers-Smith.

It is also worth noting that working in the city was a clear salary advantage, compared to the district courts.[5] The *qadi* of Chwaka, Sayyid Mansab b. Abd al-Rahman b. Muhammad al-Husayni (1828–1922), for example, earned a meagre RS 1,320 per year, despite being a highly respected scholar and even the co-founder of the Riyadha mosque in Lamu.[6] His colleague in Mkokotoni, Muhammad b. Khamis, made somewhat more, at RS 1,680 per year. We may suspect here that the salary difference between the two was rooted in actual caseload, the *qadi* of bustling Mkokotoni probably having a busier schedule than his counterpart in the more sparsely populated district of Chwaka. We may also note that both district *qadis* earned significantly less than Abd al-Bari al-Ajizi, the Egyptian teacher whose workplace was in Stone Town.

Another relatively well-paid *qadi* was Salim b. Ahmed in Pemba, who had a somewhat higher salary of RS 1,920 per year. In this case, a high salary was justified on the grounds that the government found it difficult to recruit personnel to postings in Pemba.

On the next salary step we find the court clerks, whose job description also required proficiency in Arabic, Swahili and in many instances also English. They were paid approximately RS 350 and RS 540 per year. The general salary range of the staff known in the salary ledgers as "native teachers", as opposed to other types of teachers, was somewhat higher, ranging from around RS 500 to a maximum of RS 900 per year.

By 1914, the school system in Zanzibar was still quite limited, with only five "native teachers" on the payroll, in addition to the "head teacher", the "Egyptian teacher" and one person who is simply referred to as "teacher", neither "native" nor Egyptian. The outbreak of World War I evidently had few repercussions on the growth of the

Zanzibari colonial state structure. The Department of Education, for example, grew to include nineteen "native teachers" in 1915, a radical increase from the previous year.[7]

One of the many new "native teachers" was Burhan Mkelle. Having started his service in 1908, we find him in 1915 as a so-called "Teacher, 5th grade" earning a salary of RS 40 per year. While the salary may have been a good income for the Mkelle family, his earnings were still less than half those of the "Egyptian teacher" Abd al-Bari, and less than one tenth of those of the Director of Education S. Rivers-Smith, whose salary also included generous wartime allowances for housing and vacations.[8]

Burhan's income was, as his sons noted in their biography of their father, a "small amount of income he received from the basic salary of a primary school", which due to his lack of self-indulgence, was enough to "keep two *shambas* and three houses".[9]

However, it was probably not—even at the best of times—sufficient to support an entire household alone. Burhan and several of his colleagues also taught in mosques and were probably renumerated somehow for that service. However, that did not preclude them from participating in efforts to raise their salaries and pensions.

World War I and the struggle for salaries and war bonuses: Unifying and dividing the non-European staff

The expansion of the colonial state during World War I was not accompanied by salary growth, despite the radical increase in prices, especially in the later war years. Prices skyrocketed as imported products became increasingly unavailable, and even local products became much more expensive.

The result was as expected; real salaries fell significantly. The extraordinary increase in prices during the war, combined with nonexistent pay rises, led a group of subordinate non-European staff in 1917 to send a series of petitions to the government, requesting a "war bonus" to make ends meet. These petitions are interesting for many reasons, as they are both the forerunner of what was to become an association for non-European civil servants, and they show the habitual British response of "divide and rule"—offering wartime bonuses to some groups but not to others.

The colonial government's salary, pension and leave scheme distinguished between non-European staff resident in Zanzibar and non-European staff not resident in Zanzibar. The latter were mainly Indians, as British protected subjects, and especially hired staff, such as, for example, the Egyptian teacher Shaykh Abd al-Bari. Thus, the non-European staff who served the colonial government were not hired on equal terms, as a "Goa-domiciled" servant, for example, was entitled to a longer paid leave than a "Zanzibar-domiciled" person. These differences had earlier led to a series of petitions, especially by the "Zanzibar-domiciled" staff, who requested extended, paid leave or—alternatively—to be registered as not domiciled in Zanzibar.

By 1917, the war price hike united the non-European staff in colonial service into a single front for increased salaries. In a joint letter dated 31 July 1917, the petitioners stated that:

> [...] since the outbreak of the war, the prices of the commodities have been steadily rising in Town, and since the last few months they have been further enhanced to such an extent that the cost of living is roughly 92 per cent over pre-war times. Articles of local produce and manufacture have also considerably risen in value with the result that a considerable strain is put on us all to meet these heavy expenses.[10]

The petitioners (154 signatures) added an appendix showing that the prices of necessities such as kerosene, wheat and sugar had increased up to 160 per cent from 1914 to 1917, while the price of chicken had increased a massive 200 per cent. It was, as the petitioners say, an "abnormal increase". They also noted that local employees of private companies, such as the Eastern Telegraph Company, had in fact obtained wartime bonuses.

The government-employed clerks (50 signatures) followed with a similar letter two days later. By 22 August, the teachers followed suit. In addition to the "current crisis", the teachers also invoked their special role in the future of the protectorate and their high skills relative to other groups:

> [...] we need hardly intimate to you the fact of our destined career in life, which though, honourable as profession as far as Education is concerned, is by far the most arduous function and a great health-sacrifice to its practitioners, especially in a climate like this. That is a grievous

> fact to remark that Teachers, notwithstanding the great hardships they undergo both mentally and physically, their qualifications in knowing three languages of English, Arabic and Swahili, including Mathematics etc. are very poorly compensated in their personal emoluments to such a degree that they are below the margin of many of the competent clerks in Zanzibar Government departments.[11]

The letter was signed by all the teachers at the Central Government School, including Burhan Mkelle.

In sum, these petitions may be viewed as both an expression of unity among the non-European staff in Zanzibar, across government departments and pay scales, but also as a clear expression of their disunity, insofar as the letters were sent and signed by each group separately. What it does show, however, is an emerging identity shared by the "salaried men" of Zanzibar. The fact that they are sent within days of each other clearly indicates a concerted strategy of action among the non-European staff.

In response, the Acting Chief Secretary and the British Resident were forthcoming at first, immediately granting wartime bonuses of up to 10 per cent of the salary of non-European subordinate staff, although stressing that this was "an act of grace and not a right"—in other words, it could be withdrawn at any moment, "at the discretion of the Resident", and without explanation. This was significantly less than the 20 per cent bonus given to the employees of the Eastern Telegraph Company and the 30 per cent salary increase awarded by the Bank of India. It was, of course, nowhere near enough to compensate for the actual price rise, and the government now started biding its time, awaiting a general instruction from London regarding war bonuses.

In March 1918, a new petition was sent, and this time the signatories represented all categories of non-European government employees.[12] Among the signatories, we find Burhan Mkelle, the chief *qadis* Ahmad b. Sumayt and Tahir b. Abi Bakr al-Amawi, the Egyptian teacher Abd al-Bari al-Ajizi, alongside Indian and Goanese employees—some signing their names in Latin letters, others in Arabic.

Again, the government opted for a stalling strategy, requesting guiding principles from Nairobi and London, all the while paying not a single *anna* in bonuses. By 18 October, less than a month before Armistice Day, the non-European staff sent a reminder repeating their request for extra allowances. Again, the signatories represented a wide range of ethnicities, professions and "salary classes" across the board of non-European staff in Zanzibar government employ. One may even interpret this as a "magical moment of unity" where acute shortages and price rises united employees across the multiple lines that the colonial government had introduced to divide them. It was also a successful move. In a circular dated 30 October 1918, the colonial government agreed to pay a wartime bonus also to non-European staff—and continued to do so into 1919.

This was a fleeting moment indeed. By June 1919, the Arab clerks and staff protested against being included in the category "domiciled in Zanzibar" under the new, post-war salary scheme, where "Africans" and others resident in Zanzibar were excluded from continued extra allowances:

> We the Arab clerks in the service of HHs Government [...] respectfully beg to point out that *Arabs* have never in the history of Zanzibar or British East Africa, been included in the term *Africans* [original emphasis]. [...] We humbly submit that like the Arabs residing in Zanzibar we are natives of Arabia and cannot therefore by any stretch of the imagination be included in the term Africans used in the said rule.[13]

The letter was signed by all the chief *qadis*, in Arabic and in Latin letters, and to drive the point home, they added in handwriting: "Arabs residing in Africa are not Africans but Arabs."

In other words, as the world returned to relative normality in 1919, so did the principle of divide and rule. However, as we shall see in Chapter 6, the fledgling sense of unity-in-disunity would return a few years later, when a new wave of associations swept through all levels of Zanzibari society.

The Zanzibar Non-European Civil Service Association and the Struggle over Pension Rights, 1928–1930s

As part of the drive towards development of the British colonies, the interwar period saw the reorganization of the British colonial system towards a more systematic ranking of locally hired, educated staff. As part of this, in the 1920s, the Colonial Office in London was working to streamline pension rights for both European and non-European employees in the colonies. Notes were dispatched, where the Residents and Governors were asked to outline details of their workforce—and in particular answer one main question: Who is or should be defined as a non-European civil servant?

Responses came flurrying back, as each Resident or Governor sat down to describe the particularities of the peoples serving the government in their corner of the empire. In Zanzibar, the British Resident drafted his response carefully:

> I have to inform you that in my opinion, a pensions law based on the "European Officers Pension Decree" is unnecessary and would not be suitable for the non-European officials serving in Zanzibar. Many of the elaborate provisions in the decree would rarely, if ever, be applied in practice to the non-European staff such as for example the rules governing mixed service. Transfer of officials even between Zanzibar and the mainland dependencies are extremely rare, in fact it may be safely said that more than 90% of the non-European officials of this government have served and will be likely to serve exclusively in Zanzibar.[14]

In June 1928, the Chief Secretary to the British Resident in Zanzibar received a letter from a new entity named the Zanzibar Non-European Civil Service Association. It was signed by the association's honorary secretary, Hussayn A. Bakhin.[15] The leaders of the association were clearly well aware of the ongoing process and wished to learn what changes were underway and to offer their own opinions on the matter. It is not clear exactly when this association was formed, but a safe assumption would be sometime between the petitions for wartime bonuses in 1917–18 and the mid-1920s.

The process was indeed underway, but it was a slow one. By July 1928, the government proposed a set of regulations, which included the following points:[16]

- Non-European officials are entitled to retirement. Within the category of "non-European", a distinction was made between "African" and "non-African". A non-African can retire with pension when he reaches fifty years of age or after thirty years of service, whichever comes first. If he is an African, he can retire at age fifty-five or after thirty years of service. It is unclear why this difference was introduced; apparently the government assumed that "Africans" did not age as quickly as "non-Africans".

- "African" is here defined as "a member of an African race or any tribal community permanently settled in Africa, and includes a Swahili, Somali, Comorian or a native of Madagascar". As we shall see in Chapter 6, this definition of "African" did not go down well with the many Comorian employees of the colonial government.
- Pension rights can be amassed by clerical staff drawing a salary of RS 150 per month or more, from the humblest clerk to the *qadis* and *mudirs*. Here, Burhan Mkelle clearly fell into the category of staff acquiring pension rights. By 1928, he was pushing forty-three years, and had twelve years of government service behind him. Having a pension to look forward to must have been an additional bonus.
- Pensions cannot exceed two thirds of the highest salary a person has obtained in his career.

The new regulations offered a special privilege to staff hired before 1914 and enabled some of the earliest 1890s protectorate hires to retire with a pension.[17] This included, for example, Saleh b. Ali, a long-time interpreter in the British Residency and also translator of several of the texts used in the government schools. Another early pensioner of the Zanzibar government was Sayf b. Khalfan, who had worked for the Zanzibar Government Press for thirty years and who retired with a pension of RS 94.5 per month. This special privilege also extended to the captains of the Sultan's ships HHS *Cupid* and HHS *Khalifa*, who retired after twenty-two and twenty-one years of service respectively.

Another retiree who—as was shown in Chapter 4—returned to Egypt on a government pension was Shaykh Abd al-Bari. According to his pension papers, he started his service in Zanzibar on 1 May 1905 and retired on 26 June 1930 after twenty-five years of teaching in the Government Central School. The list is also full of names of clerks, with names like de Souza, de Figueiredo, Rodrigues and de Silveira. These were clearly Goanese who had been recruited in the early days of the protectorate, and who could now retire with government pensions.

By 1931, the non-European officers' pension scheme was still a work in progress, but at least one revision was introduced. A new draft sent to the Secretary for the Colonies noted that there is "no reason for differentiating between Africans and Asiatics" when it came to retirement age, an amendment that must have pleased Burhan Mkelle and his fellow Comorians. The reasoning lays bare the colonial mindset of racial and ethnic categorization, stating that "Africans age, if anything, more rapidly than the Asiatics."[18]

The regulation of pension rights for non-European staff was finally adopted in Zanzibar in 1933.[19] The outcome, unsurprisingly, was that non-Europeans were entitled to lower pensions than Europeans (1/720 as opposed to 1/480 of total salary). In the coming years, the Non-European Civil Service Association pointed this out repeatedly, but the answer was the same: the system was not to be revised again.

One group that decidedly lost out in the new pension scheme were the lowest-ranking of all colonial employees: the street-sweepers, also known in the reports as "sanitation workers". Unlike the teachers, *qadis*, printshop workers, police officers and administrators, they were hired on a (repeated) short-term basis. Some, but not all, had a "work-book" which was meant to document their employment. When the pension scheme was introduced, many of them came forward to claim a pension for long service, only to be rejected for not having sufficient "proof" of their employment. In the ensuing debates, these men were referred to as "mainlanders" (which must be read as another term for ex-slaves) and as "old men", "not in the best physique". Some of the petitions are attached to the file and they give a sad glimpse of a group that was decidedly not included in the brave new world of organized civil service and well-regulated work. One Idi b. Hsanbari voiced his grievance as follows:

> For the last 14 years I have been a sweeper in the fish market. Two months ago, I was discharged from the service, for no fault of mine, without any bonus or gratuity. I am an old man, aged over 60 years. [...] I am without job, no other means of getting my daily bread. I sometime stayed for 2 days without food, for which an act of kindness, and I shall be forever grateful.[20]

Salary Men as Modern Men

The Non-European Civil Service Association must be viewed as one of the many associations that arose under colonial auspices and as a result of colonial ideas of how employment should be organized. Clearly, this was an association that was meant as a point of contact between employer and employee, colonizer and colonized, and not a representative organization tasked with negotiation. However, judging from the signatures on the letters from the organization, it was a very inclusive body that made no differentiation along ethnic or linguistic lines. It represented Goanese, Gujaratis, Arabs, Swahili, Comorians—so long as they were employed as civil servants.

The colonial civil service was an arena where the Zanzibari Muslim modern could come into his (and later her) own. They could form professional identities that went beyond faith or ethnicity, beyond neighbourhoods or even class. They could also lay claim to new modes of authority. That said, unity proved elusive for the salaried men of the protectorate, due for the most part to British colonial policy, but also because the associations formed held no real power and in fact had no real influence beyond direct communication with their employer. This was to prove very different for a new set of associations that emerged in this period: the ethnic and faith-based associations.

6

MODERN ASSOCIATIONS

ETHNIC AND FAITH-BASED ASSOCIATIONS IN ZANZIBAR

As described in the previous chapter, a new set of organizations arose from the colonial employment structure that emerged in the interwar years, notably the Non-European Civil Service Association. These were unions in the sense that they encompassed people who had a common employer, but not in the sense that they had any right to negotiate directly with their employer. They included people of different ethnic backgrounds (and—as the signatory lists show—many languages), but they were unable to produce unity in the sense of uniting a diverse workforce behind one common cause. That elusive unity was sought—and to some extent achieved—on a lower level, i.e. that of community, be that ethnic or religious or both. The interwar years were very much the age of associations in Zanzibar, as elsewhere in the Muslim world. Some associations were based in ethnic or linguistic origin, others in religious community. Some primarily acted as interest groups, while others sought to transform their community into Muslim moderns.

The "age of associations" was also marked by new societies that were political-ideological in nature, such as a crop of new associations (*jamʿiyāt*) dedicated to Islamic reform. The "*jamʿiyya*-model" was quickly adopted by long-standing institutions such as madrasas and

Sufi orders that chose to revamp themselves as associations. Developments in Zanzibar clearly parallel what I. Weismann pointed out in his study from Syria: a strong element of continuity between the earlier modes of organization (Sufi order/madrasa) and the new *jamʿiyāt*. In his study of Salafis and Sufis in twentieth-century Hama, he found that the Sufi orders, "the major conduit of latter-day popular piety", were superseded by the *jamʿiyāt*.[1] This superseding, the transition from personal links (often, but not necessarily based in esoteric authority links) to depersonalized formal groups, is what I here interpret as modern.

Also, in their time the new associations were from the very start associated with modernity, in terms of the organizational form itself and the causes they championed. In *al-Manar*, editor Rashid Rida championed the "association model"—or civil society organization—as one of the good lessons that Muslims could draw from the Europeans:

> Today, we see the East beginning to learn from the West how to create communal societies and corporations. The Japanese have been very successful in this field and have reached a level of maturity. The Ottomans and Egyptians remain in a state of childhood in this life of collective effort. Yet, without this effort, it is impossible for a nation to reach maturity. [...] [Voluntary] societies and corporations are the measure of a nation's progress and its life. This is indisputable. You should not be deceived by the brilliant achievement of one individual, or several, in some science or enterprise. If they do not find in their nations societies that appreciate their value and assist them into bringing to life the fruits of their brilliance, the efforts of these individuals will be wasted, and their abilities squandered.[2]

This chapter outlines the "age of associations" in Zanzibar and focuses especially on the formation and activities of the Comorian Association in Zanzibar. This was an organization that clearly had many of the functions of an "interest group" in the purely colonial sense. However, here I will view the Comorian Association as a community strategy, not in the face of colonial regulation, but as part of a broader agenda to formulate a cultural programme. To this end, the association engaged in a discourse that was both self-reflexive and taking part in a modern context.

This chapter also argues that the dividing lines between ethnic communities and "communities of commitment" were not as clear-cut as conceptual frameworks would have it. As will be demonstrated in the following, there was a considerable overlap between the "ethnic" associations and the religiously based ones, depending on what level reform was directed at: community, Zanzibari society, or a broader shift towards a "Muslim modern" East African in a global setting.

The "Age of Associations" in Zanzibar

Associations, clubs, unions: they were literally everywhere in interwar Zanzibar, organizing everything from the annual pilgrimage to groups of people with all kinds of common interests. The emergence of associations in Zanzibar started in earnest in the 1920s. Some had come into existence earlier—the most prominent being the Arab Association founded in 1911.

However, the 1920s was the decade in which an unprecedented number of groups—defined by ethnic origin, Islamic or other religious orientation, or leisure preference—could and would form an association. Sports clubs were early examples of the latter type of organization, and they represented a very popular new organizational form in Zanzibar. Here, as elsewhere in the British Empire, the colonial government considered sport a "disciplining" activity, shaping "moral" individuals into a disciplined workforce that could contribute to the economic growth of the colony. However, the colonizing powers were not alone in fostering physical activity. Throughout the Middle East, sports clubs were mushrooming and physical exercise was increasingly becoming a part of upper- and middle-class life—for men, but gradually also for women.[3] Muslim thinkers, too, emphasized the role of sports and athleticism (*al-riyāḍa*) in building the new, modern Islamic subject.[4] Moral self-improvement—as will be discussed in Chapter 7—was, by many scholars, accompanied by a notion of improving control over the body. However, the new remedy was not necessarily spiritual exercises but physical workouts. For example, the Syrian thinker Jamal al-Din al-Qasimi (d. 1914) advised several types of exercise for the believer besides the spiritual: running, rope-jumping, weightlifting, wrestling, boxing, football, gymnastics on parallel bars and—most beneficial of all—swimming.[5] A healthy body was a healthy spirit, according to al-Qasimi.

In Zanzibar, the British tended to view football as most suited to "discipline" the "African" segment of the Zanzibari population. However, as it happened, football became a popular pastime for young men of all backgrounds. As Laura Fair has shown, football really took off from 1910, and new clubs were formed faster than the reporters of the *Zanzibar Gazette* could follow. Then as now, tournaments were held at the Mnazi Mmoja grounds, drawing big crowds and producing heroes, and not least creating new arenas for social interaction across ethnic and religious divides. The colonial government struggled to keep up with the proliferation of teams (and their eager fans), and in 1926 set up the "Zanzibar Cup" as an annual event in the hope of imposing an orderly "league".[6]

Other sports were also growing in the interwar years. Cricket, tennis and sailing were the staple activities for Europeans and the urban elite. February 1928 saw the first-ever "swimming gala" take place in the sea in front of the Bayt al-Ajaib. However, as the *Zanzibar Gazette* noted, this was "still somewhat in the nature of an experiment".[7] Some of the sport clubs were ethnically based, like the Comorian Sports Club, whose leader Ibuni Saleh was known to be an able sportsman.[8]

Other organizational novelties were clearly brought by missionaries or were colonial imports—or both. One example was the Boy Scout movement, originally founded by the Universities Mission to Central Africa (UMCA). This initiative initially met with much of the same resistance as the schools; parents simply did not wish for their children to join. It was only in the 1920s, when L. W. C. Hollingsworth started promoting it in the government schools and Muhammad Salim Barwani championed it, that it gained some acceptance among parents.

Community associations

The interwar years saw the proliferation of community-based associations in Zanzibar.[9] With the exception of the Arab Association, a detailed history of all these associations has not yet been conducted, and will be hard to produce unless new material comes to light that details the internal life of each association. Suffice it here to say that the interwar years saw the emergence of a long list, which, if anything, demonstrated the many cleavages that existed within the respective communities. In addition to the Arab Association and the Comorian Association (to be further detailed below), the list included the Hadramout Association, the Coastal Arab Association (Arab Sahel Association), the Arab Hinterland Association, the Indian National Association and probably many more.

Shaaban Saleh al-Farsi noted in his account of the Zanzibari people that when the then Secretary of State for the Colonies visited Zanzibar, sometime between 1946 and 1950, he met with no less than seventeen leaders of different communities (*jumuiya 17 za makabila ya Zanzibar*).[10]

The community associations normally played the role of interest group in relation to the colonial government. Petitions for support, special treatment or exemptions from rules and regulations were frequently received, and most often rejected by the British-BuSaidi bureaucracy. A typical example was the petition by the "Arab Hadramaut Association" sent to the Director of Agriculture in February 1937. Seeking support for a *shamba* where the association could train young men for "useful agricultural work", the letter lamented that Hadramis who had contributed so much to Zanzibar had now fallen on hard times, being hit by bankruptcies, etc:

> Realizing that the prestige of the community would be harmed by so many people wandering aimlessly and mar the name of the community, the Association of Hathramat [*sic*] have decided to render such help according to the status of the persons concerned in order to train them to become useful citizens of their adopted home.[11]

The association asked the government for support for leasing the *shamba*. The offer was rejected on the grounds that the *shamba* had already been sold, but a bureaucratic comment showed the true worry of the government: if they were to offer monetary support, "other similar associations could rightly request assistance".[12]

Somewhat surprisingly given his activism in the Comorian Association, Burhan Mkelle was also a member of what was known as the Hadramout Club (or, as its membership card states: the

"Hadramout Klab", or in the Arabic headline, *al-nādī al-ḥaḍramī*). This is a strong indication that community association membership was not mutually exclusive—which in turn shows the fluidity of identity in Zanzibar at the time. It also underlines the modern aspect of the associations; these were entities which you could opt into (and out of), moulding identity both to obtain benefits but also to express something akin to "authentic selves".

The Comorian Association in Zanzibar: Islamic Reform by Community

The following history of the Comorian Association in Zanzibar argues that it had a much broader agenda than simply being an interest group *vis-à-vis* the government. Rather, its primary purpose was to change the ways in which Comorians in Zanzibar expressed and maintained their identity—as Comorians, as Zanzibaris and as Muslims.

Background: Comorians in Zanzibar, c. 1925: Conflicts and reforms

In the Comoro Islands, cultural practices such as the *aada* marriage (known in French anthropological literature as the *grande mariage*), and thus formal entry into the adult, lineage-based (and matrilineal) society, was a central identity marker, and Comorians who migrated to Zanzibar took their practices with them. The presence of a Comorian community in Zanzibar led to a practice whereby Comorian women were married to Comorian-Zanzibari men, whereupon both returned to the Comoros to "anchor" their identity through the wife's home village. As I. Walker has pointed out, in some cases the wife would accompany her husband back to Zanzibar, in others she would not. In any case, both husband and wife were then "safe in the knowledge that they could subsequently choose to retire to the home island if they so wished".[13]

Furthermore, as Walker has outlined in detail,[14] village/county (*miji*) identification was a primary marker of identity, and one that served as a contact point for new immigrants. While the former led to identity maintenance *qua* Comorian, it did not necessarily lead to cohesion among Comorians in Zanzibar. The system of county affiliation, and the ensuing rivalries, was outlined in Chapter 3, as were Burhan's mediation efforts. However, he was not the only Comorian who saw a need for greater unity. As one might expect, this system was becoming increasingly challenged in the first decades of the twentieth century, when calls for Islamic reform and Islamic unity were becoming increasingly prevalent in Zanzibar, and the challenge was coming from *inside* the Comorian community.

M. A. Saleh has viewed the confrontation as a generational conflict, between older Comorian-Zanzibaris who clung to the traditions of their forefathers and a younger generation who were embracing Zanzibari life and—implicitly—modernity:

> L'enjeu des traditions était tel qu'après la période de la grande dépression de 1929, un conflit de générations éclata ouvertement entre les jeunes et les anciens. Les premiers étaient pour la plupart des commis d'administration ou des lettrés laïcs et religieux. Ils prirent position pour la modification radicale, sinon la suppression pure et simple, de ces coutumes qui semblaient à leurs yeux, dépassées.[15]

The polarization resulted in two opposing groups: the *Yaminis* (right, representing the younger, reform-oriented set) and the *Shimalis* (north/left, representing the elders and traditionalists). As we saw in Chapter 3, this polarization also reached the Shadhiliyya, only to be reconciled by a poetic intervention by Burhan Mkelle.

For the Comorian community in Zanzibar, the question was really this: Should we continue spending money on extravagant rituals like the *harusi ya aada* and elaborate funerals, or should we start doing things differently? The latter option, then, would mean a significant loss of authority and influence for the traditional leaders of the *miji* organizations. Another potential outcome was that the Comorians become entirely assimilated Zanzibaris and lose their hard-fought status as a "community".

Another core question, linked to the first, was how Comorians should position themselves in the Zanzibari colonial context. As has been outlined by M. A. Saleh,[16] Comorians objected to being categorized as "African" in the colonial hierarchy, and those who could made use of their "Arab" lineages to claim the superior status of "Arabness". To obtain their goals, Comorians also laid claim to French protection, thus juggling two colonial identities, while at the same time situating themselves either as "Comorians resident in Zanzibar" (*Shimalis*), or assuming the hyphenated identity of "Comorian-Zanzibaris" (*Yaminis*).

The founding of the Comorian Association

The Comorian Association that will be discussed here was founded on 11 June 1924. It had a predecessor in a "Comorian Club" founded in 1917, but the complicated details of inter-Comorian strife (including personal misgivings) is too much to go into here. Rather, it is worth noting that this new association represented a clear ideological break from established Comorian practices. The rulebook of the association, printed in English, Swahili in the Latin script and Arabic, is abundantly clear about what was expected from its members. Paragraph four states that:

> Any person who has been elected member of the Association shall take oath or affirmation to the effect that he shall obey all the rules of the Association and that he shall not be a member of any of the Comorian County Societies (MJI) to which his parents may have belonged and that he shall in no case pay the traditional "KATA" (Marriage Tax) or "MUONOGELO" (Life-Tax) to any of his said county Societies.[17]

This was indeed a "breakout" group, choosing a new community over old ones, and a solemn choice to make. M. A. Saleh states that the formation of the Comorian Association was sealed by an oath made in the Comorian graveyard, where each member of the new association pledged personal fidelity to the cause.[18]

In addition to the rule against participation in county societies, the association had all the regular and formal rules of a modern association: the election procedures for president and other positions; the powers of an executive committee; and the regulations on what funds could (and could not) be used for. There were membership fees, which were initially set relatively high, but which eventually were lowered in order to recruit more members. However, there were also rules set for members to hand over preparations for family marriages and funerals to the association (who then, presumably, would contribute to the costs). Should a member choose to organize weddings or funerals with the county associations ("without reasonable cause"), he would be liable for a fine of up to RS 200.

A final rule worth mentioning, as it points forward to the discussion in this chapter (and surely also back to the conflicts among the Comorians) is rule number 15: "Every member of the Association shall try his best to be a peaceful and law-abiding citizen, and shall likewise be amicable to every other Community in Zanzibar." By 1926, the association had acquired a locale in the form of a building purchased from the Zanzibar government for RS 10,000.[19] It is not clear if this amount resulted from a funding campaign among its members or if one or more wealthy Comorians undertook to pay for it. Relations with the Zanzibar British government were apparently relatively cordial, but by 1927 the association nonetheless unanimously decided to appoint the French consul in Zanzibar as trustee for its properties, most of which were held as *waqf*. However, the relationship with the French consul turned out to be a fraught one at times. In 1934, for example, the consul decided to withdraw as trustee because of the apparent disunity within the Comorian community itself. The response from the Comorian Association was telling: they implored the consul to remain as trustee as the properties would otherwise revert to their earlier state of being under no legal jurisdiction.[20] The fact that the Comorian Association opted for its Zanzibari properties to be vested in French jurisdiction shows that they not only distrusted the British (who had relegated them to the category of "natives"), but also that links with the Comoros were close.

By 1932, when the rules of the Comorian Association were revised, its properties consisted of four plots of land and two houses. All income from these properties was to go to the Comorian School, "for the welfare and education of all Comorians residing in Zanzibar".[21]

The Comorian Association as a reformist organization

Among Burhan's papers can be found a short, two-page text entitled "A history of the Comorian reformist movement in Zanzibar" (*Taʾrīkh al-ḥaraka al-iṣlāḥiyya al-Qumriyya bi-Zinjibār*).[22] The account, clearly written in retrospect and based on Burhan's own participation in the process, places the origin of the movement squarely within the field of Islamic reform. He is even very specific as to when this drive started: "In 1343/1924, there arose among the Comorian youth and its men a spirit of community reform. In the forefront of this reform was the late Ahmad b. Muhammad Mlomri [...]."[23] In 1924–25, the purpose of these "young men"—imbued with the spirit of reform—was very clear, according to Burhan: "Together with their younger brethren, they reformed the community, purging the innovations (*bidʿa*) and outrageous taxes that some of their fathers had practised [...]." While not stating it outright, Burhan here refers to the *miji* counties and their practice of levying taxes for ritual purposes. However, it should also be noted that this text was written later in Burhan's life, when there may have existed a retrospective need to justify their efforts in more religious terms—either to place the association on the "right" side of history, or simply because Burhan had grown more reformist over the years.

The reformists first tried to enact their programme "from within", working with the *miji* organizations. This was unsuccessful, according to Burhan, and they realized that the only way to create a "fresh start" was to form a new association:

> When the people of the *nahda* [Ar: awakening, renaissance] saw that these illegitimate taxes (*al-ʿawāʾid al-mubtaʿida*) continued, and that their clubs (*hayʾātihim*) continued to grow, and people that did not withdraw from this economic system (*bi-niẓām aḥwālhim al-iqtiṣādiyya*) until the last of the competitor withdrew from the arena [i.e. they engaged in self-destructive competition], they founded the association which they named the "Comorian Association" (*al-Jamʿiyya al-Qumriyya*).

It is worth noting that Burhan here uses the term "illegitimate" or "unlawful" (*mubtaʿida*) for the charges levied by the *miji* counties. The terminology clearly indicates that the reformists viewed the old practices as both beyond Islamic orthodoxy, as well as divisive to the Comorian community.

Even more telling is Burhan's next statement that these practices were neither acceptable according to the example of the early Muslims, nor compatible with life in the "modern city" (*al-madīna al-ʿaṣriyya*). In other words, the *miji* counties, their taxes and the practices they were meant to fund were neither Islamic nor suitable for life in a new Muslim modernity as visualized by Comorian-Zanzibari Muslim moderns.

Gradually, says Burhan Mkelle, the Comorian Association was able to recruit some of the leaders from the old counties: "Then some of these upright men realized the truth of their calling and the purity of their intention to serve their cause and their homeland (*waṭanihim*)." Here, too, we can detect the dual purpose of the Comorian Association: to bring the Comorian population in Zanzibar more in line with reformist ideals, and at the same time serve the homeland for modernity. The question of what exactly is meant by "homeland" in this context will be discussed further in Chapter 8.

The Comorian Association leadership: Young and not-so-young employed men

The image of the "*Yaminis*" and its *jamʿiyya* format—the Comorian Association—as consisting mostly of young men, is not entirely correct. Its first president, Ahmad Mlomri (1873–1938), was well into his forties when he was elected. His leadership seems to have been both political and religious in nature. The choice of Ahmad Mlomri is also not surprising if we view the Comorian Association as motivated by Islamic reformist ideals. He was a widely travelled shaykh and Islamic scholar who had studied with none other than Muhammad ʿAbduh in Cairo. It is not at all unlikely that he was the one who initiated the debate in *al-Manar*, outlined in Chapter 2. He had also attended classes among reformist-oriented scholars in Syria and in the Hijaz. In Zanzibar, Ahmad Mlomri belonged to the circle of Ahmad b. Sumayt and Abd Allah BaKathir.[24] He did most of his Islamic teaching in the Barza mosque, which was at that time a powerhouse of what may be termed "reformist Sufism" in Zanzibar, and which Burhan Mkelle also attended. Another well-known reformist teacher at the Barza mosque was Sayyid Mansab b. Ali al-Husayni (to be discussed in Chapter 7). Yet another attendant was the young Abdallah Saleh al-Farsy, who later referred to Mlomri as the "shaykh of keys" to his understanding.[25]

Ahmad Mlomri died in Grande Comore in June 1938. His obituary in *al-Falaq* (which uses the *nisba* "al-Qumrī" rather than Mlomri) particularly highlighted his role as a leader of the Comorian Association, and as a close associate of many of the leading *ulama* of Zanzibar.[26] When news of his death reached Zanzibar, a special Quran recital was held for him in the Friday mosque, praying for his passage to Paradise. Burhan composed an elegy for his predecessor as president of the Comorian Association, highlighting Mlomri's erudition and scholarship, rather than his activism on behalf of his *taifa* (community).[27]

The first elected secretary of the Comorian Association was Haji Amir, known as Mzee Bwana. He too was a "salary man", an ex-colonial employee, who had served as interpreter for the British troops in East Africa during World War I. After the war, he settled in Zanzibar as a trader. Burhan found him worthy of mention in his *History of Grande Comore*, alongside other Comorian interpreters who were "diligent and truthful, and endured great danger".[28] Haji Amir's end came not in battle, nor in Zanzibar, but in 1928 on his *hajj* in Mina on the Day of Sacrifice.[29]

Yet another "salary man" in the founding circle was Muhammad b. Abd al-Rahman (d. 1943), who was another "product" of Hollingsworth's Teacher Training College and a frequent contributor to the *Mazungumzo ya Walimu*.[30] However, in the 1930s his perhaps most prominent position—and one most clearly indicating his reformist drive—was his role as "ethnographic expert" at the Peace Memorial Museum. For years, he gave talks in the museum and supplied "ethnographic data" and artefacts from the Zanzibar districts. His activities have been reviewed by S. Longair, who views him as a homegrown intellectual who supplied the museum's director, Ailsa Nicol Smith, with a view of Zanzibar history that meshed well with the British, but also as "one of its most important intermediaries and influential Arab thinkers".[31]

Burhan Mkelle was also getting on in years, having turned forty-one when he co-founded the Comorian Association. He was pushing fifty when he became its second president, sometime during or immediately after 1934, when Ahmad Mlomri had to resign from his position because of ill health.

However, Burhan remained president for only a few years. He resigned from the position in a letter dated 11 September 1937. He tendered his resignation due to "old age", and his wish to spend more time on his beloved *shamba*. Most likely, he was anticipating his imminent retirement from the Zanzibar Government Central School which, as we saw in Chapter 4, was effective from 1939. He thus respectfully asked to be "released from the duties as president of the Comorian Association".[32]

The composition of the Comorian Association leadership in its first decade exactly follows the profile which I. Weismann has shown for the new *jamʿiyāt* in Syria.[33] These were primarily men who were in salaried (and mainly colonial) employment. Their educational background was partly traditional (with the shaykhs whose knowledge was imparted in mosques and madrasas) and partly based on modernized educational material, mainly Egyptian. These were men who, as H. Kalmbach has noted for the graduates of the Egyptian Dar al-Ulum, embodied the habitus of ocularcentric teaching and discipline, both in work and life. They were neither *effendis* (European-trained professionals; doctors, engineers, specialists) nor traditional religious leaders, but representatives of a middle way. Like their counterparts in Egypt, who in Kalmbach's analysis were "significant contributors to the Egyptian project of modernity",[34] the founding figures of the Comorian Association clearly had a modernizing agenda. However, in Zanzibar one vital question remained unresolved: to whom does the modernizing project apply?

The Comorian Association and the Comorian School in Zanzibar, 1930–1945: Shaping the new Comorian Muslim?

> Oh Lord, grant our nation (*ummanā*) your rewards, and keep us from evil and misfortune
>
> [...]
>
> Ours is a model of happiness, so let us cheer for joy: Long live the Qumriyya[35]
>
> *From a song performed at the Comorian School*

The main activity of the Comorian Association was the running of the Comorian School. The rationale behind the Comorian School was to provide education for Comorian children of the same standard as was offered at the Government Central School. The aspiration to set up a Comorian School had been there since before the Comorian Association, dating back to at least 1918.[36] However, possibly due to the internal conflict among the Comorians (and possibly also due to several other requests to the French consul in Zanzibar), this did not come about until more than a decade later.

Burhan Mkelle held the role of inspector of the Comorian School for many years. This was an appointment by the French government who funded the school and whose responsibility it was that the curricula and teaching were kept up to standard. Children born to parents of Comorian origin in Zanzibar found themselves in a peculiar position after 1925. In that year, the Zanzibar colonial government included Comorians in the "natives" category, which, as I. Walker has discussed in detail,[37] had far-reaching implications for their options within the legal and educational system. In effect, Comorians were now subject to Zanzibar "native" legislation and their prospects in the educational system accordingly followed British notions of "suitability".

As a result, many Comorians opted to keep their status as French protected subjects, while at the same time pushing for "non-native" status for Comorians within the British system. A consequence was that Comorian children were not eligible for the education offered to "Arabs" by the Zanzibar colonial government. The outcome was the Comorian School, established in 1930. Rather than sending their children to the "African" government schools, the Comorians created their own, with French support, thus divesting themselves from the colonial efforts to create a comprehensive system of schools for "native" children.

Well before the establishment of the Comorian School, and well after, the Comorians in Zanzibar had a reputation for being strong educators. In the higher echelons of Islamic learning, towering figures like Ahmad b. Sumayt and his son Umar influenced two entire generations of *ulama*. As mentioned in Chapter 4, female teachers were also known to be particularly good teachers for young children. In his (quite rambling) mix of memoir and political commentary titled *Enduring Links*, Juma Aley noted that *vyoo* (madrasas for young children) were often run by "[…] middle-aged Comorian women whose way of life was reputed for their fear of God and attachment to the Quran and tradition which they imparted with such zeal and devotion to the little children in their formative years".[38] So good was their reputation that parents from other communities sought to send their children to a Comorian madrasa—often held in the homes of these formidable ladies, "with very poor light and sitting on the floor".

The Comorian School was located in Kikwajuni, in a premises known at the time as the "Saxi Building".[39] The school was intended to be a cornerstone of the Comorian community in Zanzibar and of the Comorian Association. The syllabus was the same as in the "Arab" section of the Government Central School in Stone Town, which clearly shows what level Comorians viewed as their rightful one, and what type of knowledge they wanted for their children. By the end of 1931, fifty-one boys and thirty-four girls attended.[40] The school was entirely a private undertaking, based on wide fundraising, run by the community itself, and drawing on teachers from within the community.[41] It received no support from the Department of Education, except for the sharing of syllabi from the Central School. From the French government, the financial support was initially limited to the salary of a single teacher brought in from Grande Comore, one Abd al-Rahman b. Said.[42] Later, in 1935, when the school ran into financial trouble, the French authorities agreed to provide the school with direct funding.

It is worth noting that there were probably more Comorian children being educated in Zanzibar (either in government schools or the Comorian School) than in the Comoros, where the educational system was suffering after decades of neglect by the French administration. In fact, as I. Walker has pointed out, the quality of the Comorian School in Zanzibar in the 1930s was "far superior to anything on offer in the homeland", and several families in Grande Comore opted to send their children to be educated in the Comorian School in Zanzibar.[43]

The educational aspect of the reformist agenda was a factor that in itself recruited Zanzibari Comorians to the reformist cause and to the Comorian Association. In effect, the reformists offered education as an alternative way to social advancement than the one offered by traditional Comorian *rites de passage*. Modernity, here in the form of alternative routes to social status, was a main factor that led to the relative success of the Comorian Association, albeit not without a struggle with the leaders of the traditional *miji* counties. A new form of solidarity that went beyond ancestral village belonging and alternative ritual practices that was understood to be in greater conformity with "proper Islam" led many Comorians to become "less Comorian" in the interwar years. The question then is: What did they become? Zanzibaris? Or Muslims among Muslims, no matter where? These questions will be discussed further in Chapters 7 and 8 below.

Muslim associations in interwar Zanzibar: Organized religious commitment

The faith-based associations in interwar Zanzibar differ from the community-based associations in a fundamental sense. First and foremost, being born into a community (Indian, Comorian, Hadrami) does not require a conscious choice or moral stance—the choice being rather to devote time and effort to community work. Choosing to take part in a faith-based association, however, is qualitatively different, as the latter type of organization constitutes a "community of commitment" that often means discarding aspects of identity generated by the norms and values of the first. A. Hofheinz has discussed this difference with reference to a nineteenth-century reformist Sufi community in Sudan, stating that:

> [...] a paradigmatic shift took place whereby the believers were asked to make an individual decision to turn around and leave their former ways and join a new voluntary association based on faith and individual moral commitment instead of merely following the community into which they were born.[44]

In the same way, I argue, these were fundamentally modern associations, insofar as they recruited members based on individual choice, and the ability of the individual to opt out of something and opt into something new.

Associations based on specific aspects of faith were emerging throughout the Islamic world during the interwar years. These appealed to different levels of "community"; from those recruiting from specific groups, to broader reformist orientations, via Sunni associations, to the Muslim Brotherhood and onwards to organizations that called for commitment to the *umma*—or even *al-Islam* itself. The Zanzibari reading public was well aware of this development. News about new associations and their activities featured regularly in *al-Falaq*[45] and—of course—in the Middle Eastern newspapers to which the Zanzibari elite subscribed.

The All-Muslim Association

The All-Muslim Association of Zanzibar (AMA) differs somewhat from the above "opting out/opting in" model. It was formed primarily as a "task force" in order to organize annual and recurring Islamic events and rituals such as the pilgrimage, Eid festivities and—as we shall see in Chapter 7—the *mawlid* celebrations. Several sub-committees were appointed every year to facilitate, organize, lead and—not least—fundraise for these purposes.

The *Supplement to the Zanzibar Gazette* (Arabic section) started reporting from the meetings of the association in 1926. In the 1926 report, we may read how "all Islamic factions in Zanzibar" gathered.[46] Reportedly, the factions agreed upon the need for a new umbrella association that could oversee the appointment of members to the various committees, such as the "*Mawlid* Committee", the "*Hajj* Committee", etc. The organization of formal committees (and the naming of members in the *Supplement*) may have been a colonial invention, but it was also one that spurred the formation of associations vying to be represented.

The annual Eid celebrations were the most important task assigned to the All-Muslim Association. Fundraising for the celebrations was an annual event, and benefactors had their names reprinted in the *Supplement to the Zanzibar Gazette*. The Sultan and the British Resident were the two main donors, but individuals and companies also contributed. Interestingly, the annual lists also contain the names of prominent Goanese who, as Christians, either saw this as an opportunity to show their community spirit or, perhaps more likely, saw the Eid celebrations increasingly as a national holiday for all Zanzibaris. By its all-sect membership and the increasingly "national" nature of the events they organized, the AMA had the potential to become a real unifying body in Zanzibar. However, as shall be discussed further in the following chapters, this did not happen.

The Young Muslim Men's Association

As will be discussed further below (Chapter 7), the journals of the Syrian-Egyptian intellectual Muhibb al-Din al-Khatib (1886–1969), were well known in Zanzibar, especially on matters regarding education. More relevant to this discussion, Muhibb al-Din was also among the founders of the *Jamʿiyyat al-Shubban al-Muslimin* (Young Muslim Men's Association, founded in Cairo in November 1927, with Muhibb al-Din as its first Secretary-General.[47] The YMMA (as it came to be known in Western literature) is generally considered one of the forerunners of the Muslim Brotherhood, whose founder, Hassan al-Banna, was also a member. From 1930 to 31, the YMMA in Cairo published a monthly magazine entitled *Majallat Shubban al-Muslimin*.[48]

The YMMA in Egypt was headed by (not so young) intellectuals and political figures from the *Hizb al-Watani* (Egyptian National Party) and received financial support from the royal family. The YMMA sent delegates to the General Islamic Conference held in Jerusalem in December 1931, which was the start of a long engagement of the YMMA in Palestine and of the internationalist orientation of the association.[49] Part of its oath was a pledge to strengthen solidarity between all Muslims, and the organization quickly had branches in Syria and Iraq.

As a contemporary observer, the German orientalist G. Kampffmeyer noted that the YMMA in Egypt was both nationalist and Islamic-internationalist.[50] Kampffmeyer also noted the YMMA's emphasis on moral reform, as well as the understanding of the Quran as a basis for moral culture as well as science and thought. In short, according to Kampffmeyer, the YMMA aspired to "religious and moral betterment" through breeding "a new generation of men who may be capable of the highest deeds to serve their country in every branch of modern life, in social interchanges, in education, in public life, in science, in technics, and so on".[51]

By 1932, the YMMA had a branch in Zanzibar, although the exact year of its foundation is unknown.[52] It is not clear who was involved in this association, but many of the younger generation of civil servants in Zanzibar were. One person who was actively involved with the YMMA was Salim b. Abd Allah Wadʿan (d. 1942), who at one point also served as editor of *al-Falaq*. He was a Comorian, with a Hadrami father who came to Zanzibar to study.[53] His activism also extended to the Comorian homeland, as he was among the founders of the *Jamʿiyyat Ikhwan al-Huda* (The Society of the Brothers of Guidance).

The names of the "established" generation are only incidentally associated with the YMMA in Zanzibar, in minutes from meetings published in *al-Falaq*. We also do not know exactly what the YMMA in Zanzibar propagated. That said, it is likely that it stood for the same moral regeneration as its Egyptian and Levantine counterpart; that is, abstinence from all things evil (alcohol, unlawful sex, gambling, etc.) and the promotion of all things good (Muslim unity, moral purity and conscientiousness in life and work). Thus, like the All-Muslim Association, the YMMA too had the potential to unify a new generation of young Muslim men in Zanzibar. As we shall see, this proved difficult.

Other associations

Several other associations were founded in this period, about which little is known beyond their existence. The *Jamʿiyyat al-Islamiyya* (The Islamic Association) and the *al-Jamʿiyyat al-Islahiyya* (The Reform Association) were both founded 1922. We can only assume that there were others that have faded into obscurity.

Comorian Sunnis and Other Sunnis: The Jamʿiyyat Ahl al-Sunna wa-l-Jamaʿ

One of the new associations founded in the 1920s deserves special attention, because it had the broader aim of uniting all Sunni Muslims, regardless of their community belonging and their age (i.e. it was not limited to "young" men like the YMMA). Founded in the latter half of the 1920s (some sources say 1927), the *Jamʿiyyat Ahl al-Sunna wa-l-Jamaʿ* (*Jamʿiyyat al-Sunna*, for short, and in Swahili) was an association that emerged from the environment around the Gofu mosque/ Madrasa BaKathir and the Barza mosque, and the employees in colonial service discussed above. In this sense, the *Jamʿiyyat al-Sunna* recruited from much the same pool as the Comorian Association, which, as we have seen, also consisted of *ulama* and civil servants. However, unlike the Comorian Association, the *Jamʿiyyat al-Sunna* voiced a reformist stance that reached beyond community.

A brief history of the *Jamʿiyyat al-Sunna* and its activities has been recounted elsewhere and will not be repeated in detail here.[54] Rather, my purpose is to investigate the overlap between an "ethnic" association and one founded in faith. In short, the *Jamʿiyyat al-Sunna* ran several schools and also provided teachers for secular subjects, including English-language training. It was also an active *daʿwa* reformist agent in Unguja and Pemba.

The first president of the *Jamʿiyyat al-Sunna* was Sayyid Mansab b. Ali (1863–1927).[55] His reputation as a scholar "with ideas that Unguja's scholars were not accustomed to"[56] gave the association a decidedly reformist orientation. It should also be noted that Sayyid Mansab b. Ali was of Comorian origin, being a grandson of Mwinyi Mkuu Sultan Ahmad of Moroni (d. 1875). He was thus very much part of the "Comorian *ulama*" of Zanzibar Town, which most likely played a part in the proximity that developed between the Comorian Association and the *Jamʿiyyat al-Sunna*. Upon Sayyid Mansab's death in 1927, Burhan Mkelle composed an elegy for him, which again emphasized piety over social and political engagement:

> He inherited honour from his father—Ali, and was covered in the cloth of piety (*taqwā*)
>
> He walked the straight path of the Sharia—and did not stray from it in life
>
> From his youth he was appointed *khaṭīb* for us—we were covered in pearls during his sermons.[57]

For the purposes of this discussion, it should also be noted that both Burhan's colleague in the GCS, Abu ʾl-Hasan Jamal al-Layl, and his close friend Abu Bakr b. Abd Allah BaKathir (to be discussed further in Chapter 7), were among the founding members of the *Jamʿiyyat al-Sunna*.

There was, in other words, significant overlap between the members of the Comorian Association and the *Jamʿiyyat al-Sunna*. Most of the leading members of the Comorian Association were also members of the *Jamʿiyyat al-Sunna*, including Ahmad Mlomri and Burhan Mkelle. When the Comorian Association opened its new library in 1926,[58] members of the *Jamʿiyyat al-Sunna* were present and were greeted specifically for being active reformist agents. Burhan Mkelle gave the welcome speech:

> Your founding of the *Jamʿiyyat al-Sunna* was [with the purpose of] promoting welfare (*al-maṣāliḥ*) and drawing together [people from] every Sunni *madhhab* to be involved and devote themselves to that purpose. We [i.e. the Comorians] are part of this *madhhab*, and our dearest wish (*ḥubbnā*) is to fulfil its every requirement. We answer when called [to it], and our hearts know neither doubt nor flinching (*wa-qulūbnā bi-lā taraddud wa-lā aḥjām*).
>
> We wholeheartedly thank your delegation for being here tonight and united in this purpose as we open our library (*maktabatnā*). There is no need for a celebration of this opening as we will be rewarded by pride and honour of having the *Jamʿiyyat al-Sunniya* present at the opening [...] In conclusion, we pray for the forgiveness of God Almighty upon us, and you, and all the Muslim, and upon our two societies to rise to fulfil their aims (*jamʿiyātnā ilā al-qiyām bi-mā rabaʿa maʿhim*). [We pray for] *complete harmony between the individuals in each unit until they become like one single association, united in good relations and mutual interest* [my emphasis] (*ḥattā taṣīr ka-jamʿiyya waḥida fī ḥusn al-ʿalāʾiq wa-mubādilihi al-maṣāliḥ bi-baʿḍihim al-baʿḍ*), and participate in all the events—religious or worldly—that they are called to take part in by their association, for great benefit and advantage.[59]

Burhan evidently viewed the two associations as having one single purpose: welfare and unity—to the extent that he envisions a future where the two associations are one. This may seem unexpected coming from the leader of one of the "ethnic" associations, but is in fact not so. As we have seen, Burhan strongly emphasized the reformist agenda of the Comorian Association too, albeit with the additional purpose of improving the "*watan*"—their homeland.

The social and intellectual links between the two associations were based first and foremost on personal friendships and mosque affiliations, especially the Gofu and Barza mosques. Also worth noting, with reference to Chapter 5 above, is the fact that both associations had several teachers (including Burhan) and other civil servants among their members, pointing to the "salaried men" as key actors in the formation of associations. One may say that schoolteachers were indeed a "new elite" by virtue of their common employer. However, their real modernizing agenda was formulated not only in curriculum choices, nor in fora like the Non-European Civil Service Association, but in the Islamic call to reform and welfare.

Moreover, and somewhat more surprisingly, the *Jamʿiyyat al-Sunna* found its recruits among people with a certain Sufi *tariqa* background. As we saw in Chapter 3, Burhan himself was a life-long member of the Shadhiliyya. Other members, like Abu Bakr BaKathir and Abu ʾl-Hasan Jamal al-Layl, came from a background in the Alawiyya. The uniting factors were the goals of the *Jamʿiyyat al-Sunna*, which its members could agree upon irrespective of their community or *tariqa* background. These were outlined as follows in a speech made by Burhan Mkelle, where he lamented the departure of the earlier "great scholars" of Zanzibar who were "among the foremost of the Islamic world". Their mantle is now assumed by the *jamʿiyya*, the modern version of an established tradition. While the departed scholars are invoked in this speech, the planned activities of the *Jamʿiyyat al-Sunna* point very much to the future. Seeking a good relationship with all the other *madhhabs* is listed first, then follows teaching and guidance, and—not least—*daʿwa*:

> It is not unknown to you, esteemed brothers of the *Ahl al-Sunna wa-l-Jamaʿ*, that we here in Zanzibar used to have scholars who were among the best scholars in the Islamic world. They were our foundations in organizing affairs of our *madhhab*. When we were gathered around them, we benefited from their light and their thoughts. And we would seek their advice and their fatwas whenever any issue would arise regarding religion and *madhhab*. They would respond with seriousness, forbearance and strength of opinion.
>
> Then, in the past years, God chose for them to enter the Final Abode, in mercy and sanctification of their souls. We lost them and we lost our companions, and our Association was not in existence when they passed away. Nor do we have anyone to do what they were doing for

us. By losing them, we were like a body out of balance. And our words were all dispersed and nearly blew away. And were it not for the efforts of the men of the Sharia and the madrasas, the honour of the *madhhab* would have waned from people's hearts.

But today, praise be to God, God has appointed men for us to set up the *jamʿiyya* that we were hoping to follow [in the footsteps of] these *sāda* [the earlier and now departed great scholars of Zanzibar]. We have had an urgent need for our association, the *Jamʿiyya Ahl al-Sunna wa-l-Jamaʿ*. They have made it their overall purpose to safeguard the interests of the *madhhab* and to maintain its honour and that of its founder forever. Among the rules we wish to build this *jamʿiyya* on is that of friendship and association among its members, as in the Noble Hadith:

[Hadith, 5688] The Messenger (SAWS) said, You see the believers as regards their being merciful among themselves and showing love among themselves and being kind, resembling one body, so that, if any part of the body is not well then the whole body shares the sleeplessness (insomnia) and fever with it.

We intend to realize many goals through the activities of the Association, now and in the future. We seek a relationship between the *Jamʿiyyat al-Sunna* and all the other Islamic *madhhabs* and to establish preaching and guidance at religious forums.

Furthermore, [it is the intent of the *jamʿiyya*] to spread the Islamic *daʿwa* to the extent of its capacity in the future.[60]

The Age of Associations in Zanzibar and the Islamic World: Reform of the Community—But Which Community?

The above statements show the emphasis placed by the *Jamʿiyyat al-Sunna* on Sunni unity in Zanzibar and maintaining the position of Sunni *madhhab*. However, the speech also stresses something else and something that is clearly elusive: improved relationship with the other *madhhabs* and a general emphasis on "Islamic *daʿwa*" to all. We see, in other words, a vaguely worded ambition that aims at both maintaining Shāfiʿi-Sunni values following the loss of the "great scholars", while at the same time forming an inter-*madhhab* unity in favour of "*daʿwa*".

This was to prove more difficult than the above speech might indicate. The tendency in Zanzibar was towards fragmentation rather than unity, at least if we are to judge by the number of associations. By the late 1930s, the plethora of associations and clubs was becoming bewildering to even the best-informed Zanzibari. At the same time, the established ones saw it in their interest to prevent new groups from forming associations dedicated to almost the same cause.

A typical voice is that of an anonymous letter-writer to the Arabic section of *al-Falaq*, signing under the name "al-Shambawi" (the countryside-person), who objected to yet another "Muslim Association". This one was formed on 29 December 1937 in the "Sunni Mosque".[61] The man behind the initiative was one Ustadh Ghulam ʿAli and the otherwise unidentified Imam of the al-Bahriyya madrasa. Al-Shambawi points out that there already existed—and had existed for "a number of years"—an inclusive organization known as the All-Muslim Association, the one described above as organizer of Eid celebrations. In his letter, al-Shambawi points to this organization as the only one where all Muslim communities on the island are represented, thus there is no need for another. If generational differences should be a point, he continues, there is also the Young Muslim Men's Association.

Al-Shambawi goes on to express hope that the founders of the new "Muslim Association" will:

> reconsider their movements and approach all proper and leading Muslims of this country to cooperate with them in the suggested cause unless, of course, the aim is to create some sort of competition and rivalry with the already existing associations and not to benefit Islam and its followers.

The author expresses, in a somewhat overbearing tone, that "we already have many Muslims associations" and goes on to list them: "the Arab Association, the Comorian Association, Jumiyyat Islamiyya, Jumiyyat el-Khayri, Jumiyyat Hadramiyya, and the Jumiyyat Ahl al-Sahil and Jumiyat Shuban al-Muslimin".[62]

It is interesting to note that "al-Shambawi" here equates the Arab, Comorian and Hadrami ethnically based associations with groups that are clearly formed for a distinct, Islamic purpose. Most likely, this was a common understanding in Zanzibar at the time: "Arab"—and by inference, Hadrami and Comorian—meant "Islamic", in this context Sunni.

A more open question is what was meant here by "Arab"—as indeed it was throughout the twentieth century in Zanzibar.[63] The

Ibadi Arabs (through the Arab Association) were clearly also the main drivers of reformism in Zanzibar, as A. Ghazal[64] has shown. However, as an identity, this was a less open category, insofar as "opting to become an Ibadi Arab" was less of an option than the dual membership "Hadramout Club"/Comorian Association that we have seen Buhan Mkelle held.

Another equally confounded reader wrote to *al-Falaq* in January 1938. This anonymous author signed his letter simply "A Muslim", perhaps an indication of an inclusive reformist outlook—perhaps just an easy nickname to further his cause.[65] In any case, the writer had seen the news about the formation of a new "Muslim Association" in Zanzibar, and was "surprised" to learn about this, as were "undoubtedly many Muslims in this country for according to my information no legally constituted representative meeting was convened to inaugurate this institution". He added: "The opinions [of the new association] represent the founders only, not all Muslims." In conclusion, he stated that the existing organizations should have been consulted before yet another was established.

As indicated above, Zanzibar was far from the only place with an overabundance of associations. In Egypt, where, as we have seen, Zanzibaris sought inspiration for educational reforms, H. Kalmbach has noted that new associations were formed with increasing frequency, many of them with names containing one form or another of the word *akhlāq* (moral, referring to a moral rejuvenation).[66] Kalmbach also noted that despite the overwhelming success of the Muslim Brotherhood in Egypt, by the end of the constitutional period, James Heyworth-Dunne[67] in the late 1940s could still document 135 Islamic organizations whose primary work was religious and/or charitable—very much confirming C. Mayeur-Jaouen's statement about the "moral turn" taking place in the interwar period. Here, Zanzibar was clearly part of the general development in the Muslim world.

Unity and Fragmentation in Associations: Personal, Community, or National Reform?

The proliferation of new associations inevitably led to calls for unity. However, as we have seen with the history of the Comorian

Association, even the community-based associations were the result of divisions that were not necessarily healed by founding an association. Traditional leaders did not give in that easily, neither in Zanzibar nor elsewhere. In the Zanzibari-Comorian case this meant the *Shimalis*, who quickly founded their own organization to act as a "counter-*jamʿiyya*". The rivalry (and probably back-stabbing and dirt-slinging) was both confusing and exasperating to the French consul, with whom the Comorian Association had vested the jurisdiction of its properties. In 1934, when matters came to a head, the French consul threatened to withdraw French protection. In his letter to the French consul in Zanzibar, Ahmad Mlomri, as President of the Comorian Association, was simply reporting the plain truth when he pointed out that "Practically all the local Associations have opposing parties among their respective communities."[68]

The polarization of the Comorian community in Zanzibar is best viewed as a mirror of a broader trend in the Muslim world. Tradition, understood as religious practice and the structures that existed to authorize, organize and finance such practices, was coming under increased criticism. The criticism would refer both back to the *salaf*, the early Muslim community, and to the demands upon each believer in modern life—a sentiment we saw echoed in Burhan's statement on the purpose of the Comorian Association.

In effect, then, the "reformist" faction of the Comorian community (the *Yaminis*), represented by the Comorian Association, aligned with organizations like the *Jamʿiyyat al-Sunna*. Or, put in another way, reformists sought out other reformists with whom to align their activities, but also their politics.

The quest for unity (organizational, religious, political, national) was high on the agenda for both the Comorian Association and the *Jamʿiyyat al-Sunna*. In a poem written probably in the late 1930s, Burhan expressed his views on unity and the goals to strive for—not wealth for the sake of wealth, but rather striving for improvement:[69]

> The hopes of all the island's parties are to cooperate with each other graciously
>
> And for old feuds to be set aside and reconcile the disputes over matters of wealth and responsibilities

> Wealth in the possession of the ignorant is of no benefit, to him nor his relatives (*ʿashīratihi*). Rather, it is like nothing
>
> He will be easily led astray by a swindler (*khabb*) ensnaring people to be led like livestock (*al-naʿm*)
>
> The homeland (*waṭan*) will find no benefit in its wealth in its striving for grand schemes as they appear

The original cause of the Comorian Association was—at least as narrated by Burhan Mkelle—not merely to further community interests, but to actually change the practices and identities of the Comorians in Zanzibar. The outcome, somewhat paradoxically, was a "streamlining" of (at least large parts of) the Comorian community into the general reformist tide that arose in Zanzibar and in the broader Islamic world. In the end, the argument that was voiced by the reformists was not one of Comorian traditions versus assimilation, but one of Islamic reform overall, as Muslims in the modern world. *Islah* (reform), it seems, was where *taifa* (community) integrated—but into what? Into a cultural identity that was uniquely (and nationalistically, and thus modern) Zanzibari? Or into a community of Muslim moderns anywhere? Before we turn to the most complicated question concerning the process towards a modern national identity, we must first turn to what changes these Muslim moderns actually propagated and implemented in interwar Zanzibar.

7

MODERN ISLAMIC PRACTICES

ZANZIBAR IN THE AGE OF CULTURE WARS

In Zanzibar in the early 1920s, the most high-profile Sufi of them all, Ahmad b. Ṣumayt, publicly went to have his smallpox vaccination in the colonial health clinic rather than placing his trust in fate, miracles, angels, saints—or God. He followed, in other words, the logic of Rashid Rida outlined in Chapter 2: trusting in God but tying the camel. The public example of Ahmad b. Sumayt did not, however, register far beyond the immediate circle of the Muslim moderns in Zanzibar Town. Throughout the 1930s, and well into the 1940s, resistance against the vaccination of schoolchildren (especially girls) was a recurring phenomenon throughout the protectorate.[1] It only abated slightly in 1945 when the colonial authorities made smallpox vaccination mandatory and threatened criminal charges against parents who refused. Beliefs die hard, and practices even harder. Those who set out to change them must have a clear message, strong arguments, the *zeitgeist* on their side, and—not least—powerful allies. Culture wars are hard fought and won harder still.

In this chapter I address a set of core questions. How did the *qadis*, teachers, community activists and *jamʿiyya* leaders assert their views of proper Islamic practice? How did their arguments line up with the fundamental reshaping of the self which in Chapter 2 we saw Rashid

Rida argue for to Zanzibaris as early as 1904? How did they go about "selling" this message in their respective communities and in Zanzibar overall? I seek to answer these questions in four ways:

1) By outlining the Zanzibari community of Islamic scholars, teachers and educationalists that served as community leaders. These men were frequently called upon to perform ritual tasks and implicitly thereby to endorse them.
2) By examining views on education as formative of moral individuals, as voiced by this segment of society.
3) By tracing lasting changes to ritual practice, notably the public celebration of the Prophet's birthday, the *Mawlid al-Nabi*.
4) By highlighting the efforts to curb practices, such as "excessive" funerary practices, and examining the ways in which these were defined.

Practices Challenged, Traditions Defended: The Muslim Modern and the Struggle for "Hearts and Minds" in Zanzibar

Anthropologist David Scott has alerted historians to the "darkness of the enlightenment"—and the ensuing "tragedy of colonial enlightenment".[2] The debates outlined in this chapter took place within a colonial context. However, my point here is not to argue for or against the darker sides inherent in the colonial project. Rather, I take it for granted that the "colonial enlightenment" as implemented in Zanzibar—the faith in schools, medical clinics, roads, museums, proper accounting and organization—was in fact one ideology on offer in a far greater "modernity market" that Zanzibaris could pick and choose from. Rather than viewing the colonial project as a tragedy, as Scott poses it, this chapter views the colonial project as an intervention among interventions; powerful, indeed, and oppressive, and with long-standing consequences for the colonized, but in no way able to fully attain the "hearts and minds" even of its most diligent employees. Instead, hearts and minds could be swayed by Islamic moral guidance, instilling in believers several different visions of a future Islamic community. The notion of the individual moral core as a cornerstone of society was one that was emerging throughout the Islamic world, with many voices being heard and heeded in Zanzibar also.

The Wahhabi voice as perceived in Zanzibar

On the global stage, the loudest, most distinctive call for "hearts and minds" came from the Wahhabi invasion of Mecca and Medina in 1924 and the subsequent establishment of the new Saudi state. The behaviour of the Wahhabis in the Hijaz, as well as their views on Muslim expressions of personal piety, reverberated in both the European and Middle Eastern news and created new factions among Muslim intellectuals. Famously (or infamously), Rashid Rida chose to take the side of the Wahhabis, and for a time set up shop in Jiddah to make the Wahhabi message palatable to a wider audience.[3] Wahhabi religious doctrines were also discussed in Zanzibar, as we shall see, but their presence in the Hijaz first and foremost impacted on the Zanzibari pilgrims who were now the guests of the Saudi state. The official perception of the Saudi state seems to have been one of fear mixed with a hint of disapproval.

Before the *hajj* in 1926, the *Zanzibar Gazette* deemed it necessary to remind the pilgrims that the Wahhabi religious police (*muṭawaʿīn*) were "more impolite (*afaẓẓa*), rude (*akhsan*) and more extreme (*aqṣā*) than the *muṭawaʿīn* of Oman".[4] Pilgrims were advised to refrain from smoking during their entire stay in the Hijaz, let their beards grow and trim their moustaches—all to avoid provoking the Wahhabis.

The pilgrims, upon their return to Zanzibar, also had stories to tell. Their homecoming was reported every year in *al-Falaq*, sometimes with anecdotal news about the Saudi governance of the *hajj*. In 1939, an Egyptian pick-pocket who had operated inside the al-Haram mosque was swiftly dealt with by the Saudi justice system. *Al-Falaq* reported the incident with an overtone of awe mixed with horror:

> With their characteristic swiftness the Saudi judiciary authorities did not allow a day to go by before visiting the deserved punishment upon the wrong-doer. His right hand was amputated in the presence of thousands of pilgrims and hung around his neck to deter others from similar escapades.[5]

The intellectual foundation of Wahhabism was also discussed in Zanzibar. A trace of controversy can be found in the November 1927 issue of *al-Manar*, when the Zanzibari Muhammad Abdallah Qarnah (Gurnah)[6] posed the following question to the editor, Rashid Rida:

> What is your opinion on a person who believes and openly declares that whosoever relies on the books of Ibn Taymiyya, the well-known imam, that his opinions (*qawluhu*) are not to be quoted or his works accepted/permitted, nor should he be appointed to be among judges or witnesses? On the pretext that this violates the consensus on sixty issues in the *madhhab* of the Ahl al-Sunna wa-l-Jamāʿ.[7]

Not unexpectedly, Rida responds that there is no reason why a scholar who relies on Ibn Taymiyya should not hold the office of *qadi*, nor be a witness in court. However, Rida emphasizes, the main criterion is that the scholar is a *mujtahid*—capable of forming his own opinion, and not relying solely on the opinion of others, including Ibn Taymiyya. The way the question from Zanzibar is phrased indicates that debate had been ongoing over Ibn Taymiyya's opinions, which are here placed in opposition to the generic Sunni position (the *Ahl al-Sunna wa-l-Jamāʿ*). However, it is not clear who the person relying "on the opinions of Ibn Taymiyya" was and who wished to exclude him from office.

One area where the scholars of Zanzibar clearly departed from the Wahhabi view was over the use of music and song. As we have seen, *mawlid* events featured not only recitals, but also secular songs like a national anthem. Even the—by all accounts—strictly puritanical Sayyid Barghash hosted concerts that featured selections from European operas.[8]

A prominent example of the Zanzibari endorsement of music as part of Islamic culture was the musical orchestra Ikhwani Safaa, founded in 1905 under the tutelage of Sayyid Ali b. Hummud and which is still active to this day. By the end of World War I, the Ikhwani Safaa was already an established and important part of Zanzibari cultural life, playing *taraab* music on public and private occasions. It was founded on the premise that no drunkenness or vice should be part of its performances, and that the ensemble should consist of men only (the latter was the case until after the 1964 revolution; it has since featured very famous female lead singers). During the interwar years, the Ikhwani Safaa regularly performed on secular occasions, like Sultanic *barazas* for prominent guests, but it also had a "clientele" among the urban elite Islamic scholars. For example, Ahmad b. Sumayt was known to attend their performances and invited them to play in his country house.[9] The *Jamʿiyyat al-Sunna*, too, approved of the Ikhwani Safaa and invited the orchestra to its gatherings.[10]

Al-Fath *and the Zanzibari Muslim Hearts and Minds*

Another important voice in the vision for a new Islamic society was Muhibb al-Din al-Khatib (1886–1969), a Syrian-born intellectual and publisher who made his career in Egypt. He became influential through his role in the Salafiyya Bookstore (*al-Maktaba al-Salafiyya*)—later co-located with Rashid Rida's *al-Manar* bookshop. According to Henri Lauzière, the bookshop was reformist-oriented, and came to use the term "Salafiyya" as a broad and multi-faceted reform programme.[11] Muhibb al-Din was also a prolific writer, on topics regarding literature, language and Arab and Islamic history. Earlier research has identified his works as Arab nationalist in tone,[12] others as an example of a wide Islamic cultural orientation.[13]

Muhibb al-Din was, in the words of S. M. Rizvi, a "secondary intellectual" in the broader world of Islamic reformist-oriented writers in the twentieth century. In many ways, he was, as Rizvi states, part of "the generation that served as a link in the chain of continuity of Islamic thought in the twentieth century Middle East"[14]—a position he very much had in common with Zanzibari "employed intellectuals" like Burhan Mkelle. Both men were, as M. Hatina phrased it in the title of the 2008 edited volume, "guardians of faith in the modern world".[15] H. Lauzière has stated of Muhibb al-Din that he "embodied the overlap between Salafi inclinations and Islamic modernism".[16]

Muhibb al-Din's most lasting influence came through the three main journals he edited: *al-Qiblah*, *al-Zahra* (monthly) and *al-Fath al-Aghar* (weekly).[17] *Al-Fath*, which Burhan and several of his contemporaries subscribed to, was first issued in Cairo in 1926, and continued publication until 1951. Unlike Rashid Rida's contemporary journal *al-Manar*, *al-Fath* was not a "one-man show", but rather a publication where Muhibb al-Din allowed multiple voices from all over the Muslim world, under his own editorship.[18] B. Lia, in his account of the Muslim Brotherhood, calls *al-Fath* the most important of Muhibb al-Din's journals.[19]

Among the most active contributors to *al-Fath* in the late 1920s was Hassan al-Banna. Another was Shakib Arslan, who we shall return to later in this chapter. The explicit intention of *al-Fath* was to "circulate the news and views of the Islamic worlds, to describe the good qualities of Islam and to refute the accusations levelled against Islam."[20]

The "attackers" here were perceived to be liberal, westernized Egyptian intellectuals. The defenders' views were often expressed in debates over education, a topic that, as we have seen, was also high on the agenda in Zanzibar. The profile of *al-Fath* was overtly political, viewing the Muslim world as one *watan* (homeland), as demonstrated by its reports from all corners of the globe. It also published regular reports from the YMMA in other countries, presumably including Zanzibar. During the 1930s, *al-Falaq* in Zanzibar reprinted many articles from *al-Fath*.

Views on colonial modernity

In Zanzibar, there were times when the colonial modernizing project was fully aligned with that of Muslim reformists, others when they were clearly clashing. They existed side by side, pushing for change, guided on the one hand by British developmentalism and on the other by an emerging Islamic morality. As will be shown below, the twain could, in fact, meet, and often did, but they could also clash—as was the case when the *Mombasa Times* in 1938 made the mistake of running a serialized version of H. G. Wells' 1922 bestseller, *A Short History of the World*. The text contained passages that may be read as insults to the Prophet Muhammad. The outrage in Mombasa reverberated in Zanzibar, where the editor of *al-Falaq* wrote a note entitled "Sacrilegious remarks". Fuming that while novelists, Darwinists and socialists (in that order) like H. G. Wells perhaps did not know any better, the editor of the *Mombasa Times* certainly should, he concluded:

> What surprises us most is the lightheartedness with which the *Mombasa Times* has quoted the despicable and hated paragraph in his journal published as it is in the heart of the Muslim world, knowing as it must have that it was bound to injure the Muslim feelings.[21]

Conversely, a case of moral-intellectual alignment can be found in the apparent endorsement by chief *qadi* Tahir al-Amawi and *Jamʿiyyat al-Sunna* founding member, Isa al-Barwani, of the Indian jurist Syed

Ameer Ali (1849–1928).[22] Upon the latter's death in England in 1928, the two leading Zanzibari scholars hosted a Quranic reading for his soul in the Friday mosque in Malindi, attended by Muslims "of all *madhhabs*" and Prince Abd Allah Al BuSaidi, the son of Sayyid Khalifa.[23] Syed Ameer Ali was best known upon his death as one of the main architects behind the Anglo-Muhammadan law as codified in India, through his 1897 book simply entitled *Muhammedan Law*.[24] He was also known for his 1919 appeal to the League of Nations, where he spoke on behalf of "Islamic States" and their right to self-determination in the new, post-World War I world order.

Partners in Progress: Changing Practice through Moral Guidance

Several studies have appeared in the past twenty years that detail the "translation" or "localization" of reformist ideas voiced by the Wahhabis, the "Egyptians", Indian printing presses and others to various parts of the Muslim world.[25] Others have highlighted the role of the Sufi orders in "filtering" the Wahhabi/Salafi message to make its core ideas acceptable in diverse local contexts. The Sufi orders, represented by their teachers and scholars, were, in other words, central to the localization of the overall Salafi message—with the adaptations needed to make it palatable.[26] In short, to return to S. Kaviraj's idea of multiple "modern accents" outlined in Chapter 1 of this book, several parties were engaged in formulating the Islamic modern accent. In the following, I portray the relationship between Burhan Mkelle and one main "formulator" of the East African modern accent, Shaykh al-Amin al-Mazrui. While close friends, they did not always agree on how this accent was best presented to the public.

Shaykh al-Amin al-Mazrui (1891–1947) and Burhan Mkelle

Shaykh al-Amin al-Mazrui, resident in Mombasa, is best known as a reformer through his editorship of the journals *Sahifa* (published from 1930) and *al-Islah* (published from 1932). *Sahifa* was the first independent Swahili-language printed paper, appearing in *ajami* Swahili (Swahili in the Arabic script)—two pages were handwritten by Shaykh al-Amin, printed to 100 copies and then appeared weekly.

Al-Islah was expanded to eight pages and appeared in *ajami* Swahili and Arabic. Both publications contained what K. Kresse has called "public critique, commentary and other forms of communal self-questioning",[27] and at times borrowed from—and fed into—ongoing debates in international journals like *al-Manar* and *al-Fath*.

As Kresse has analysed in detail, Shaykh al-Amin's publications were first and foremost marked by their educational stance, and their direct communication to population segments well beyond the learned religious elite. Like Burhan Mkelle, Shaykh al-Amin frequently argued for improved education, be that secular or Islamic, but his social critique went further and opened up debates on the position of women, and the pros and cons of Western culture and political systems. Kresse has analysed Shaykh al-Amin's writing in light of ongoing debates in the Middle Eastern press, and compared it to the work of the Lebanese writer and historian Shakib Arslan (1869–1946).[28] The life and career of Shakib Arslan was very different from that of al-Amin and Burhan Mkelle, as Arslan led a truly international life, especially after having been exiled from his native Lebanon in 1918. As H. Lauzière has pointed out, he "epitomize[d] the de-territorialized Muslim activist".[29]

As Kresse has shown, in both Arslan and Shaykh al-Amin we find recurring concepts like "striving", "work", "science", "knowledge" and "action", which underline their orientation towards self-transformation, and the building of a new, modern individual whose very moral fibre was to shape society—rejecting closed intellectual debates over theological or legal questions. Kresse especially singles out the conceptual pair of knowledge (*elimu*) and work/action (*kazi*/*kitendo*) as central to Shaykh al-Amin's writing.[30] These are also very resonant in Burhan's poetry—especially in the texts meant for students. Formulated in Arabic, the terms *ʿilm* and *ʿaml* occur frequently, but are most often tied to a supplication whereby God is implored to endow these traits upon the students. In both cases, they refer back to the characteristics of the righteous as formulated by Sayyid Fadl (introduced in Chapter 1).

Furthermore, Mkelle's songs composed for students, whether in the Government Central School or the Comorian School, convey the overall message that hard work and dedication will bring about knowledge, which in turn will benefit the community. Moreover, all three writers underpin their critiques (or, in Burhan's case, exhortations and encouragement) with Islam, and its need to reform and modernize—but on its own terms.

Burhan Mkelle clearly admired his friend Shaykh al-Amin, and their friendship seems to have been one based on shared experience and religious outlook. The two travelled on *hajj* together, and al-Amin was present during the discussion with the "sons of Najd and Hijaz" outlined in Chapter 4. Burhan Mkelle composed a poem in praise of his "brother, his dear friend" on the occasion of al-Amin's visit to Zanzibar in September 1923. Here, he praised the arrival of al-Amin as a blessing and a joyous occasion.[31]

Most likely, Shaykh al-Amin and Burhan Mkelle found in each other mutual inspiration in their common efforts to strengthen education for Muslims in East Africa. Burhan's approach was clearly more "hands-on", spending most of his day in classrooms, teaching in his Malindi madrasa or writing Arabic textbooks to improve the curriculum in the Government Central School. Al-Amin too, lamented the poor instruction given in Quranic schools, and repeatedly pointed out how other communities (like the Goans, Indians and upcountry Kenyans) had advanced well ahead of the Mombasa patricians.

Shaykh al-Amin and Burhan were both acutely aware that they were living in a changing world. The transformation was partly technological, as we saw in Chapter 1, and the skills needed to operate these technologies were core to future success. However, as both al-Amin and Mkelle point out, the transformation was first and foremost social. Long-standing traditions were no longer adequate responses, neither for the Muslims *qua* Muslims, nor *vis-à-vis* other communities who forged new, "updated" responses.

Burhan and Shaykh al-Amin also had a common employer: the British colonial government. Al-Amin was appointed *qadi* of Mombasa in 1932, and then chief *qadi* of coastal Kenya from 1937 until his death. Although Burhan's stint as a government employee was much longer (thirty-one years), they both represent what K. Kresse has called "ambivalence"—being both critical and integral to the British developmentalist agenda. As Kresse also argues, al-Amin's primary interest seems to have been with his community and its well-being (in every sense of the word: economic, educational, spiritual and political). The same can be said about Burhan, whose professional task it was to oversee the spiritual well-being of the youngsters of the community, i.e. the students.

As we saw in Chapter 6, Burhan and his compatriots in the *Jamʿiyyat al-Sunna* were also in agreement with Shaykh al-Amin on another key institution contributing to knowledge: the library. In his essays in *Sahifa*, Shaykh al-Amin repeatedly pointed to the libraries established by the Indian communities in Mombasa as being as vital to progress as their schools and hospitals:

> [...] we see the prosperity of the Indians in their many shops and their big businesses, and their very good schools and "libraries" filled with books of all disciplines, and their [own] newspapers which appear in the mornings and evenings, and their hospitals which assist us with free medication.[32]

However, an extant letter[33] shows that Burhan and Shaykh al-Amin were not always in full agreement. Their difference seems to have been more over form than actual content, as Burhan wrote to Shaykh al-Amin:

> I inform you that the issue of your newspaper *Sahifa* reached me, the volume that contains an article on prayer for rain, and I was very happy about it[34] because in this issue you promoted the revival of the Prophetic Sunna and admonish those who do not care about its revival. However, despite this joy, I disliked one aspect that you raised in your propagation, with regard to its intensity/harshness (*min haythu al-shidhdha*). I think there is no need for admonition as such severe advice because people often become repulsed by receiving advice given to them with severity and condemnation and if it contains exaggeration. That is why I don't see how you can reach your goal with *al-Sahifa* quickly unless you change the direction you follow now. Rather, what I see you reaching most quickly is the indignation of the public. May God forbid you to do that, as this is not your intention. But that which I prefer—and I am not instructing you—is that you use a softer tone in your admonitions. For it is not hidden from you what God Most High said, as conveyed by his Messenger: "Invite all to the Way of your Lord with wisdom and kind advice, and only debate with them in the best manner" (Q 1:125).[35]

In the same letter, Burhan also takes issue with Shaykh al-Amin for stating that prayer to the Prophet is not part of the Islamic faith. He warns Shaykh al-Amin that people will speak ill of him, which again will defeat the purpose. Interestingly, Burhan also adds that although he sympathizes with the Wahhabi message, he insists that prayer to the Prophet has its origin (*bi-aṣla*) in the religion. "Your Wahhabism is stronger and more forceful than mine (*wahhabiyyatika aʿẓam wa-aqwā min wahhabiyatī*)", Burhan writes—while implicitly also saying that Shaykh al-Amin would do well to keep some of his opinions to himself.[36]

In other words, Burhan is saying that efforts towards change will be more successful if one does not speak too harshly or appear too radical (even if one's actual opinion may be so), which will cause a backlash and people will refuse to listen. Rather, says Burhan, although he agrees with Shaykh al-Amin on principle, he advises a softer approach in order to reach the widest possible audience.

Higher Education and the Formation of Moral Individuals

There is much in Burhan Mkelle's career and writings that indicates a broader view of reform than merely that of education, the Comorian community or even Zanzibar. As we have seen in Chapter 4, he exchanged views with the Wahhabi scholars of Mecca (often finding himself in agreement with them), and he was an avid proponent of Arabic as a compulsory language for all Zanzibaris. We have also seen that his private library shows a wide range of literature, from classical legal Islamic manuals to Sufi poetry, to modern Egyptian authors like Jurji Zaydan and Shakib Arslan. The latter was quoted frequently by Burhan in his historical writings, as an authority figure on Islamic history.

Burhan Mkelle also composed poetry in Arabic in praise of such distinct modernist figures as the author and translator Sayyid Mustafa Lutfi al-Manfaluti of Egypt (1876–1924),[37] who was mostly known for his short stories, his emotionally laden style and for giving an Arabic-language voice to nineteenth-century French short stories.[38]

Last, but not least, he corresponded with publishers of journals that were clearly reformist-oriented. One case in point is a long Arabic letter from Burhan to Muhibb al-Din al-Khatib as editor of *al-Fath*. The date of the letter is not known, but in the text Burhan refers to Ibn Saud as "king of Hijaz and Najd", which indicates that it was written before the 1932 unification of the two kingdoms into Saudi Arabia. Most probably, the letter is dated around 1929–30:[39]

> Reference is made to issue number 1859184 of the *Fatḥ* [*al-Fatḥ al-Aghar*], entitled: "When will the Muslims have schools, and what is the way to that end?" signed by the virtuous Muhammad Fath Allah Darwish. In [that article] can be found a suggestion which the author made to King Abd al-Aziz Al Saud. I praise God Most High for the clarity of this advice in your newspaper, which specializes in the service of the Islamic religion, supporting and defending it. The proposal is that the king [i.e. Ibn Saud] found an Islamic University in Mecca, to be open for entry for the sons of Muslims, of all races, who will graduate as qualified men, skilled in professions that are useful to themselves, and to their homelands. [...]
>
> God willing, His Majesty the King will open this proposed university, and make it into an institution that does not violate the spirit of the Islamic religion in any way. He [Ibn Saud] needs to be mindful of the good of Muslims all over the world, as well as of what is mentioned today in the pious calls for security and peace in the Hijaz, and enjoin for its people what is right, enjoining five prayers at the right time. True Muslims know that this university—should it become a reality—will be an antidote to the disease that has spread rapidly among the sons of Muslims and [is] destroying them. There is only one reason for this [disease] in the Islamic world, and that is (because) they leave their Islamic faith when they are sent to Arab universities, to receive education in modern sciences that benefit them and their families. [...] Most of the graduates from these universities have lost their Islamic ethics (*akhlāq*) which they learnt for years in the madrasas.
>
> This type of learning has led them astray, and they have learnt only vanity. Undoubtedly, if they would hold on to the morals of their forefather [...], their moral standing in society would not be compromised [...] no matter what they gain of academic titles, and they will reach the point where sons follow generations in perfect harmony. But if they become atheists—as is the case for some of them today—they will not be appreciated by their own people, or their country-

> men, but viewed with distaste and antipathy, because the Muslims, who have a pure Islamic upbringing, cannot tolerate the disdain of these atheists. When [the young men] receive these degrees, they will view their countrymen with nothing but contempt and disrespect—even their own parents who sent them to school and who sent them off to seek modern education, spending not insignificant amounts [on that], even when they had not a single dirham. Then, the fathers will be worried when they see their sons [turn out] different from what they intended, and they feel that they have brought upon themselves an unforgivable sin. [The fathers] feel that they have committed an unforgivable crime, they regret the waste of efforts, and lose faith in education. [...] Wherever such disparity in morals occurs between fathers and sons, a gap will open between them, and disobedience and discord will remain for the rest of their lives.[40]

The aim here is clearly to support the foundation of an "Islamic University" in the Hijaz, under Saudi tutelage. This was an idea that had been launched before World War I by the Ottomans, and by 1913 preparations were well underway for the founding of the "Salah al-Din al-Ayubi University" in Medina. From the start, this was very much envisioned as an Islamic-internationalist institution, and among its most outspoken proponents was Shakib Arslan. However, the outbreak of war and the collapse of the Ottoman Empire meant that the original plans were shelved—only to be revived once more after the Saudi takeover.[41] Prominent, but ideologically different figures like Shakib Arslan and Rashid Rida both championed the Saudi cause as a future educational power—although Arslan added the reservation that the Wahhabis were at times too extreme in their doctrine.

Like many of his contemporaries, Burhan saw the seed of this dream reborn in the *al-Maʿhad al-ʿIlmī al-Saʿūdī* (the Saudi Scholastic Institute) opened in Mecca in 1926/27, which lasted until the opening of the Islamic University of Medina in 1961. This was an institution established by the nascent Saudi state to train primary school teachers—an undertaking that would be close to the heart of Burhan Mkelle and Shaykh al-Amin. By 1927, the new institute taught subjects such as Arabic grammar, language-related topics, arithmetic, book-keeping, geography, engineering, morals (*al-akhlāq*) and—perhaps more surprisingly—the French language.[42] However, these were supplemented by religious education which had the clear ambition to spread and legitimize the tenets of Wahhabism. Not unexpectedly, the institute did not become popular among Hijazi in the early years, being run by Wahhabi teachers on a Wahhabi curriculum. Only after 1928, when it was placed in the care of Rashid Rida's non-Najdi associates—notably Taqi al-Din al-Hilali—did it attract Hijazi students.[43] During this period, it is also reported to have recruited students from overseas, especially from Indonesia—despite the fact that the overall objective of the institute remained clear: to propagate the creed of Wahhabism. *Tawhid* was a core subject in this regard and was taught directly from Muhammad b. Abd al-Wahhab's *Kitāb al-Tawḥīd*,[44] a work that had been the target of polemics from more Sufi-oriented scholars since it was first publicly known. Religious instruction accounted for up to 40 per cent of the weekly classes.[45]

This ideological core would conceivably have been enough to put off East African teachers like Burhan Mkelle and Shaykh al-Amin, both hailing from strong intellectual traditions rooted in Sufi teachings, despite their above profession of "Wahhabism". The widely published excesses during the Saudi takeover of Hijaz would have been another natural deterrent. However, the "other face" of the institute was compelling enough to merit support. The secular part of the curriculum was expanded during the period 1928–35, in a style that borrowed much from the Egyptian Dar al-Ulum (and many of its graduates). As M. Farquhar has argued, the very modernity of the teaching style at the Saudi Scholastic Institute (fixed syllabi, textbooks and—to use H. Kalmbach's term—ocularcentric learning) also influenced the Wahhabi doctrines taught there, if not in content, then in style.[46] In other words, Burhan, like Shakib Arslan, was willing to overlook very obvious doctrinal differences for the greater good of an Islamic university that could produce graduates whose morality (*akhlāq*) was not compromised.

That said, it is also worth noting Burhan's statement that the new Saudi king would do well to create an "institution that does not violate the spirit of the Islamic religion in any way" and "be mindful of the good of Muslims all over the world". We may read here some wishful thinking that Ibn Saud would honour the ideas set forth by his Ottoman predecessors—or at least tone down the most explicit Wahhabi *daʿwa* aspect of Saudi education.

Burhan was here also very much in line with Hassan al-Banna, the founder of the Muslim Brotherhood. According to the study by B. Lia, it was precisely the YMMA's views on Islamic education (or rather its lack thereof, according to al-Banna) that caused him to break from the organization.[47] Al-Banna viewed the YMMA's increasing emphasis on Western, secular education as a problem because it alienated young people from Islam, and from their "roots". Burhan was also in line with many intellectuals in the Middle East who viewed students returning from schooling in Europe with scepticism. By 1920, Western-style education was generally viewed as having great potential, but also as an inherent danger to society. "Foreign" knowledge was deemed as "stumbling stones" or even "poison", while at the same time necessary for the development of society.[48]

It is also worth noting that Burhan nowhere in his letter makes specific reference to Zanzibar or East Africa, but rather refers to a non-situated "generational gap". He paints a picture of young men losing the orientation of their cultural compass and, in turn, the respect of their home community. Of course, it may be argued that Burhan would wish his statements to be non-specific for the sake of publication in *al-Fath*. On the other hand, the tone of the text indicates that Burhan is speaking from experience, and from a Zanzibari experience where the need for reform is as urgent as in the Middle East. He is, in other words, placing both his own community (Comorians in Zanzibar)—and perhaps also the Swahili coast—on a par with the Muslim experience of Western-oriented education throughout the world.

Akhlāq and the moral turn: The Muslim modern as individual and community ideal

The apparent support for Saudi Arabia as the host for a modern Islamic university is not the only notable aspect in Burhan's letter. Also striking is the argument for the need for moral individuals to produce a moral, truly modern Islamic society. A. Hofheinz has pointed out how "the moral turn" was not only embraced by emerging Salafi thought, but also played into Sufism. From being primarily a spiritual practice (aimed at producing enlightenment), emphasis was increasingly placed on ethical aspects of faith (*li-l-takhalluq*).[49] The emphasis on morals, in Hofheinz' analysis, accentuated individual responsibility for one's actions over scholastic jurisprudence. The self-improvement project inherent in this development—or what C. Mayeur-Jaouen has called "the slide from *adab* towards *akhlāq*"[50]—can be read in Burhan Mkelle's statements in the letter above.

Burhan, like Shaykh al-Amin, was adamant that no community would benefit from simply imitating the ways of others—the reference here clearly being to the Europeans. Reform, al-Amin stated in many of his essays, must be based in the traditions and customs of the coastal Muslim community, or else they risk becoming like the crow—forever imitating and in the end "stuck between somewhere neither here nor there".[51]

The same sense of moral decay was voiced by Burhan's colleague in the GCS and in the *Jamʿiyyat al-Sunna*, Abu ʾl-Hasan Jamal al-Layl. In a poem dated 1943, he lamented the decay of *akhlāq* among the young people.[52] "When did the pride of our ancestors disappear?" he asks, noting that youngsters nowadays watch football rather than attending prayers. Men take their wives out in public and eat with them in restaurants, and they even go to the cinema together (!). Abu ʾl-Hasan's lament is less overtly political than that of Shaykh al-Amin, but in essence the same: emulate the examples of your forefathers, the water from whose wells is no longer directly available; all the more reason to savour what drops we have.

We see the same sentiment voiced in Burhan's letter above. Students who obtain their education at Western universities (or universities established in the Middle East with Western curricula and no Islamic moral foundation) do so at the risk of their own souls, says Burhan, and of their futures as moral members of the community. They will be left lacking in *akhlāq*—the ethical foundation needed to represent Islam in modern society. They have learnt only vanity, which does not a community make.

Changing Practice by Means of Public Rituals

In 1924, the *Mawlid al-Nabi* (celebration of the Prophet's birthday) was inaugurated as a high-profile public event in Zanzibar.[53] Before this time, *mawlid* events had been held every year throughout the islands (and indeed throughout East Africa), organized locally in mosques, smaller public spaces and in private homes. However, the Zanzibar *mawlid* was not the first such celebration to become a major event. This honour went to the *mawlid* in Lamu, instituted around 1900, on which much literature exists.[54]

By 1928, the Zanzibari public *mawlid* event had already become immensely popular. The report in the *Zanzibar Gazette* from 1928 states that somewhere between 25 and 30,000 people attended the event in the Mnazi Mmoja "recreation park". The evening started out with a 21-gun salute, whereupon the Sultan had "refreshments" with the imams, *qadis* and other dignitaries. At 10 p.m., the Sultan, the British Resident and the Crown Prince made their way to the Mnazi Mmoja grounds, where they were welcomed by Shaykh Tahir al-Amawi, the head of the "Maulid Committee". Verses from the Quran, and then the *Mawlid al-Barzanji* were recited, verse by verse, by alternating reciters. The *Gazette* reporter noted that:

> The sight of the thousands of people packed into serried rows, listening with rapt attention to the chanting of the various verses from the Koran and Maulidi el-Burzanji by the successive occupants of the rostrum, the deep-toned responses of the congregation, the multicoloured lights, illuminated arches, and fluttering red and green bunting, all served to render the ceremony a deeply impressive one, and great credit is due to the Organizing Committee for the excellence of the arrangements.[55]

The quest for moral unity: The *Mawlid al-Nabi* as public event

In the early 1920s, unity was a central topic on several levels of Zanzibari society, and this continued throughout the interwar period. We have seen the term used at the community level in the foundation of the Comorian Association, where the purpose was to unite rivalling Comorian factions under a reformist umbrella. Likewise, we have seen the term used by the *Jamʿiyyat al-Sunna*, where the purpose was religious unity among Sunni Muslims. The efforts of the new generation of teachers may also be viewed as a drive towards unity, albeit one with a slant towards education.

The new communal *mawlid* celebrations may also be viewed as part of this effort, establishing common grounds for religious worship that would be socially and religiously acceptable to most communities, while at the same setting a standard for how rituals like the *mawlid* ought to be performed. No loud or ecstatic chanting, no excessive movements or shifts in rhythm or style—and above all a focus on the narrative and devotional expression inherent in the text by al-Barzanji. The result was, as the *Gazette* reported, "a deeply impressive" ceremony, and one which could also be fully acceptable to the British administrators.

Repeated articles and op-eds in *al-Falaq* and in the Arabic *Supplement to the Zanzibar Gazette* in the 1920s also appealed for unity among residents in Zanzibar. We may glimpse this quest for unity in the report in *al-Falaq* and in the *Supplement* where the participation of all Zanzibari factions in the selection of the Organizing Committee is stressed. In a report on a meeting held in the offices of the Arab Association in August 1926, the *Supplement* states that it was attended by "all the Islamic factions in Zanzibar" (*jamīʿ firaq al-Islāmiyya*).[56] The purpose was to establish committees for the various events to be hosted during the *mawlid*.

The emphasis in the report on the participation of all factions, and the relative diversity in the names of the appointed committee members, show a drive towards unity through diversity. Among the appointed organizing members were Umar b. Sumayt (the later chief *qadi*, who was then in Zanzibar as a "private person"), Burhan Mkelle, Tahir al-Amawi, and the Egyptian Arabic-teacher Shaykh Abd al-Bari, alongside names that show an Ismaili background. That said, the very fact that the Arab Association hosted the meeting still shows that this was very much in the hands of the Arabic-speaking and Arabic-literate urban elite.

When it comes to the actual *mawlid* recitals, the annual reports usually made a point of noting the diversity of the reciters, as, for example, in 1939 when it was stressed that "Arab, Ithnaasheri, Bohra, Memon and Native school boys" gave the recitals.[57]

While the number of attendees at the *mawlid* event may be exaggerated, the overall impression is that of a very public, well-organized and "state-sponsored" event. The public nature of the event was even more clear by 1929, when students from the Government Central School were among the reciters of the *Mawlid al-Barzanji*.[58] The unifying element—as well as the modernizing drive—was even more explicitly on display by the 1930s, when students from the Government Girls' School also participated. The girls did not perform in these public events, but were present in the audience, demonstrating their proper *heshima* as educated young girls.[59]

The *Zanzibar Gazette* "*mawlid* coverage" tended to convey a sense of a fair or market. Reporting routinely mentioned the "brilliantly illuminated" grounds, the presence of tents and sweets, and the "thousands" of people in attendance. However, this was a fair with a highly and increasingly official overtone. The Sultan (or one or many senior princes) "graced the occasion" with his presence, as did the British Resident and the upper echelons of the British administration. Ahead of the recitation, addresses were read in Arabic, Swahili and English.

From the early 1930s, the Zanzibar national anthem was sung upon the arrival of the dignitaries, the Arabic lyrics of which were composed by Burhan Mkelle.[60] The singing of the national anthem, the increasingly prominent role of the Sultan and the Sultan's family and the reporting itself indicate that the *mawlid* was becoming (or was promoted as) a national event—one that projected Zanzibari cultural identity above all. Whether or not this amounted to a Zanzibari national identity will be discussed further below (Chapter 8).

The composition of the annual *mawlid* committees gives another indication of the unifying ambition of the ritual. Published every year in *al-Falaq*, the committees were sub-divided into groups responsible for recitation, fundraising, reception (of the dignitaries), etc. By the 1930s, the list of committee members featured in the *Gazette* (of up to fifty members) shows that efforts had been made to include all Muslim sects and communities. At times it was pointed out directly, as for the 1938 committee, when the committee leader, Ghulam Ali Khaderbhay, reminded the assembled representatives about the words of the Prophet: "One Muslim is the brother of another Muslim."[61]

That said, there were also disagreements between the members of this committee, most probably expressed within committee meetings (of which there are no records). However, some dissent was expressed publicly in the form of letters to the editor of *al-Falaq*, complaining about lack of preparation and the like. A distinctly modern side note here is an op-ed in *al-Falaq* where the author—who signed as Abu Salih—suggests broadcasting the event on the radio.[62]

It would be overly simplistic to state that the Mnazi Mmoja *mawlid* was launched solely for the purpose of unity and for building a form of national culture that was acceptable and attractive to the Arab (and Arabic-literate) elite and the non-Arabs, as well as to the British. It would be equally simplistic to read the *mawlid* celebration as an unhesitating endorsement of public religious recitals *per se*. On the contrary, several members of the Zanzibari scholarly milieu argued forcefully against, for example, Quranic recitations that were overly musical or appealed to the senses rather than to the *aql*, the mind. One very explicit criticism was penned by Muhammad b. Ali al-Barwani, whose book *Riḥla Abū Ḥārith* was introduced in Chapter 3. Observing Quranic recitals while travelling in Egypt, he quoted and clearly condoned the Egyptian newspaper *al-Muayyad*:[63]

> In my opinion, reciting the Quranic verses in the familiar way common among Muslims was the greatest reason for their decay (*inḥiṭāṭhim*) from centuries ago until now because this rendering of the Quran is like a song that affects the feelings of the soul of the listener by the effect of the sound and its rhythm, but [obscures] the intended meaning." [...] What we have now is a vicious circle where the Revelation of God has become fashioned into styles like the Jarkā, Sirkā, Hijazi and Iraqi[64] and so on. [...] Like a stroke of lightning from the sky, it strikes at all the listener's senses. [...] By the manner in which it is composed, and the way the reciter alters his voice and adds various strange movements (*al-ḥarakāt al-gharība*),[65] he takes it from recital to pure singing (*al-ghināʾ*) and thereby the listener loses all that could be gained from reading the Quran and listening to it. If the Quran is the book of God, revealed to our Prophet Muhammad (SAWS) to guide people, strengthen their morals (*akhlāqihim*) and reform their way of life (*maʿāshihim*), then this is being reversed (*yanqalabu*) by the manner and extent by which it is performed.[66]

Likewise, Abu Harith was highly critical of some types of *mawlid* rituals. In Giza, he observed a *mawlid* which caused him to make the following remark: "I am amazed at those who have a mind and [still] believe that these vanities (*al-abāṭīl*) and delusions (*al-aḍālīl*) are part of the religion."[67] The fact that his book, as we have seen, was endorsed by Ahmad b. Sumayt, Abu Muslim al-Rawwahi[68] and Burhan Mkelle can only lead to the conclusion that this was a widely held view among the Arabic-literate milieu in Zanzibar.

Burhan's *Diwan* includes several *mawlid* texts that were used for general *mawlid* celebrations and taught to the children in the Government Central School, expressing praise and love for the Prophet while at the same time instilling a sense of common ground as Muslims. Two very evident examples are the ones referred to as "Song no. 1" and "Song no. 2" in the Burhāniyyāt collection:

Burhan Mkelle, Song no. 1[69]

Praise is for the one who gifted Ahmed to the world
And sent him with truth and guidance, Who then proclaimed the verses of the Quran
My brothers in Islam, Hold fast onto the rope of Allah
You have been named "Muslims", Be congratulated, for you have the Quran
On the Prophet's birth anniversary, You have gathered, O noble folk
For singing praise and eulogies, And to recite the Quran
It was in such a night, That the Messenger of Allah was born
The land of the Qibla took pride therein, A land where the verses of the Quran were revealed
This congregation is rightly justified; It is the recipient of mercy and reward
Allah has looked towards you with divine illumination, He is the
One who revealed the Quran
May Allah prolong for us, The days of our Caliph
And may He prolong for us our days of ease, Which we spend adhering to the rules of the Quran
Prayers be upon the Chosen One, And upon the pure progeny
And also, the good companions, All of whom are the companions of the Quran

Burhan Mkelle, Song no. 2, to be recited after the narration of the Prophet's birth (SAWS)[70]

The Creation attained pride—Ever since the truth became clearly manifest

By the appearance of Mustafa—The Prophet who came with truth
And then Islam prospered—Its face bright and smiling
Polytheism sunk into oblivion—Its voice turning into a whisper
O brethren, thanks are for the One—Who gave death, and gave life
And He guided us, until we became guided—And He ruled by command and prohibition
So, know that we all—Live by the Book of Allah
Ever since we acknowledged him as the Leader—And ever since he emerged as a firm pillar
It is only because of him—That we walk upon the straight path
O Lord, make our end good—You are eternally Self-Sufficient
Prayers be upon Tāhā—As long as the Pleiades shine
And upon the progeny, and companions—And thereafter upon the pious folk

Another is the poem known as "Badr al-Naẓīm" (The Full Moon) which in a highly pedagogical manner lays out the birth and life of the Prophet, from his birth to his community in Medina. This poem, which his sons tellingly placed as the first in their edition of their father's poetry, was taught to children in the government schools and instilled in the young readers the Prophet as a model to be emulated.[71]

The Zanzibari *mawlid* celebrations of the 1920s and 1930s were not unlike the way in which the *mawlid* is marked in present-day Zanzibar. The impact of the colonial-Sufi reformist alliance may, in other words, be observed almost a century later, primarily by the fact that ritual observance was made public, communal and available (at least in theory) to all.

More moral unity: *Mawlid al-Miʿrāj* as public event

Only four years after the introduction of the public *Mawlid al-Nabi* celebrations, another ritual was being moved from the privacy of mosques and homes and into the public domain. In the *Supplement to the Zanzibar Gazette*, we may read about a new public ritual; the marking of the *miʿrāj*, the Prophet's ascent to the heavens.[72]

The event took place in the Friday mosque in Malindi. On 27 Rajab 1346H/20 January 1928, the Prophet's night journey (*laylat al-miʿrāj*), was marked as a public event organized by the "Jamiyyat al-Sunna", almost certainly a reference to the organization described in the previous chapter.[73] The *Gazette* report states that it was the first event of this kind to take place in Zanzibar, with an estimated 4,000 people in attendance.

The report also features a long account about the Prophet's night journey through the heavens, authored by the *Gazette* editor Harold Ingrams and Shaykh Tahir b. Abi Bakr al-Amawi. In addition to bringing readers information about the night journey itself, the authors also express satisfaction with the event: "[...] the arrangements made for its performance (the first of its kind, so it is said, to take place in Zanzibar) were excellent, including the illumination of the Mosque which was cleverly conceived and striking in effect".[74] The actual ritual is described at length, and painstakingly names all the religious leaders involved. Celebrations started with a reading of Quran 17:1, which is the verse that outlines the history of the Prophet's nightly journey from Hijaz to Jerusalem, accompanied by Gabriel during the night between the 26th and 27th of Rajab.[75] Abu Bakr b. Abd al-Allah BaKathir then started the recitation of the *miʿrāj* (although the actual text is not named) assisted by Abu 'l-Hasan Jamal al-Layl, Burhan Mkelle, Sayyid Hamid b. Mansab b. Ali and Shaykh Muhammad b. Umar al-Singani/Shanjani.[76]

Proceedings ended at 10.00 p.m. with thanksgiving. From there, the attendees proceeded to a reception, organized by yet another group of Zanzibari scholarly "heavyweights": Tahir b. Abi Bakr al-Amawi, Said b. Dahman, Muhammad b. Ali b. Khamis al-Barwani, Sharif Abd Allah b. Ahamd al-Hamidi and Sharif Muhammad Mansab. The composition of this group is interesting, and one that was clearly drawn from the Sufi orders in Zanzibar Town, Shadhili, Qadiri and Alawi. It is also clearly a "reformist" group, the core being made up of the members of the *Jamʿiyyat al-Sunna*.

The entire event was sanctioned and financed from the highest level, as the *Gazette* goes on to emphasize:

> Nearly every mosque on the island witnessed the observance of this ceremony, and His Highness the Sultan is graciously pleased to lend his support in the shape of considerable monetary assistance [...] In Zanzibar, the occasion is observed with every circumstance of reverence and devotion by all who hold to tradition.

A central part of the *miʿrāj* story concerns how the Islamic prayer cycle was established; the Prophet meets face to face with God and "negotiates" the number of daily prayers from fifty to five. The *miʿrāj*, in other words, is a ritual that marks both the establishment of the Islamic prayer cycle on earth (and thus orthodoxy), and a fantastic, fantasy-like world of winged creatures, spirits, sacred trees and time-travel (and thus leaning towards magic and mysticism).[77] The latter has made it a contested ritual in Islamic history, as it almost certainly also was in 1920s Zanzibar.

That said, there is no doubt that the *miʿrāj* as a textual corpus was well known in East Africa, and that the event was celebrated privately and in local mosques—like the *Mawlid al-Nabi*—before it made its debut as something approximating a national event.[78] By far the most widely used and well-known *miʿrāj* text was the *Qiṣṣa al-isrāʾa wa-l-miʿrāj* by al-Barzanji, of which two manuscript copies can be found in the Riyadha mosque library,[79] and one nineteenth-century copy in the Zanzibar Institute for Archives and Records.[80]

While the *Gazette* report does not note it, the recitation of the *miʿrāj* story tends to be held in a different tone to that on the Prophet's birth and life. As C. Ahmed has noted, the latter is celebratory, and the congregation participates fully in joyous choir responses, dressed for celebration and with accompanying festive foods.[81] The *miʿrāj*, in contrast, is understood to be more instructive, laying out the narrative of the journey and—in the Swahili context—accompanied by a line-by-line translation.

It is interesting to note in the *Gazette* report that the support of the Sultan is emphasized. It is explicitly stated that in Zanzibar and Oman the Ibadis do not celebrate the occasion. On the contrary, say the authors, the Ibadi view is that "the ascent up to heaven is an unauthorized elaboration of the story, miraculous enough in itself, of the journey the Prophet made in a single night from Mecca to [Jerusalem]".

The first observation to be made here is that the group of "A-listers" from the intellectual milieu in Stone Town clearly endorsed the introduction of the *miʿrāj* recitation as a public, organized event. Secondly, the same group was clearly associated with the *Jamʿiyyat al-Sunna*. One may ask why this group found it pertinent, and indeed necessary, to seek high-level support (financial and organizational) for the introduction of yet another new public ritual at this particular point in time. The answer, again, is probably to be found in the quest for a religious foundation for cultural unity.

The End of Superstition and Excessive Practices

As outlined in Chapter 2, magic in all its forms has often been viewed by modernizers (European or Islamic) as public enemy number one. How can there be a moral Muslim subject where superstition reigns and when individual responsibility is superseded by amulets, incantations and the like? We have seen (in Chapter 2) that at least some Zanzibaris were sceptical towards practices like healing by 1904, and sought the opinion of Rashid Rida.[82] By the interwar years, debates were expanded to a wide range of practices that were deemed incompatible with modern, moral lives. Here, they took their cues from the Rashid Rida brand of modernity, but also from the rising influence of Saudi Arabia.

The introduction of new rituals under state auspices was but one part of the changes in religious practice in interwar Zanzibar. A qualitatively different mode of change was state campaigns to curb existing practices, especially rituals and traditions that were deemed "excessive". To forcibly end existing practices was—and is—beyond the capability of any *jamʿiyya* or even the most revered religious authority. For this, the reformists (whatever their organizational form) needed the support of a political authority. This was something reformers were alert to elsewhere in the Islamic world too. The Syrian thinker Jamal al-Din al-Qasimi (d. 1914), for example, explicitly stated that the *ulama* alone could not end all *bidʿa*. For change to ensue, the support of the Governor, or even higher political authority, was essential.[83]

In Zanzibar, the powers that be were the colonial government. There existed throughout the interwar years sufficient "common ground" between the government and the religious establishment to form such alliances. One such shared objective was to rid Zanzibari society of "un-Islamic" or "un-modern" behaviour. Other more or less willing partners in this alliance were the ethnic and faith-based associations, which were perceived by the British as "channels" for the new policies to reach the population.

The Pemba campaign and the legal limits of mourning

R. Loimeier has analysed the so-called "Pemba Campaigns" held in 1935–36, with a view to understanding the relationship between the *ulama* and successive Zanzibar governments.[84] While I agree fully with his conclusion that the learned elite and the British government were very much in agreement on the core issues of the campaign (and indeed on many overriding issues also discussed in this chapter), I offer here an analysis of *why* this was so. As Loimeier has argued, the British concern was primarily with the excessive expenditure incurred by funerary feasts and *khitima* prayers for the dead, which in turn generated competition within the communities.[85] But what were the concerns of Muslim moderns over these long-standing rituals? Why exactly did their interests align with those of the colonial power? In the following I take my cue from M. Janson, who, in a study of present-day religious debates between traditionalists and reformists in Gambia, views death and funeral rites as an opportunity for social change.[86] As she points out, these rites force communities to "think, reflect and debate about what 'being Muslim' involves".[87]

The main bone of contention in the 1930s Pemba campaign was the practice of extensive prayers for the deceased to ease their "trials of the grave"[88] and thus ensure their painless passage to Paradise. In Zanzibar—and especially in Pemba—this had been taken to extremes, with prayers and Quran recitations evolving into large feasts.

From the point of view of Islamic practice, such prayers included the recitals while preparing the deceased for the funeral (washing and shrouding), recitals underway and during the burial, and then the series of *khitima* readings at various point afterwards (usually on the third, seventh and—the most widely practised, the *arobaini*—fortieth day after death). The question of just how much the living can do to help the dead obtain the acceptance of God is one that is hotly debated in recent Islamic debates, as F. Becker has shown in an interesting analysis that also discusses pre-Islamic funerary practices.[89] The Salafi/reformist view today is that the living, in fact, can do but very little to assist their kin or friend on their passage to Jannah, beyond the supplications that are recited when preparing for the funeral and at the gravesite. Once the deceased is buried, the living should focus on remembering the good deeds of their loved one. The emphasis, thus, is on the departed individual, who is primarily responsible for his or her own onward journey. Present-day Sufis, on the other hand (and especially Qadiris), maintain that not only are the living able to intercede on behalf of their dead even after the burial, but doing so is an act of utmost love and care that will be noted by God. The emphasis is thus on the communal responsibility to care for its members also after death and beyond the funeral.

The Zanzibari "funeral question" was evidently one that caught the attention of the reading public. In May 1930, it was brought before Rashid Rida in *al-Manar*.[90] The petitioner was the same Muhammad Abdallah Qarnah (Gurnah) who three years previously had consulted Rida on the followers of Ibn Taymiyya. Now he raised six questions on ritual practice, two of which were directly related to funerals:

1. Is it lawful for a Muslim to set aside money in a will or a *waqf* for prayers to be recited after his/her death?
2. Are *dhikr* permitted during the funerary procession?

The very fact that these questions were submitted to *al-Manar* shows that the topic was being debated in Zanzibar. It is not clear from the tone of the question what Mr Gurnah himself thought about the issue: "Was there, during the era of the Messenger of God (SAWS) or the Rightly Guided Caliphs, any mention of *dhikr* during the funeral procession? If you say: No, is it permissible? Or is it a *bidʿa* (unlawful innovation)? And is it beneficial, or not?" The deliberation of Rashid Rida is typical of the modernist stance. Regarding setting aside funds in a will for posthumous *soma* (readings), Rida acknowledges that this is a point where opinions differ between scholars, but his own position is spelled out very clearly. Prayers are useless except when sincerely performed by a faithful, living believer, to God, without intercession. Prayer on behalf of others, living or dead, has no effect. Thus, it follows for Rida that it is not permissible to set aside money for prayers after death.

On the question of *dhikr* during the funeral procession, Rida is even more explicit: "Some people of the *tariqas* and others used to recite *dhikr* on the occasion of the funeral by raising their voice and some of them add reciting verses from the Burdah. All of this is *bidʿa*." While he does go into various scholarly opinions on raised versus low voices during *dhikr*, this is only marginal to Rida's fundamental position, namely that prayers and recitals on behalf of others are—at best—secondary to the prayers performed by the believer during his lifetime.

It is not immediately clear how this clear-cut response was received in Zanzibar (or even if Gurnah received the answer he was looking for). It would be a hard sell to argue that the living could not in any way influence the fate of their relative after death. Rather, the consensus was that of present-day Sufis: the obligation of the living is, by means of supplications and prayers, to plead for the departed to be accepted by God. Indeed, as we saw in Chapter 3, Burhan Mkelle was buried with the Shadhili *Mashīshiyya* prayer at his gravesite and his soul was given the *talqīn* (the guidance for the encounter with the angels). This is a pattern that with some variation is widely practised in Zanzibar (and large parts of the Muslim world) to this day.

Rather, the 1930s debate in Zanzibar concerned the *manner* in which these prayers were to be recited and what social events they were to form part of. It was, in other words, not so much a debate over theology, as it was one of behaviour—*heshima*. It was also a debate that sought to establish unity within cultural practice; when argued by the urban elite this was to be based in modern definitions of what was—and what was not—Islamic.

Forms of intercession: Modern funerary practices

As several studies have pointed out, Swahili funeral rites were often accompanied by *ngoma* (drumming), loud chanting and high-pitched voices (ululation). These practices have been criticized all over the Swahili coast in the twentieth century, until recent times.[91] As Liazzat Bonate has described in her study of northern Mozambique, the debate centred first on the use of drums, and then on the use of loud chanting, hand-clapping and the general use of rhythm during funerals.[92] The two factions—in Mozambique as elsewhere, but with local variations—consisted of the *sukutis* (Ar: silent) and the *dhikris* (from the chanting of *dhikr* in a rhythmical fashion). The former would practise quiet supplications during the funerary rites—but still with the clear intent of aiding the departed in his or her new residence in the grave. The latter would have the same intention, but express this in loud chants, the use of hand-clapping and sometimes high-pitched ululation, depending on local custom. This would also extend to the *khitima* readings after the burial. The Pemba campaign targeted both the funerary practice itself and the associated practice of large gatherings, after the funeral and at *khitima* readings, paid for and hosted by the family of the deceased.

In a short undated poem, Burhan left no doubt about his own opinion:

> The dead cannot be prepared [for Paradise] by the living
> Nor should money or food be exchanged
> This is the practice of the Jahiliyya, devoid of *karām*
> End the practice of wailing, and let the true religion be heard![93]

The primary concern for the British was the overspending related to funerals. In January 1936, the Deputy District Commissioner in Pemba blamed the "competitive spirit" for the excessive *khitima* readings, combined with easy access to credit on the security of *shambas* or clove crops, for the excessive feasting taking place in connection with funerals throughout the island.[94] The British also quickly latched on to the inter-Islamic debates surrounding these practices, but typically interpreted the issue within the framework of straightforward permissibility or impermissibility. The Pemba Deputy DC noted, probably after conferring with legal scholars in Pemba, that excessive *khitima* readings are "strictly against the regulations of Islamic law".

In the months that followed, meetings were held. *Qadis* were consulted. Notes and reports were written, but burials and *khitima* readings continued unabated. One of those consulted was Shaykh Tahir b. Abi Bakr al-Amawi, one of the two Sunni *qadis* in the Zanzibar High Court. He gave his opinion in a one-and-a-half-page *raʾy* (view, or opinion).[95]

Shaykh Tahir started his opinion by referring to the general injunction against wastefulness ("God abhors the profuse, for the profuse are brothers of the devil") and praise of the "thrifty". Then he notes the legal injunction against living beyond one's means, which specifically forbids feasting on borrowed money. Tahir then turns to *ngoma*, the use of drums. This, he says, is simply forbidden (*fa hiyya ḥaram*). Therefore it follows that any expenditure for this purpose is forbidden. Tahir then goes on to describe which celebrations and celebratory spending are acceptable in Islamic law, such as showing hospitality, and celebrating the birth of a child by killing two goats for the birth of a boy and one for a girl—as long as this is not done on borrowed money.

Shaykh Tahir, like so many of his fellow *qadis* and religious leaders in East Africa—and, as we have seen, Rashid Rida—reserved a special ire for the habit of marking funerals with "high-pitched" wailing and prolonged feasts offered by the family of the deceased. This, stated Tahir, is no less than "pre-Islamic ignorance" (*afʿāl al-jāhiliyya*). Here, Tahir refers to hadith that condemn the feeding of the "wailing congregation"[96] and even the readers of *khitima* or the *arobaini* (fortieth-day prayer readings). It follows that any expenses of this kind paid from the estate of the deceased are completely unacceptable if the estate is not solvent. Even if the estate is solvent, says Tahir, it is only legal if all heirs agree, and then only up to one third of the total estate.

Tahir then explains how the heirs are obliged to reject the will of the deceased if his wishes contradict Islamic law, such as being covered in silk for his burial, the erection of a tomb, etc. However, as one would expect from a *qadi*, Tahir also emphasizes the point that wills cannot be set aside at will by lay people: "A will cannot be made null and void unless the Kathi sees to it."

The *qadi* (with or without British prompting is not clear) also sought other authorities in the matter. Attached to the file is a second legal opinion published in the Al-Azhar journal *Nur al-Islam* and translated into English.[97] It concerns the legality of ceremonies related to burial and goes a step further than Shaykh Tahir.

Again, the general injunction against feasting is stressed; nor should the bereaved family host large gatherings. On the contrary, states the unknown author, the people *around* the bereaved should make food for them, because grief can stop people from cooking and eating, and they forget their meals "and consequently they become weak". Thus, rather than providing a feast, the mourners should be provided for. It is especially forbidden to kill animals on the threshold while carrying the body out of the house. This is outright pre-Islamic. Other feasting on happy occasions is legal, so long as it is according to one's means (and provided men and women do so separately). Women may use tambourines and dance and chant, "but not with the high-pitched tone which is forbidden for both men and women". Thus, adds the writer, what is going on nowadays—"big feasts, dancing and chanting at high tone and mixing men and women"—all of it is unlawful.

As J. Glassman has discussed, the debate over perceived "un-Islamic" practices was a recurring one in the *Mazungumzo ya Walimu*. However, in the early 1930s, voices could still be heard that viewed rural practices as something to be preserved, "as symbols of national pride and solidarity"[98]—in other words, an argument along the lines of cultural heritage.

Formulating a Zanzibari Modern Accent

The debate surrounding the Pemba campaign indicates that to the parties that entered into an alliance with the British, this was less about Islamic legal permissibility and more about creating a specific, locally based form of morality. Shaykh Tahir and the al-Azhar shaykhs were bound by their profession to express their argument in legal terms; Burhan expressed the same in poetry. They presumably all read Rashid Rida's opinion, which laid out the case in no uncertain terms. What they sought was a blueprint for a common Muslim identity that was to be distinctly Muslim, modern—and with a distinct Zanzibari accent.

In this modern context, where the colonial state was both an employer, a potential adversary (in the case of education) and partner (in the case of the *mawlid* celebrations and the Pemba campaign), an ongoing and highly self-reflexive discourse sought to define this accent. Should it be a Wahhabi accent? As we have seen, the two friends Burhan and Shaykh al-Amin disagreed over how best to convey this message to the public. We may even read Burhan's objection to his friend as saying that the Zanzibari modern accent should not be a wholesale Wahhabi one, but one which retained a more Zanzibari pronunciation.

The new, public and (at least in principle) multi-ethnic Zanzibari *mawlid* may be viewed as another attempt to formulate such an accent.

It was a way to express a broader orientation within the Islamic world and a search for common denominators—a common *adab* metamorphosed for modernity. In the Zanzibari context, this meant projecting a new ideal of *heshima*, one that could fuse individual and communal respectability with unity. These common denominators were cultural (related to manners, etiquette, dress code, etc.) but they were also explicitly religious and consequently concerned with morals and values. In this context, the Prophet may even be understood as "the great unifier"; the figure around which Burhan and his colleagues proposed that all the communities of Zanzibar, the nation—and beyond Zanzibar: the *umma*—should rally.

8

WATANIYYA?

TOWARDS A MODERN ZANZIBARI CULTURE

The previous chapters have highlighted the efforts of the Muslim moderns to create a new ideal, a person imbued with moral fibre, able to choose, self-aware—while not compromising on *akhlāq*. The question that has been left hanging is by far the most difficult to answer: *Who exactly were they talking to?* To their immediate *taifa*—community, be that Comorian or Arab, or even Sunni Muslims? To Zanzibaris in general, irrespective of ethnic or religious background? Or even to the general Muslim world, of which Zanzibar was a part? Who was to be shaped into Muslim moderns and what was the Zanzibari version they strove for?

The question is difficult to answer because it interlinks with ideas about Zanzibari culture, identity, nationality and nationhood, all of which have been highly contested both before and after the interwar period.

Islamic traditionalism—or more precisely: Arabic-language traditionalism evoked as *adab*—was, in twentieth-century history writing, often labelled as reactionary, and incapable of producing nationalist thought. "Real" nationalism was perceived as being entirely secular in nature, as Amal Ghazal pointed out in her book on Ibadi-Omani nationalism in Zanzibar. She quotes William Cleveland, who viewed the traditionalist line of thought as not only stagnant, but the "enemy of progress".[1] In contrast, the rise of secular, political nationalism in the broader African context, derived from colonial schooling, has unhesitatingly been viewed as "nationalist". C. Decker and E. McMahon have pointed to the paradoxical rise of a generation of African leaders:

> Colonial education reinforced the notion of separate development, but it also offered a platform for social change, political mobilization, and—ultimately—national liberation. Nothing emphasizes this inherent contradiction more than the fact that the majority of African nationalist leaders were products of colonial schools.[2]

In other words, secular education led to secular nationalism which led to liberation of what were to become secular nation states. In this chapter I argue for a somewhat different type of nationalism which was expressed in different terms. Rather than pointing to instances of resistance or outright anti-colonialism, in line with the understanding of modernity as a culture (introduced in Chapter 1) I argue for the rise of a *cultural nationalism* in Zanzibar, based on a specific common denominator: an understanding that envisioned Islam as core, but reformed in a way to serve the believer in the present. In other words, love for one's culture, one's homeland—expressed as *hubb al-watan*—becomes part of *akhlāq*. It becomes part and parcel of what is expected of a good Muslim modern.

In political terms, I see this as a set of ideas that had the potential to grow into a unified Zanzibari identity, if not a unified nation. In other words, I view the interwar period in Zanzibar as an era of "culture wars", very much in line with what took place in the broader Muslim world. This corresponds to the "war of words" that J. Glassman posits,[3] but formulated in the language of morality. Rather than viewing this solely as an elitist exchange to maintain hegemony (or negotiate a way into the elite), I approach these ideas as a self-reflexive discourse that ultimately aimed to formulate an inclusive Zanzibari culture.

Wataniyya and Cultural Identity

Amal Ghazal has shown the nascent Zanzibari nationalism in the interwar period, expressed in the concept of *al-wataniyya*. She points to

Islam and modern Arabism as the two main pillars of Zanzibari nationalism. Arabism, she argues, must here be understood in the broadest possible sense and include the many grievances of the Arab populations in the mandate period, and perhaps most especially in Palestine. The situation in Palestine was closely covered in *al-Falaq* and events were organized to raise money for the suffering brothers there. This broad understanding of Arabness was, as A. Ghazal has shown, also cultivated in Zanzibar, and led to a position of resistance against colonial rule.

Al-wataniyya was, in Ghazal's analysis, less about hegemony and more about a patriotic duty to build, improve and construct the homeland. In other words, this project was closer to what C. Mayeur-Jaouen called an effort to transform *adab* to include also individual morality—to create a morally reconstructed person whose hard work was to result in a better future.

However, as was outlined in the introduction to this book, Arab identity in interwar Zanzibar remained a very open category, despite persistent British efforts to create a fixed hierarchy. "Arabness" meant privileges that caused many to self-identify as Arab based on language and culture. The predictable result was an 80 per cent increase in the number of people self-identifying as Arab between 1924 and 1931.[4] At the same time, Arabness, viewed from the "inside", had its own exclusion mechanisms, as M. Limbert has pointed out.[5] Although many of the Ibadi Omani intellectuals were propagating Arab nationalism, that did not mean that any Arabic speaker should be defined as Arab. On the contrary, the demarcation line still came down to genealogy. Limbert points to the need to exclude the *akhdām*, the servant classes who were also immigrating from South Arabia to Zanzibar and who in most cases spoke Arabic much better than the land-owning Arab families there.

Another complicating factor is that pointed out by N. Bertz, who has studied the relationship between nation, race and diaspora in Dar-es-Salaam from a somewhat different angle. Arguing from the basis of interwar movement between India and East Africa, he sums up by saying that moving towards decolonization, India "'nationalized' its disparate diasporas, which contributed to marking Indians overseas as possessing different national origins from the majority population among which they lived".[6] The rise of Arab nationalism in Egypt, the Levant and North Africa could mean that "diaspora-Arabs" in Zanzibar (however defined) were "nationalized" into the greater Arab cause, thus marking out Arabs more distinctly as "foreign" in the longer run.

Furthermore, the term "nation" means different things to different people in any society, and during the interwar years, this was very much the case in the Islamic world. T. Mitchell made this clear in his study of 1920s Egypt, concluding that "nationalism was not a singular truth, but a different thing among [those] different social groups".[7] Hilary Kalmbach, in her analysis of the Dar al-Ulum in Egypt, has pointed to the importance of including socio-cultural processes in an analysis of late nineteenth- and early twentieth-century Egyptian nationalism: "Graduates of Dar al-Ulum [...] had mixed civil-religious expertise that enabled *fin-de-siècle* nationalists to create a national culture that was modern *and* authentically Egyptian."[8]

Closer to Zanzibar, and more specific to its ethnic and religious context, J. Brennan has described a related process taking place in Dar-es-Salaam through the lens of *taifa*—the Swahili Arabic loanword today commonly understood to mean "nation", but in the first half of the twentieth century more widely understood as "race".[9] He has analysed in great detail how terms such as *taifa*, *kabila*, *watan*, *rangi*, *mila* and *desturi* were all reformulated by African nationalists in the twentieth century, as part of a process whereby Africanness was formulated in the late colonial and post-colonial era.

What factors could form the basis of shared identity and belonging in interwar Zanzibar? Common descent within groups is clearly one, residency in the city another. Common religion and shared practices further had the capacity to shape a Zanzibari identity, as we have seen expressed in the public *mawlid*. However, from this to nationalism is a leap that, as we have seen, the *jamʿiyāt* of Zanzibar struggled to make. The core of the discussion in Brennan's analysis was how the concept of "nation" was to carry "assimilative cultural characteristics, implying the potential realization that a nation state could theoretically house multiple races".[10] This chapter asks how the Muslim moderns of Zanzibar proposed to formulate nationhood.

A note on wataniyya, qawmiyya and nationalism

The Arabic term *wataniyya* literally means something along the lines of love for—or pride in—one's *land*, the territory of one's origin, i.e. approximating to the English term *patriotism*. This fits well with the usage we see in non-political texts from interwar Zanzibar, where authors like Umar b. Sumayt and Abu Harith express joy upon returning to the "watan", the territory of Zanzibar, or encountering fellow "*abnāʾ al-waṭan*", sons of the homeland abroad. This meaning of *watan* is imbued with emotional attachment which a person feels to the homeland, the place where a person feels at home. As Mandana Limbert has pointed out in a study of *watan* defined in early twentieth-century Oman and Zanzibar, the definition of homeland determined where a person would pray the full prayers (in his self-defined homeland) or the travel prayers (when away from his homeland).[11]

That said, *watan* is a notoriously difficult term to pin down, and its meaning has shifted in the past hundred years according to the tides of Arab nationalism, or that pertaining to specific nation states like Egypt, Oman, Lebanon, etc. Likewise, political leaders have invoked *wataniyya* in highly varying contexts, and with very different meanings. It is also at times hard to distinguish from the term *qawmiyya*, which refers to love or strong concern for the *nation*, in the sense of one's people—regardless of whether this *qawm* is organized in a state or demarcated by borders. As we shall see, this term, too, features in the writings of Burhan Mkelle, but here the usage is more ambiguous, and may refer to a particular group (in the case of Burhan: Comorians) or to Zanzibaris in general.

However, in modern usage, the term *qawmi* clearly incorporates the meaning of both the nation as a people who share a certain history and/or culture, and the state structure that organizes them—as, for example, in fixed phrases such as *al-amn al-qawmi* for "national security". This is clearly not the usage that was current in interwar Zanzibar.

Without going further into philological details or the long theoretical debate of what nationalism is and is not, I wish here to point out the difficulties these concepts pose for an analysis that argues for the formation of a national *culture*. Linguistically speaking, one would think that a national culture would be formed around its *qawm*—its people as a collective identity. Nonetheless, it is the term *wataniyya* that has come to mean what in traditional Western scholarship is referred to as nationalism: the integration of territory, people and political institution into one unit, often supported by what Laurie A. Brand has called a "national narrative".[12]

My purpose here is explicitly not to argue for or against the emergence of a European-style or European-defined type of nationalism. The purpose is to argue for the emergence in Zanzibar of a deliberate and self-reflexive cultural programme that concerned Muslims throughout the Islamic world in this period. It is for this process that I here use the term *wataniyya*.

Al-wataniyya *as Expressed by Burhan Mkelle*

The interwar years saw the end of the Ottoman Empire and the end of the Caliphate. With the former potential superstructure gone, Muslims from Borneo to Dakar were increasingly coming to the realization that M. Feener has stressed as specific to the era of globalization: "'our' questions increasingly resemble 'their' questions, regardless of how one might delineate these two essentialized groupings".[13] There was, in other words, a convergence of conversations, as the previous chapters have aimed to show, unfolding in Zanzibar. When we now turn to examine who they actually spoke to, the unavoidable question becomes exactly how this "our" and "their" was, in fact, delineated by Zanzibaris in the interwar years.

There is no straightforward answer to this. Burhan Mkelle, as we have seen, was an avid proponent of Arabic as core to becoming a "good citizen", even in Swahili-speaking Zanzibar. Yet he himself was not an Arab, linguistically speaking. As we have seen in Chapter 3, he had to learn Arabic the hard way, through studying. Moreover, he found it an arduous process, made more difficult by traditional Arabic grammars. If anything, he self-identified as a Comorian. Throughout his career as an academic, teacher and scholar, Burhan repeatedly and publicly invoked his Comorian origin, in action and writing. As we have seen in Chapter 6, he was among the founders of the Comorian Association and its second president. He was inspector of the Comorian School in Zanzibar. As a community leader, he functioned as a "hub"[14] for a close-knit group of Comorians in Zanzibar. As a Sufi shaykh, he represented the Shadhiliyya, the "national order" of the Comoro Islands and Comorians in diaspora. He wrote a lengthy work in Arabic entitled *Taʾrīkh jazīrat al-qamar al-Kubrā* (History of Grande Comore).[15] The one time he did travel, he used the "Comorian network" and visited the leader of the Comorian Association in Mombasa, Ali b. Said, while underway to the *hajj*. His closest friends and associates were part of the Zanzibari-Comorian network. He lived in the Malindi quarter of Zanzibar, which was home to many Comorians. Burhan's *Diwan* (collected poetry) contains poems of praise for several of his fellow Zanzibaris of Comorian descent, including Ahmad Mlomri, Sayyid Mansab b. Ali, as well as notable Comorian-Zanzibaris like father and son Ahmad and Umar b. Sumayt and the founder of the Riyadha mosque in Lamu, Habib Saleh. Finally, Burhan carried a French passport, which was a marker of Comorian identity in Zanzibar.

Comorian Islamic Reform—Zanzibari-Comorian Wataniyya?

The Comorians in Zanzibar were so-called "domiciled in Zanzibar", according to colonial parlance. By 1930, close to half of them, including Burhan himself, were Zanzibar-born. This makes this extract from the Comorian School song open to several interpretations:[16]

> O Comorian youth, stand firm in culture and be praised for that
> And worship your God, the Majesty over all creatures
>
> Know that Muhammad is his Messenger, leading you to guidance
> He is the generous one to be followed and our intercessor on the Day of Resurrection
>
> Be faithful to your nation (*qawm*)—expressing love of the homeland/ patriotism (*ḥubb al-waṭan*)
> Abide by good manners (*khalq al-ḥusn*), and by that you will succeed

This song was sung in the mornings in the Comorian School and expresses both the Islamic dedication expected from the students—and the identity to be fostered there. The first is clearly that of being a good Muslim: worship God and follow the Prophet, emulate his example and abstain from vices to avoid punishment on the Day of Judgement. The tone of the poem is clearly to instil morals: how to be an upright person, because being so will allow you to succeed in future endeavours. Part of this is to follow one's culture, which is most likely a way of warning students from taking after the ways of the Europeans. This echoes Shaykh al-Amin al-Mazrui, who clearly advocated a form of "cultural nationalism" that was defined in contrast to the European model of modernity and government.[17] Moreover, the student should remain faithful to their nation (*qawm*) and express their *hubb al-watan* (love for the homeland). The question, then, is what does Burhan mean by these terms? Most likely, *qawm* here refers to "Comorian people wherever they are", given that the song itself addresses "Comorian youth".

The reading of *hubb al-watan* is somewhat more open, but for the sake of argument I read it now as love for the Comoro Islands—i.e. not for the land of residence, but for the land of ancestral origin. In this reading, the song is one that aims to induce Islamic ideals in diasporic Comorian youth in the Comorian School in Zanzibar. Admittedly, this reading is somewhat paradoxical, as Burhan and the Comorian Association precisely rejected the traditions brought from the island. However, that does not necessarily preclude him from encouraging pride in one's origins.

Before moving on, it should be noted here that Islamic reform may be perceived somewhat differently by a community that views itself as diasporic, than by a community that views itself as autochthonous or indigenous. As N. Mobini-Kesheh has discussed with reference to the Hadramis in Indonesia, the anti-colonial sentiments inherent in the reformist ideology may be readily adopted by, say, a Malay Indonesian in Java, but the same ideological material may also be utilized by diasporic (or minority) groups as an argument for assimilation, or even for fitting predetermined, colonially imposed categories with regard to language, education or social/religious practice.[18] Furthermore, the adoption of a reformist stance may also imply a claim to moral authority *vis-à-vis* other groups, indigenous or otherwise. In other words, Islamic reformism (whether expressed as Salafi/modernist sentiments or within the Sufi episteme) could—and very much still can—serve widely different purposes. It can be where diasporic communities completely dissolve, or where their boundaries are strengthened.

When Burhan writes about "the Comorian reformist movement in Zanzibar", questions arise as to who are the targets for "reform" and what is the actual long-term ambition of that reform. These questions take on different significance for a Muslim minority in a Muslim-majority society than they do for the overall population. M. Laffan, in his study of nationhood in colonial Indonesia,[19] outlines the complexity of the positions in which the Hadrami community there found themselves under Dutch rule: as "allies" to the colonial government as well as a Pan-Islamic threat; as "natural leaders" of local Muslims (due to their perceived closeness to the Prophet and to the Arabic language) as well as "foreigner traders" to be envied and resented. When the Hadramis of Batavia—now Jakarta—(and the Malay world overall) increasingly adopted successive strands of Islamic reformism, their efforts may be viewed as attempts to gain favour with the colonial authorities, and achieve religious authority *vis-à-vis* the Malay population. However, the same move can be interpreted as an attempt to find an alternative source of identity, oriented towards the Middle East (and especially the Hadrami "homeland"), thus distancing themselves from the cultural environment in which they lived—and perhaps also, as Bertz noted for the Indian population of Dar-es-Salaam, being "nationalized" by the homeland.

How did this look from the Comorian-Zanzibari point of view? Turning first to the efforts of Burhan and his compatriots in the Comorian Association, their reform efforts can clearly be understood within the framework of contemporary British colonial policies. Although Burhan explicitly stated that he and his reformist friends opposed costly marriages and funerals because they were *bid'a*, the strong incentives for being categorized as "Arab" within the British colonial system cannot be disregarded. In other words, Islamic reform can be understood as an entryway into a specific "ethnic category" (as designated by the colonial authorities).

However, the "becoming Zanzibari/Arab-Zanzibari" motive goes beyond the utilitarian drive to fit a certain colonial "category". Islamic reform here means bringing the Comorian community more closely in line with the Islamic practices in urban Zanzibar—especially those aspects perceived to produce progress and development. *Grande mariage* and the matrilineal transmission of land were neither recognized by Zanzibar courts nor practised by other communities, nor perceived to be "forward-looking" in the sense of leading to progress.

From a regional historical perspective, this would mean that Comorians in Zanzibar (like in Mombasa) gradually adopted practices that were acceptable not only to the legal system but also socially—and not least with a view to a common future. In other words, what Burhan called "the Comorian reform movement" can be understood as a drive towards *assimilation*, and an appropriation of practices and values that brought Comorians in line with contemporary and, not least, a future vision of Zanzibar. In this vision, the minority is envisioned as dissolved into the future modern nation, in this case, the Zanzibari nation.

This interpretation may be strengthened by a reading of Burhan's *History of Grande Comore*, where he explicitly evokes the contributions that Comorians have made to the Zanzibari government, naming military leaders and police, as well as a long list of religious scholars. In this reading, reform served to emphasize the impact of the original homeland on the new—implicitly perhaps also acknowledging the opportunities offered there.

The same argument is made by Burhan's close associate, Ibuni Saleh, in his 1936 *History of the Comorians in Zanzibar*. Here Saleh very much highlights the contribution of the Comorians to the "development" of Zanzibar.[20] He argues that Comorians born and raised in Zanzibar "consider themselves as good Zanzibaris as anybody else could claim to be".[21] At the same time, he acknowledges the benefits of French patronage, although it seems unclear here whether Saleh added his praise of the French "lest I should be misunderstood".[22] His preface, on the other hand, can be read as an exhortation to Comorians in Zanzibar to accept and seek modernity:

> It is unnecessary at this stage to remind them [the Comorians] that the tide of time is moving rapidly and that they must, if they wish to preserve their dignity and retain their position, move on with the times, otherwise they will surely be overwhelmed and drowned. Such is the prediction of their fate in Zanzibar if they fail to appreciate the difficulties confronting them in the near future.[23]

Zanzibari reform—Zanzibari *wataniyya*?

The step from building a modern, future Zanzibar as a Comorian-Zanzibari and doing so as a Zanzibari Muslim is a small one, but was a very significant one during the colonial era. The question is whether the Muslim moderns—Comorian or otherwise—saw themselves shaping a new Zanzibar *qua* Zanzibaris, envisioning a future of cultural unity. If we read Burhan Mkelle's song for the Comorian School above somewhat differently, we may interpret his *hubb al-watan* to be directed towards the land of residence rather than that of ancestry—i.e. towards Zanzibar. In such a reading, the forward-looking gaze is fixed on Zanzibar, the homeland, which is the place where "you will succeed". The *qawm*, on the other hand, becomes more akin to heritage, something to take pride in, but within the framework of the real homeland.

In the previous chapter, we saw the "call for unity" of all the island's factions, and the ways in which reform of Islamic rituals and practices were understood to promote this unity. The Government Central School was another arena, as we saw in Chapter 4, where the "new" Zanzibari was to be moulded. We have also seen that the Comorian Association saw it as an ultimate goal to "be one" with the broader *Jamʿiyyat al-Sunna*. Lastly, the Mnazi Mmoja *mawlid* may well be understood as an event underscoring unity above all: unity among the many Islamic factions of Zanzibari society and implicitly building towards a Zanzibari cultural identity. The latter was a theme that Burhan returned to repeatedly in his writings about the *Jamʿiyyat al-Sunna*, and much of his devotional poetry may also be read as appeals to unity in love and respect for the Prophet.

However, here it is pertinent to raise the question of whether these future model citizens and associations were to be Zanzibaris as opposed to hyphenated Zanzibaris whose ancestral identity was to be maintained. In a song that Burhan composed for use in the Zanzibar Government Central School, where (despite its clear biases) young men of different backgrounds attended, the verses leave little doubt that the aim of the youngsters should be to create a better Zanzibar. We see the same moral tone here as in the song for the Comorian School. Again, we see the notion that Islamic moral codes, modelled upon the Prophet, will bring not only success for the individual, but for the *watan*—which in this case can mean only Zanzibar:

> Oh Lord, bestow knowledge upon this homeland (*waṭan*)
> So Zanzibar over time be lifted by her honourable sons[24]

There is no doubt that individuals like Burhan Mkelle, Abu 'l-Hasan Jamal al-Layl, Abdallah al-Hadrami and the rest of the "new intelligentsia" had much to gain by remaining in the good graces of the British-BuSaidi Sultanate, which was their main employer. As we have seen, they had their salaries and pensions to gain, but also their paths to influence—through the emerging media, and not least through the younger generation of Zanzibaris. There is little doubt that most of the drivers of Islamic reformism tended to express loyalty to the Zanzibar Sultanate and to highlight their links to the powers that be. During his career, Burhan Mkelle wrote several poems of praise for Sayyid Khalifa b. Harub, upon his ascension and upon his travels to and from Zanzibar. He also offered poems of praise for the "Sahib al-Dawla" Nasir b. Sulayman al-Lamki[25]—and even a poem offering condolences for Sayyid Khalifa upon the death of his wife Matuka in 1940.[26] We have also seen that he composed the lyrics for the Zanzibar national anthem—the "Sultan's March". While these poems should be read in light of the obvious motive of remaining close to the Muslim ruler of Zanzibar, we should also keep in mind the Sultanate itself as a political institution. The resistance to colonialism that Amal Ghazal has shown also meant that the Sultan was the most obvious future guarantor of modernity, progress and development in Zanzibar.

Islamic reform—Islamic *wataniyya*?

Returning to Burhan Mkelle's song for the students in the Comorian School, a third reading is possible that points solely to an Islamic identity, regardless of territorial or ethnic background. The direct link between faith and love of homeland that Burhan makes is also a reference to an oft-quoted line that is said to originate in a hadith: "One of the signs of faith is love of the homeland."[27] Here, homeland may be understood as anywhere in the world where Muslims reside, in other words, a de-territorialized form of *watan* that emphasizes Muslim unity across geography, sects and *madhhabs*. This is moving closely towards what colonial and other contemporary observers knew as Pan-Islamism.[28]

There are strong indications that Burhan's (and his companions') activities were directed towards an alignment with the Pan-Islamic, *umma*-oriented notion of community. Burhan, in his letter to Muhibb al-Din, is clearly concerned with the education of young Muslims overall—although we may also read into his letter concerns that he has seen play out in Zanzibar, and perhaps even more particularly among young Comorians in Zanzibar. Here, like Shaykh al-Amin, he seems to be very much in line with the political ideas of Shakib Arslan, whose main argument was that Muslims needed to develop a nationalist sentiment *qua* Muslims.[29] According to Arslan, the communal strength of the *umma* could only be realized when Muslims founded their national aspirations on their Islamic history, culture and heritage. In Arslan's world, there were neither Sufis nor Salafis, orthodoxy nor transgression, but a series of Muslim societies that were "backward" because they had lost their historical interconnectedness and thus also a clear view of their shared future. This opinion was most clearly expressed in Arslan's 1930 article, "Why Muslims Lagged Behind and Others Progressed",[30] which there is every reason to assume was also read widely in Zanzibar.

We may also view Ibuni Saleh's somewhat "on-the-one-hand/on-the-other-hand" statements in his *History of the Comorians in Zanzibar* as pointing in the same direction. In one way, he points not towards Zanzibari or any form of Arab-Swahili nationalism, but rather towards an alternate, extra-Zanzibari identity, much in the way of the Hadramis in Jakarta. By emphasizing a different origin from, for example, the Omani or Hadrami Arabs, Comorians would do well to position themselves as part of a greater Islamic world, or "transnational network", where the moral narrative of modernity was being played out.

Finally, it is worth noting that unlike in the Dutch East Indies or the Middle East (especially Egypt), the activities of Burhan Mkelle's circle do not seem to have a clearly expressed anti-colonial element—or at least it was not immediately perceived as such by the

British in Zanzibar. The British in Zanzibar certainly ramped up surveillance, especially in the 1930s, due to fears of both rising Arab nationalism and communist activities. In 1929, the British authorities in Zanzibar asked to be included in the monthly security briefs from the "Arab States" (i.e. the Gulf), and that of the Bombay Presidency Police Secret Abstract of Intelligence.[31] Still, the Zanzibari situation does not seem to have given cause to the moral panic voiced by L. Massignon, who, observing from North Africa in 1932, lamented at length "the problem of nationalism".[32] That said, the British surveillance was clearly very aware of tendencies that might arise, typically in relation to the *hajj*, and noted, for example, the presence of Shakib Arslan (referred to as "the notorious Nationalist") during the 1929 pilgrimage.[33]

The Failure of an Islamic Modernity in Zanzibar after World War II—Or Cultural Unity, Political Divide?

Kai Kresse has argued that Shaykh al-Amin's journal *Sahifa* remained a "little newpaper", never able to create a common platform for the entire coastal community.[34] In terms of theology, he might have done well to follow the advice of Burhan Mkelle, discussed in the previous chapter, by refraining from harsh condemnation and "extreme" statements such as outlawing prayers to the Prophet. However, another and more prosaic reason for the very limited circulation of *Sahifa* was the limited audience it appealed to.

Kresse analyses al-Amin's writings in light of the other communities that feature in them—the Indians, the Goans, the up-county Kenyans—and argues for a perspective whereby al-Amin casts them in Mombasa as "different but equal", i.e. as fellow men and women to learn from. In other words, social hierarchies are being cast anew, and knowledge can—and should—flow in all directions, each community learning from the other. The community that seeks change must seek it where it is most beneficial, be that in British technology and schooling systems, Indian business models and what would today be called corporate social responsibility, or just the hard work displayed by many. However, there is no doubt that al-Amin only speaks to the community of coastal Muslims, aiming mainly to instil the new form of Islamic morality we have seen repeatedly in this book. His intended audience does not extend, for example, to Muslims of other backgrounds—or, one may argue, even the new Muslims converting by means of Sufi networks or commoners.[35] As F. Becker has outlined for the southern Tanzania coast and hinterland, "new Muslims" made autonomous choices as to how the religion was to be practised—irrespective of what the likes of Shaykh al-Amin or Burhan might say or do.[36] In other words, the reform they propagated did not (or at least not explicitly) aim to dissolve pre-existing social, ethnic and linguistic lines that existed—even those that existed among Muslims.

The nationalizing of diasporas after World War II

As World War II came to an end, Zanzibar was still very much a British-BuSaidi protectorate, and while the "time of politics" was beginning, there were in fact few administrative or political changes towards greater independence or self-governance. The 1940s also saw the death of a generation, including Shaykh al-Amin and Burhan Mkelle. Meanwhile, what was described above as "secular nationalism" was rising in other parts of the Muslim world and across the Indian Ocean, leaving the different communities in Zanzibar open to becoming "nationalized" by the independence struggles in their respective countries of origin. This is, as outlined above, what N. Beertz has shown for the Indian community in Dar-es-Salaam.

In the post-World War II Comoro Islands, changes were unfolding that actualized the still-lacking unity-in-diversity that had been very much part of the interwar Islamic reformist discourse. In 1946, the islands were granted administrative independence from Madagascar. New political institutions were introduced, and the archipelago formally became a *territoire d'outre-mer* in its own right. Colonial subjects of these territories were granted French citizenship, even if resident in another colony—as we have seen with Burhan Mkelle and the Comorians of Zanzibar.[37]

The new administrative position of the Comoros in 1946 meant that the archipelago was entitled to representation in the French parliament. Two candidates emerged for the single seat. The first was Said Mohamed Cheikh (1904–1970),[38] a descendant of Mwinyi Mkuu, born in Mitsamiouli, Grande Comore. After schooling he won a scholarship for further education in Madagascar where he studied medicine and graduated, in 1926, as the first Comorian doctor. This may have been where he got in touch with anti-colonial movements then emerging in Madagascar. After World War II, he went into politics and emerged as a candidate for the single seat allocated to the Comoros in the French Fourth Republic. The second candidate was Prince Said Ibrahim b. Said Ali. He too was educated in Madagascar and entered the civil service. Prince Said was originally the candidate of the elders, but they eventually rejected him in favour of the older Cheikh (then aged forty-two), who had more support on the other islands. Said Mohamed Cheikh was thus elected unopposed and represented Comoros for the first five-year period.

As M. Saleh has pointed out,[39] the two candidates for the first Comorian seat in the French parliament very much echoed the *Yamini/Shimali* divide in Zanzibar in the interwar years. Cheikh was the reformist candidate, propagating an agenda of progress and development, whereas Prince Said originally represented traditional power structures and Comorian customs. It is not surprising, then, that Burhan Mkelle chose to salute Cheikh with a statement on the occasion of the latter's departure for Paris:

> This is the medical doctor Said Mohamed b. Cheikh Mansab.
>
> This envoy travelled to Paris, the capital of France, and this time he achieved his mission.
>
> Now he is returning to his homeland and to his position.
>
> We pray God for his safety and purity in his state and his travels.[40]

While the *Yamini* modernists had achieved relative success in Zanzibar, at a time when independence was not on the horizon, no such resolution was in sight in the soon-to-be independent Comoros.

In other words, while the struggles over Islamic reformist identity remained a "culture war" in Zanzibar, in the Comoro Islands it played out in a very real political struggle over representation. While this elicited a poem of praise in Zanzibar (which shows merely that Comorians in Zanzibar followed developments in the Comoros closely), it did not elicit similar demands for representation *qua* Comorians in the British-BuSaidi state.

The story is very different if we turn to Arab nationalism. Contrary to Comorianness, Arabness in Zanzibar was an established hegemonic discourse, favoured by both the British and the BuSaidis. However, as discussed here, rather than straightforward political nationalism making political demands, this had the form of a cultural programme that was far from clearly formulated in terms of whom it spoke to. The potential of inclusivity and exclusivity remained unresolved in the Zanzibari discourse of Islamic reform, as formulated in Arabic and with frequent references to ongoing debates in Egypt and the broader Middle East.

Cultural unity—divided nation?

Iain Walker has pointed out with reference to the Comoro Islands that the African post-colonial nation hardly counts as a success story.[41] However, in its post-revolutionary history, Zanzibar has fared much better than the Comoros, insofar as *coups d'état* and violence have largely been absent, although post-election violence and widespread allegations of fraud have plagued Zanzibari elections since multi-party elections were introduced in 1995.[42] Despite the drawn-out debates over the nature, purpose and future of its union with the mainland, it is hard to characterize Zanzibar in its current post-revolutionary iteration as a failed state. Retrospectively, it is possible to view this lack of complete fragmentation in Zanzibar as founded on the relative success of the cultural programmes that were formulated in the inter-war years.

The very ambiguity inherent in this form of cultural nationalism, and the vague (or even inconsistent) definition of who should be the targets of Islamic reform, meant that broader alliances were hard to establish and political mobilization—let alone unity—remained elusive. On the other hand, the cultural programme that was espoused by the Muslim moderns did in fact succeed, insofar as Zanzibar to this day is marked by precisely the rituals, the teachings and the associations that they established—despite successive waves of change: the period of decolonization, the 1964 revolution, and the emergence of Saudi-style Wahhabism and modern Salafism from the 1990s.

9

CONCLUSIONS

THE BEGINNINGS OF A MODERN MUSLIM ZANZIBARI CULTURE

Zanzibar anno 2024 is a state within the union of Tanzania, a semi-independent territory with its own president, flag, parliament, laws and education system. It is also very much a 2024 society, marked by all the trappings of modernity, most notably mass tourism with all its effects on labour migration, the natural environment, cultural heritage and monuments, and the culture itself. It is also predominantly a Muslim society, where men and women hold on to practices which they perceive as core to their faith, be that in dietary habits, dressing style, the celebration of Eids and *mawlids*—or in healing by *soma* (readings) or the recurring practices linked to life-cycle events.

This book has sought to locate a vision laid out a hundred years before the omnipresence of beach hotels and Islamic guidance circulating on WhatsApp and in Swahili. How did the interwar generation view the modern Zanzibari, the new Muslim who was to lead the way to progress and development?

The Paradoxes of Progress: On Cultural Change

This book has examined a set of self-reflexive discourses from the Zanzibari interwar period. This discourse was produced by and between men who I have called "Muslim moderns" (rather than outright defining them as Sufis, Salafis, Wahhabis or any other religious label), because their discourse was informed by something new, something their elders and teachers (like Ahmad b. Sumayt and Abd Allah BaKathir) did not incorporate into their writings and actions. This "something new" was a moral narrative of modernity, an orientation towards a future somehow envisioned as better than the past.

The reader has now spent around 200 pages in the company of a group of people who I claim "spoke modern", and who—I also claim—wanted their fellows to speak the same way. What I have aimed to show is that men like Burhan Mkelle, Shaykh al-Amin, Ahmad Mlomri and many others participated in an ongoing moral narrative that aimed at nothing less than transforming the Zanzibari self. In this sense, they were modern. They spoke, I claim, modern.

Let us now first examine the accents they used in their "modern-speak". As many of the textual sources that form the basis for this argument were written in Arabic, it comes as no surprise that their accent was heavily infused with Arabic. However, this was not the Arabic of the land-owning Omani aristocracy (or rather, by this time, the former land-owning aristocracy). Nor was it that of the classical tradition of Islamic scholarship. It was, however, definitely Islamic, and decidedly Shafiʿi Sunni.

It was also heavily Manarist. This is not to say that the Zanzibari Muslim moderns necessarily followed the Manarist line in all matters of law or politics. However, they were aligned with the Manarist view of religion as fully compatible with modern science, and as a knowledge system understood as something that evolved (and could intentionally *be* evolved) over time. This shift was, as we saw in Chapter 2, a prolonged one in Zanzibar, as indeed anywhere in the world—and is perhaps still ongoing.

A second detectable accent is that of the Dar al-Ulum in Cairo. This is particularly clear within the educational field, where a new pedagogy for teaching Arabic was introduced. Knowledge was no longer to mean knowing by heart, but knowing how to *use* that knowledge, to be a person with agency, capable of self-transformation.

Thirdly, our actors also spoke with the accent of the salaried employee. This was primarily a result of the bureaucracy set up by the British colonial state, so in that sense one could argue that this was a hint of a British accent. However, like D. Commins, I argue that the very fact of being employed by a depersonalized bureaucracy, receiving monthly salaries and concerning oneself with issues such as pension rights, gives for a new sense of identity as something that can be cultivated and—not least—organized by the individual.

Fourthly, our Zanzibari Muslim moderns spoke with a wide range of different accents depending on their origin. In this book, we have focused particularly on Comorians who sought "loose" aspects of their Comorianness in favour of a more generalized Zanzibari, Muslim identity. In this context, Comorianness becomes heritage, a memory of an origin past to be celebrated and honoured, rather than a set of customary practices defining identity. The modern accent, in this regard, will retain a "heritage" twang, one kept purposefully to highlight cultural origin. The Comorians were not alone in this endeavour. As we have seen, many other groups in Zanzibar formed similar associations. People of Arab descent, for example, were first and foremost represented by the elite Arab Association, but by the 1920s by a proliferation of alternative organizations. While the inner workings of these associations have not been examined in detail in this study, they too sought in various ways to mould a modern form of Arabness in the Zanzibari context, referencing different origins and different notions of what origin implied. Although Arabness retained prestige and access to resources, people who for various reasons self-identified as Arabs were faced with the same choice as the Comorians: whether to retain or loose aspects of distinct cultural practices in favour of reform, understood as a future Zanzibari identity. This was particularly acute for those of Hadrami origin; as fellow Shafiʿi Sunnis, they were not ritually set apart in the way of the Ibadi Omanis. The same is the case for one of the most understudied, yet influential communities in Zanzibar, the Bravanese—alongside many others.

The Wahhabi way of speaking modern could also be detected in Zanzibar during the interwar years. However, as we have seen, it would have to be "toned down", lest people turn against it. The early accent of the Muslim Brotherhood, as expressed by *al-Fath*, is another inflection that comes across in the writings of Burhan Mkelle and Shaykh al-Amin.

Together, these made up a disinctly Zanzibari accent, formed through a discourse that took place in a modern context.

In the same vein, I have also examined a set of actions, such as the reformulation of the *mawlid* celebrations and and the efforts to teach Islamic subjects in new ways. The Zanzibari Muslim moderns shared many traits with their compatriots in the Middle East, such as their educational background (a melange between traditional Islamic and modern education), regular employment and access to new media, such as journals and newspapers. This is not to say that their notions of self-transformation were entirely moulded upon Middle Eastern models. Rather, as we have seen, this was a discourse that at times proposed solutions grounded in the emergent state of Saudi Arabia, and at others elevated selected locally grounded traditions, such as the *mawlid*, to the level of national culture, while outrightly rejecting others, such as funeral rituals.

In this study I have also examined a series of cultural programmes, formed on the basis of cultural exchanges in what was clearly a modern Zanzibari context. We have seen educational efforts within the colonial school system, organizational changes in the form of a new crop of *jamʿiyāt* (associations), and an ongoing debate over how best to organize education, from provision for the youngest children up to universities.

The cultural programmes formed in this period focused on improvement, such as "educating oneself" or becoming "civilized". These were core concepts to the generation of Zanzibari authors, teachers and activists who figure in this book. We have seen how they formed associations for this purpose, how they argued for educational institutions that could produce moral subjects, and how they denounced practices which they deemed incompatible with being "civilized" in the modern Islamic way.

Some of these Muslim moderns were educated in the Islamic sciences, like Shaykh al-Amin al-Mazrui. Others were employed men in various branches of the colonial system, like Burhan Mkelle and his fellow Comorians in the Comorian Association. Their ideas were very much in line with those of Jurji Zaydan, whose books we have seen appear on the shelves of a figure like Burhan Mkelle. Being a person of *adab* no longer meant only outwardly mastering social forms. To the Muslim modern it meant continous improvement of the self, of being a person of moral character (*akhlāq*).

The Muslim moderns of Zanzibar clearly did not make a puritanist turn, where morality would serve solely to improve the individual in the eyes of God. This was not a puritanist-Salafi movement, although it certainly adhered to some of its ideas, such as the rejection of what it termed *bidʿa* practices. This was not a rejection of their Sufi teachers and elders, even though there were certainly points where opinions could differ (such as, for example, the possibility of God allowing miracles in our day and age).

Rather, on the contrary, as we have seen in the case of the *Jamʿiyyat al-Sunna*, the aim was to *develop* and implement their teachings for a new era. This was a process whereby ideas of Zanzibari civility became formulated in the "modern accent" of Rashid Rida and his fellow modernists. To the Muslim modern, having *adab* and *heshima* amounted to the same: a moral, respectable, rational individual whose acts were guided by the *choice* to do good.

Rather than an individualist self-improvement programme, the Muslim modern ideal was explicitly voiced as an improvement of society, one person at a time—for Zanzibar to be "lifted by her honourable sons", as Burhan Mkelle formulated it. The core aim was to build a moral *community*, one that could achieve the overarching goals of progress and development.

As C. Mayeur-Jaouen has pointed out, and as I have noted in Chapter 1 of this book, *adab* came to be understood as having also a moral dimension, which increasingly came to be formulated in terms of identity. Who are we to be, in this, our morally strengthened community? We have seen in this book how this could mean the improvement of young children in the government school, the Comorian community, the Sunni Muslims—or even the ambition of progress for the Muslim world in general. Here, as this book has shown, the "target audience" remained unclear.

While the Muslim moderns clearly aimed to reach the widest possible audience (especially clear in the case of the *Jamʿiyyat al-Sunna*), one may argue that they ran into a problem on how to disseminate their ideas—or how to establish an arena for knowledge exchange. As we have seen, Burhan Mkelle would carefully correct his friend

Shaykh al-Amin for being too harsh in his criticism of all things traditional. Rashid Rida was even harsher, and simply called traditional healers "charlatans" whose knowledge was essentially useless.

As has been shown in this book, the Muslim modern in Zanzibar came from within the Sufi episteme. The actors may have distanced themselves from organized Sufism, preferring the non-initiatory format of the *jamʿiyya*, but as we have seen they were also very much associated with long-standing Sufi circles—and were, as in the case of Burhan Mkelle, even buried with Sufi *dhikr* prayers.

Like their teachers, who were themselves reformist-oriented Sufis, the Muslim moderns emphasized textual transmission and production over oral, while at the same time organizing rituals that were decidedly oral and communal. Furthermore, their emphasis on rational knowledge over magic or esoteric text usage led to an increased emphasis on understanding the Arabic language for access to the Revelation. Without such access, an individual could not strive for moral self-improvement and, consequently, society could not develop. Proper knowledge in itself, in the sense of non-esoteric, modernist, rationalist religious knowledge and corresponding professional skills, was perceived of as imperative for future progress in Zanzibar. The Muslim moderns in Zanzibar shared much with Sayyid Fadl, as outlined in Chapter 1, including the local/present and transregional/historical qualities pointed out by W. C. Jacob. They particularly shared a seemingly unshakable faith in knowledge, to be acquired, imparted and used for a specific purpose.

In many ways, one may say that the "culture wars", viewed in the 100-years-later rear-view mirror, actually succeeded in creating a kernel of Zanzibari identity. Observers of present-day Zanzibar Town tend to view the urban conglomeration as cosmopolitan, multi-ethnic or multi-cultural. However, most agree—as do most residents—that there exists something that unifies Zanzibaris across their differences. This unifying element, as K. Larsen has argued, is cultural, and goes beyond ethnic group (or *kabila*, as Larsen proposes): "[…] Zanzibar as a complex society, socially and economically differentiated, yet culturally unified and imbued with expected as well as actualized forms of rank and stratification".[1] In other words, one could argue that the self-reflexive discourse on Muslim identity, during an era when all Zanzibari identities were "in play", was sufficiently inclusive to become if not a unified political nationalist stance, then at least a shared culture within which separate groups could assert their distinctiveness.

* * *

At the end of this study, some questions remain wide open. The pathways signposted by the interwar Muslim moderns somehow led to the Zanzibar revolution of 1964, and the relegation of Islamic modernist cultural programmes to the attics of African nationalism and socialism, only to reappear in the 1990s in the puritanist garb (literally and figuratively) of Salafism. One may argue that the cultural programmes, as laid out by the interwar generation, lacked a political dimension. They lacked a clear "implementation plan" for how their Muslim modernity was to accommodate all Zanzibaris—women and men, former slaves and former slave owners, Sunnis, Ibadis and Shias, Hindus and Christians, those who had a connection to the Arabic-speaking world and those who did not, those who subscribed to an esoteric world view and those who did not, Sufis and Salafis, urban and rural, Pembans and Ungujans.

One conclusion is that the future Zanzibari culture envisioned by the "*jamʿiyya*-generation" did in fact come to fruition on the cultural level, but failed on the political. The reason for this was the same as in the rest of the Islamic world: the message (expressed as moral guidance) was clear, but the intended audience was not. The orientation towards the future was expressed in the terminology of "progress" through societal moral improvement, but it failed to adress the essential question: Who are we?

NOTES

EPIGRAPH

1. Translated by A. K. Bang and Taha Shoeib from the original Arabic. Reproduced in Muhammad Ahmad Hamid, *Al-ʿAṣr al-dhahhabī li-Zinjibār*, Amman: Jordan, 2021, 269–271. All further translations are by A. K. Bang unless otherwise indicated.

1. IN SEARCH OF THE ZANZIBARI MUSLIM MODERN: ON MODERNITY, PROGRESS AND DEVELOPMENT

1. S. Lindqvist, *"Exterminate all the Brutes"*, London: Granta, 1997.
2. A. Mbembe, *Out of the Dark Night: Essays on Decolonization*, New York: Columbia University Press, 2021, 120.
3. D. Walcott, "The Schooner 'Flight'" (9: "Maria Concepcion and the Book of Dreams"), in: D. Walcott, *The Star-Apple Kingdom*, New York: Farrar, Straus & Giroux, 1979; here quoted from https://allpoetry.com/The-Schooner-%27Flight%27
4. T. Asad, "Conscripts of Western Civilization?", in: C. Gailey (ed.), *Dialectical Anthropology: Essays in Honor of Stanley Diamond*, Vol. 1, Gainesville: University Press of Florida, 1992, 333–351.
5. A. Sheriff, *Slaves, Spices and Ivory in Zanzibar*, Oxford: Oxford University Press, 1987; A. Sheriff & E. Ferguson (eds.), *Zanzibar under Colonial Rule*, London: J. Currey, 1991.
6. F. Cooper, *From Slaves to Squatters: Plantation Labor and Agriculture in Zanzibar and Coastal Kenya, 1890–1925*, New Haven: Yale University Press, 1980.
7. P. W. Romero, "'Where Have All the Slaves Gone?' Emancipation and Post-Emancipation in Lamu, Kenya", *Journal of African History*, 27:3, 1986, 497–512.
8. J. Glassman, *Feasts and Riot: Revelry, Rebellion and Popular Consciousness on the Swahili Coast, 1856–1888*, London: J. Currey, 1995.

9. L. Fair, *Pastimes and Politics: Culture, Community, and Identity in Post-Abolition Urban Zanzibar, 1890–1945*, Athens, OH: Ohio University Press, 2001.
10. J. Prestholdt, *Domesticating the World: African Consumerism and the Genealogies of Globalization*, Berkeley: University of California Press, 2008.
11. E. McMahon, *Slavery and Emancipation in Islamic East Africa: From Honor to Respectability*, Cambridge: Cambridge University Press, 2013.
12. E. Stockreiter, *Islamic Law, Gender and Social Change in Post-Abolition Zanzibar*, Cambridge: Cambridge University Press, 2015.
13. J. Prestholdt, *Domesticating the World*. See especially chapter 4, 88–116.
14. J. Prestholdt, *Domesticating the World*, 162–163.
15. R. Loimeier, *Eine Zeitlandschaft in der Globalisierung: Das islamische Sansibar im 19 under 20 Jahrhundert*, Bielefeld: Transcript Verlag, 2012, 96.
16. W. H. Ingrams, *Zanzibar: Its History and its People*, London: Stacey International, 2007 (first published 1931), 179.
17. B. Anderson, *Imagined Communities: Reflections on the Origin and Spread of Nationalism*, revised ed., London: Verso, 2006 (1st ed., London: Verso, 1983). On the role of print in the Arab and broader Islamic world, see A. Ayalon, *The Arabic Print Revolution: Cultural Production and Mass Readership*, Cambridge: Cambridge University Press, 2016; N. Green, *Bombay Islam: The Religious Economy of the West Indian Ocean, 1840–1915*, Cambridge: Cambridge University Press, 2011; R. Schulze, "The Birth of Tradition and Modernity in 18th and 19th Century Islamic Culture: The Case of Printing", *Culture and History* (Special issue: J. Skovgaard Pedersen (ed.), *The Introduction of the Printing Press in the Middle East*), 16, 1997, 29–72.
18. A. Ghazal, *Islamic Reform and Arab Nationalism: Expanding the Crescent from the Mediterranean to the Indian Ocean (1880s–1930s)*, London: Routledge, 2010.
19. For an overview of the emergence of print culture in Zanzibar, see S. Reese, "'The Ink of Excellence': Print and the Islamic Written Tradition of East Africa", in: S. Reese (ed.), *Manuscript and Print in the Islamic Tradition*, Studies in Manuscript Cultures 26, Berlin: De Gruyter, 2022, 217–242: A. K. Bang, "Double Sided Print: Silent and Communal Reading During the Rise of Islamic Print in East Africa, 1880–1940", in: K. Barber & S. Newell (eds.), *Print Cultures and African Literature, 1860–1960*, Cambridge: Cambridge University Press (forthcoming). See also A. K. Bang, "Authority and Piety, Writing and Print: A Preliminary Study of the Circulation of Islamic Texts in Late Nineteenth- and Early Twentieth-Century Zanzibar", *Africa: Journal of the International African Institute*, 81:1, 2011, 89–107.
20. L. Halevi, *Modern Things on Trial: Islam's Global and Material Reformation in the Age of Rida, 1865–1935*, New York: Columbia University Press, 2019.
21. F. Zemmin, *Modernity in Islamic Tradition: The Concept of "Society" in the Journal* al-Manar *(Cairo, 1898–1940)*, Berlin: De Gruyter, 2018.
22. *Supplement to the Zanzibar Gazette*, 11 February 1928.

23. B. Reinwald, "'Tonight at the Empire': Cinema and Urbanity in Zanzibar, 1920s to 1960s", *Afrique & Histoire*, 5:1, 2006, 81–109.
24. L. Fair, *Reel Pleasures: Cinema Audiences and Entrepreneurs in Twentieth-Century Urban Tanzania*, Athens, OH: Ohio University Press, 2018, 43–47.
25. A. Greenwood, "The Colonial Medical Service and the Struggle for Control of the Zanzibar Maternity Association, 1918–47", in: A. Greenwood (ed.), *Beyond the State: The Colonial Medical Service in British Africa*, Manchester: Manchester University Press, 2016, 85–103.
26. A. Ghazal, *Islamic Reform and Arab Nationalism*, 53.
27. C. Decker, *Mobilizing Zanzibari Women: The Struggle for Respectability and Self-Reliance in Colonial East Africa*, New York: Palgrave Macmillan, 2014, 87–92.
28. E. Stockreiter, *Islamic Law*.
29. E. McMahon, "'Marrying Beneath Herself': Women, Affect, and Power in Colonial Zanzibar", *Africa Today*, 61:4, 2015, 27–40.
30. J. Robbins, "God is Nothing but Talk: Modernity, Language, and Prayer in Papua New Guinea Society", *Amercian Anthropologist*, 103:4, 2001, 901–912, 902.
31. W. Keane, *Christian Moderns: Freedom and Fetish in the Mission Encounter*, Berkeley: University of California Press, 2007.
32. W. Keane, "Secularism as a Moral Narrative of Modernity", *Transit: Europäische Revue*, 43, 2013, 159–170, 160.
33. B. Wittrock, "Modernity: One, None, or Many? European Origins and Modernity as a Global Condition", *Daedalus*, 129:1, 2000, 31–60.
34. J. Robbins, "God is Nothing but Talk", 902.
35. R. W. Hefner, "Multiple Modernities: Christianity, Islam, and Hinduism in a Globalizing Age", *Annual Review of Anthropology*, 27, 1998, 83–104; S. N. Eisenstadt, "Multiple Modernities", *Daedalus*, 129:1, 2000, 1–29; S. Eisenstadt (ed.), *Multiple Modernities*, New Brunswick, NJ: Transaction, 2005. For a discussion, see E. Fourie, "A Future for the Theory of Multiple Modernities: Insights from the New Modernization Theory", *Social Science Information*, 51:1, 2012, 52–69.
36. S. Kaviraj, "Modernity and Politics in India", in: S. Eisenstadt (ed.), *Multiple Modernities*, 137–161, 138.
37. T. Asad, "Conscripts".
38. D. Scott, *Conscripts of Modernity: The Tragedy of Colonial Enlightenment*, Durham, NC: Duke University Press, 2004, 113–115.
39. A. Tayob, "Decolonizing the Study of Religions: Muslim Intellectuals and the Enlightenment Project of Religious Studies", *Journal for the Study of Religion*, 31:2, 2018, 7–35.
40. A. Tayob, "Decolonizing", 19.
41. C. Mayeur-Jaouen (ed.), *Adab and Modernity: A "Civilizing Process"? (Sixteenth–Twenty-First Century)*, Leiden: Brill, 2020.
42. C. Mayeur-Jaouen (ed.), *Adab and Modernity*, 27–32.

43. E. McMahon, *Slavery and Emancipation*.
44. R. Pouwels, *Horn and Crescent: Cultural Change and Traditional Islam on the East African Coast, 800–1900*, Cambridge: Cambridge University Press, 1987.
45. W. Keane, *Christian Moderns*.
46. R. Loimeier, "What is 'Reform'? Approaches to a Problematic Term in African Muslim Contexts", *Journal for Islamic Studies*, 32, 2012, 7–23, 10.
47. J. Glassman, *War of Words, War of Stones: Racial Thought and Violence in Colonial Zanzibar*, Bloomington: Indiana University Press, 2011.
48. R. Loimeier, "Memories of Revolution: Patterns of Interpretation of the 1964 Revolution in Zanzibar", in: W. C. Bissell & M-A. Fouéré, *Social Memory, Silenced Voices and Political Struggle: Remembering the Revolution in Zanzibar*, Dar-es-Salaam: Mkuki na Nyota, 2018, 37–78, 61.
49. In addition to the ones quoted above, see also R. Loimeier, "Is There Something Like 'Protestant Islam'?", *Die Welt des Islams*, 54:2, 2005, 216–254.
50. A. K. Bang, "Esoteric Authority and Sufi Networks of the *ḥajj*: Two Zanzibari *ḥajj* accounts, 1898–1951" (forthcoming).
51. Central studies in this debate include: A. El Shamsy, *Rediscovering the Islamic Classics: How Editors and Print Culture Transformed an Intellectual Tradition*, Princeton: Princeton University Press, 2020; H. Lauzière, *The Making of Salafism: Reform in the Twentieth Century*, New York: Columbia University Press, 2016; and S. Haj, *Reconfiguring Islamic Tradition: Reform, Rationality, and Modernity*, Stanford: Stanford University Press, 2009.
52. M. M. Ringer, *Islamic Modernism and the Re-Enchantment of the Sacred in the Age of History*, Edinburgh: Edinburgh University Press, 2020, 6.
53. F. Piraino & M. Sedgwick (eds.), *Global Sufism: Boundaries, Structures, and Politics*, London: Hurst, 2019.
54. The list is too long to be given in full here. For examples, see I. Weismann, "The Politics of Popular Religion: Sufis, Salafis and Muslim Brothers in 20th-Century Hamah", *International Journal of Middle East Studies*, 37:1, 2005, 39–58; O. O. Kane, *Beyond Timbuktu*, Cambridge, MA: Harvard University Press, 2016; M. van Bruinessen & J. Day Howell (eds.), *Sufism and the "Modern" in Islam*, London/New York: I. B. Tauris, 2013; and A. K. Bang, *Islamic Sufi Networks in the Western Indian Ocean (c. 1880–1940): Ripples of Reform*, Leiden: Brill, 2014.
55. R. Gauvain, *Salafi Ritual Purity: In the Presence of God*, London: Routledge, 2012.
56. On this, and on what follows, much research exists. See A. H. Nimtz, *Islam and Politics in East Africa: The Sufi Order in Tanzania*, Minneapolis: University of Minnesota Press, 1980; B. G. Martin, *Muslim Brotherhoods in Nineteenth-Century Africa*, Cambridge: Cambridge University Press, 1976; C. Ahmed, "Networks of the Shādhiliyya Yashruṭiyya Sufi Order in East Africa", in: R. Loimeier & R. Seesemann, *The Global Worlds of the Swahili: Interfaces of Islam, Identity and Space in Nineteenth and Twentieth-Century East Africa*, Hamburg: Lit Verlag, 2006, 317–342; and A. K. Bang, *Islamic Sufi Networks*.

57. R. Loimeier, *Between Social Skills and Marketable Skills: The Politics of Islamic Education in 20th-Century Zanzibar*, Leiden: Brill, 2009; A. Ghazal, *Islamic Reform and Arab Nationalism*; A. K. Bang, *Islamic Sufi Networks*; R. Loimeier, *Islamic Reform in Twentieth-Century Africa*, Edinburgh: Edinburgh University Press, 2016.
58. D. J. Morgan, *The Official History of Colonial Development*, Vol. 1, *The Origins of British Aid Policy, 1924–1945*, London: Macmillan, 1980; M. A. Havinden & D. Meredith, *Colonialism and Development: Britain and its Tropical Colonies, 1850–1960*, London: Routledge, 1993.
59. S. Constantine, *The Making of British Colonial Development Policy, 1914–1930*, London: Routledge, 1984; E. R. Wicker, "Colonial Development and Welfare, 1929–1957: The Evolution of a Policy", *Social and Economic Studies*, 7:4, 1958, 170–192.
60. C. Decker & E. McMahon, *The Idea of Development in Africa: A History*, Cambridge: Cambridge University Press, 2021. As an example, Decker and McMahon point to the fact that while 600 technical specialists were assigned to British African colonies in 1919, their number had increased to 2,000 by 1931 (*The Idea of Development*, 110).
61. From the declaration of the Zanzibar Protectorate in July 1890 until its formal end in December 1963. On the British period in Zanzibar and East Africa, and the preceding period of BuSaidi rule, see, for example, L. W. Hollingsworth, *Zanzibar under the Foreign Office, 1890–1913*, London: Macmillan, 1953; N. R. Bennett, *A History of the Arab State of Zanzibar*, London: Methuen, 1978; and M. F. Lofchie, *Zanzibar: Background to Revolution*, Princeton: Princeton University Press, 1965. See also the contemporary accounts given by R. N. Lyne, in *Zanzibar in Contemporary Times*, London: Hurst & Blackett, 1905, and W. H. Ingrams, *Zanzibar: Its History and its People*.
62. S. Longair, *Cracks in the Dome: Fractured Histories of Empire in the Zanzibar Museum, 1897–1964*, London: Routledge, 2015, 3.
63. C. Decker, *Mobilizing Zanzibari Women*, 47–67.
64. E. Stockreiter, *Islamic Law*.
65. R. Loimeier, *Between Social Skills*.
66. C. Decker, *Mobilizing Zanzibari Women*.
67. W. C. Bissell, *Urban Design, Chaos, and Colonial Power in Zanzibar*, Bloomington: Indiana University Press, 2011.
68. J. Glassman, *War of Words*.
69. L. Fair, *Pastimes and Politics*.
70. W. C. Jacob, *For God or Empire: Sayyid Fadl and the Indian Ocean World*, Stanford: Stanford University Press, 2019, 153.
71. W. C. Jacob, *For God or Empire*, 185.
72. N. Arnold, *Wazee wakijua mambo! / Elders Used to Know Things!: Occult Powers and Revolutionary History in Pemba, Zanzibar*, PhD Thesis, Indiana University, 2003; E. McMahon, *Slavery and Emancipation*; K. Larsen, *Where Humans and Spirits*

Meet: The Politics of Rituals and Identified Spirits in Zanzibar, New York: Berghahn Books, 2010; L. Mackenrodt, *Swahili Spirit Possession and Islamic Healing in Contemporary Tanzania: The Jinn Fly on Friday*, Hamburg: Verlag Dr Kovac, 2011.

73. S. Haj, *Reconfiguring Islamic Tradition*.
74. N. Gardiner, "Stars and Saints: The Esotericist Astrology of the Sufi Occultist Aḥmad al-Būnī", *Journal of Magic, Ritual, and Witchcraft*, 12:1, 2017, 39–65; N. Gardiner, *Esotericism in Manuscript Culture: Aḥmad al-Būnī and his Readers through the Mamluk Period*, PhD Diss., University of Michigan, 2014; N. Gardiner, "Forbidden Knowledge? Notes on the Production, Transmission, and Reception of the Major Works of Aḥmad al-Būnī", *Journal of Arabic and Islamic Studies*, 12, 2012, 81–142.
75. R. Loimeier, *Eine Zeitlandschaft in der Globalisierung*.

2. PROLOGUE: THE MAGIC AND THE MODERN—ZANZIBAR, 1904

1. *Al-Manar*, 7:10, 388, 16 Jumada I 1322/30 July 1904. Here quoted throughout from the version of *al-Manar* online at https://shamela.ws/book/6947
2. The lengthy discussion of the prophetic ability to know the unseen and the existence of the *Mahdi* is also interesting reading, and posits Rida's view as more rationalist than, for example, Ahmad Zayni Dahlan, who also doubted the *Mahdi*, but on grounds of weak and inconsistent hadiths.
3. R. Loimeier, "Traditions of Reform, Reforms of Tradition: Case Studies from Senegal and Zanzibar/Tanzania, in: Z. Hirji (ed.), *Diversity and Pluralism in Islam: Historical and Contemporary Discourses among Muslims*, London/New York: I. B. Tauris, 2010, 135–162. Loimeier refers to the early reformist efforts in Zanzibar as a "false start", which only gained hold mainly though the work of Shaykh al-Amin al-Mazrui.
4. W. Keane, "Secularism", 164.
5. A. Marcus-Sells, *Sorcery or Science? Contesting Knowledge and Practice in West African Sufi Texts*, University Park: Pennsylvania State University Press, 2022.
6. Y. Kumek, "The Sacred text in Egypt's Popular Culture: The Qur'ānic Sounds, Meanings and Formation of Sakīna (Sacred Space) in Traditions of Poverty and Fear", in: O. O. Kane (ed.), *Islamic Scholarship in Africa*, London: J. Currey, 2021, 204–232.
7. K. Larsen, "By Way of the Qur'an: Appeasing Spirits, Easing Emotions and Everyday Matters in Zanzibar", in: Z. Hirji (ed.), *Approaches to the Qur'an in Sub-Saharan Africa*, Oxford: Oxford University Press, 2019, 317–339. On the use of the Quran for magical or occult purposes, see also N. Arnold, *Wazee wakijua mambo! / Elders Used to Know Things!*, esp. chapter 2.
8. K. Larsen, *Where Humans and Spirits Meet*.
9. Ministry of Endowments and Religious Affairs, Electronic Library, Manuscripts. https://elibrary.mara.gov.om/en/zanzibar-library/manuscripts/

10. L. Declich, *The Arabic Manuscripts of the Zanzibar National Archives: A Checklist*, Supplemento No. 2 Alla Rivista degli Studi Orientali, Nouva Serie, Vol. LXXVIII, Pisa/Roma (Instituti Editoriali e Poligrafica Internazionali): Academia Editoriale, 2006.
11. ZIAR-ZA 2/4L. L. Declich, *The Arabic Manuscripts*, 49.
12. For examples, see ZIAR-ARC-5/23, 5/24, 5/25, 5/26.
13. MPRINT-MIC-CSMC-20.
14. For a discussion of the *Duʿa al-sabāsīb al-sabʿa* written around 1930, see A. K. Bang, "Islamic Incantations in a Colonial Notebook: A Case from Interwar Zanzibar", *Cahiers d'Études Africaines*, LIX (4), 236, 2019, 1025–1046.
15. https://elibrary.mara.gov.om/en/zanzibar-library/manuscripts/book/?id=8426 This is a modern handwritten copy of the *Al-Sir al-ʿAliy fī Khawās al-Nabāt al-Sawāḥilī*, by al-Kharusi. The copy is undated, but the lined paper and pen indicate a production some time around the 1940s/1950s.
16. https://elibrary.mara.gov.om/en/zanzibar-library/manuscripts/book/?id=8608 This manuscript has an index at the end.
17. https://eap.bl.uk/collection/EAP466–1/search See also A. K. Bang, "The Riyadha Mosque Manuscript Collection in Lamu: A Ḥaḍramī Tradition in Kenya", *Journal of Islamic Manuscripts* (Special issue: A. Regourd (ed.), *Manuscripts of Yemen, Circulation of Ideas and Models*), 5:2/3, 2014, 125–153.
18. Several hadiths make this exception in the case of scorpion or snake bites. Some also emphasize that the Prophet allowed the performer of *ruqiya* to be compensated for using the Quran for this purpose. See, for example, Sahih Bukhari, 7, 71, Hadith 632: "Some of the companions of the Prophet passed by some people staying at a place where there was water, and one of those people had been stung by a scorpion. A man from those staying near the water, came and said to the companions of the Prophet, 'Is there anyone among you who can do Ruqya as near the water there is a person who has been stung by a scorpion.' So one of the Prophet's companions went to him and recited Surat-al-Fatiha for a sheep as his fees. The patient got cured and the man brought the sheep to his companions who disliked that and said, 'You have taken wages for reciting Allah's Book.' When they arrived at Medina, they said, 'O Allah's Apostle! [This person] has taken wages for reciting Allah's Book.' On that Allah's Apostle said, 'You are most entitled to take wages for doing a Ruqya with Allah's Book'"; Sahih Bukhari, 7, 71, Hadith 637: "I asked ʿAisha about treating poisonous stings (a snake-bite or a scorpion sting) with a Ruqya. She said, 'The Prophet allowed the treatment of poisonous sting with Ruqya.'"
19. L. Saif, "From *Ghāyat al-ḥakīm* to *Shams al-maʿārif*: Ways of Knowing and Paths of Power in Medieval Islam", *Arabica*, 64:3/4, 2017, 297–345; N. Gardiner, *Ibn Khaldūn versus the Occultists at Barqūq's Court: The Critique of Lettrism in al-Muqaddimah*, Ulrich Hartmann Memorial Lecture, Vol. 18, Berlin: EB Verlag, 2020; N. Gardiner, "Forbidden Knowledge?".

20. J. Bussow, "Muḥammad ʿAbduh: The Theology of Unity (Egypt, 1898), in: B. Bentlage, M. Eggert, H. M. Krämer & S. Reichmuth (eds.), *Religious Dynamics under the Impact of Imperialism and Colonialism: A Sourcebook*, Leiden: Brill, 2017, 141–159.
21. N. Gardiner, "Stars and Saints"; N. Gardiner, *Esotericism in Manuscript Culture*; N. Gardiner, "Forbidden Knowledge?".
22. N. Gardiner, *Esotericism in Manuscript Culture*, 6.
23. Lithograph of *Shams al-maʿārif al-kubrā*, Beinecke Rare Book and Manuscript Library: https://collections.library.yale.edu/catalog/32304220
24. A. Ayalon, "Arab Booksellers and Bookshops in the Age of Printing, 1850–1940", *British Journal of Middle Eastern Studies*, 37:1, 2010, 73–93, 80. The print in question is possibly this one: https://collections.library.yale.edu/catalog/32304220
25. See https://www.worldcat.org/title/shams-al-maarif-al-kubra-wa-lataif-al-awarif/oclc/20121408/editions?start_edition=31&sd=desc&referer=di&se=yr&editionsView=true&fq=
26. The head of the authorizing committee was Ibrahim Hasan al-Inbabi, who is also endorsed in the publication. The 1926 version has been digitized by McGill University and can be accessed here: McGill University Library, et al., *Shams al-maʿārif al-kubrā wa-laṭārif al-ʿawārif*. Miṣr: Muṣṭafā al-Bābī al-Ḥalabī. JSTOR, https://jstor.org/stable/community.32953776 (accessed 2 June 2023).
27. W. I. Ingrams, *Zanzibar: Its History and Its People*, 477.
28. *Al-Manar*, vols 10 and 11, 16 Safar 1321/13 May 1903.
29. E. Czerniak & M. Davidson, "Placebo: A Historical Perspective", *European Neuropsychopharmacology*, 22:11, 2012, 770–774.
30. D. A. Stolz, "'By Virtue of your Knowledge': Scientific Materialism and the *fatwās* of Rashīd Riḍā", *Bulletin of SOAS*, 75:2, 2012, 223–247. For a broader exploration of Rida's contact with and views on European and Christian thought, see U. Riyad, *Islamic Reformism and Christianity: A Critical Reading of the Works of Muhammad Rashid Rida and his Associates (1898–1935)*, Leiden: Brill, 2009, and L. Halevi, *Modern Things on Trial*.
31. D. A. Stolz, "By Virtue of your Knowledge", 232.
32. D. A. Stolz, "By Virtue of your Knowledge", 241. Stolz is here referring to Rida's *Tafsīr al-Qurān al-Ḥakīm*, not to a debate in *al-Manar*.
33. C. Bolton, "'Useful' Knowledge and Moral Education in Zanzibar Between Colonial and Islamic Reform, 1916–1945", *Islamic Africa*, 12:1, 2021, 27–54, 31. Bolton discusses further how many of the ideas applied by British colonial educationalists in Zanzibar were derived from educational programmes for Native and African Americans in the American South.
34. S. Haj, *Reconfiguring Islamic Tradition*.
35. A. K. Bang, *Sufis and Scholars of the Sea: Family Networks in East Africa, 1860–1925*, London: Routledge, 2003, 137–139.

36. Conversation with two madrasa teachers, Zanzibar Town, October 2021.
37. E. Bever & R. Styers (eds.), *Magic in the Modern World: Strategies of Repression and Legitimization*, University Park: Pennsylvania State University Press, 2018.
38. F. Robinson, "Religious Change and the Self in Muslim South Asia Since 1800", *South Asia: Journal of South Asian Studies*, 22, 1999, 13–27, 9.
39. D. F. Reynolds (ed.), *Interpreting the Self: Autobiography in the Arabic Literary Tradition*, Berkeley: University of California Press, 2001.
40. O. El Shakry, *The Arabic Freud: Psychoanalysis and Islam in Modern Egypt*, Princeton: Princeton University Press, 2017, 2–3.
41. S. Federici, *Caliban and the Witch: Women, the Body and Primitive Accumulation*, New York: Autonomedia, 2004.
42. S. Federici, *Caliban and the Witch*, 141–154.
43. S. Federici, *Caliban and the Witch*, 155.

3. THE EXEMPLARY MUSLIM MODERN: BURHAN MKELLE (1884–1949) IN ZANZIBAR

1. Saʿid b. ʿAli al-Mughayri, *Juhaynat al-Akhbār fi taʾrīkh Zinjibār*, Oman: Ministry of National Heritage and Culture, 2001, 533.
2. Many, but not all of Burhan Mkelle's poems are reproduced in Muhammad Ahmad Hamid, *Al-ʿaṣr al-dhahhabī li-Zinjibār*. For references to poems quoted here that are not reproduced by Hamid, see Sources and Bibliography section of this volume.
3. On the Sumayt family in Zanzibar, see A. K. Bang, *Sufis and Scholars of the Sea*.
4. Ahmad Burhan Mkelle, Biographical fragment, Arabic. I am grateful to Dr Ridder Samsom for providing me with a digital copy of this MS.
5. MKELLE/DIWAN-1, 1.
6. MKELLE/DIWAN-1, 1.
7. MKELLE/DIWAN-1, 6.
8. On Shaykh al-Amin al-Mazrui, see Chapter 7.
9. MKELLE/DIWAN-1, 10. The "Jalalayn" is a common reference to two *tafsir* (Quranic exegesis) texts by Jalal al-Din al-Mahalli (d. 1459) and his student, Jalal al-Din al-Suyuti (d. 1505). It was widely taught in higher level madrasa classes in Zanzibar
10. MKELLE/DIWAN-1, 2–3.
11. MKELLE/DIWAN-1, 3.
12. MKELLE/DIWAN-1, 15.
13. MKELLE/DIWAN-1, 12.
14. MKELLE/DIWAN-1, 5.
15. MKELLE/DIWAN-1, 5.
16. MKELLE/DIWAN-1, 9.
17. MKELLE/DIWAN-1, 2.

18. We know that Burhan's father Adam came from Ikoni, mainly because Burhan himself occasionally used the *nisba* "al-Ikoni".
19. I. Walker, "Identity and Citizenship among the Comorians of Zanzibar, 1886–1963", in: A. Sheriff & E. Ho (eds.), *The Indian Ocean: Oceanic Connections and the Creation of New Societies*, London: Hurst, 2014, 239–265, 244.
20. MKELLE/TARIKH-ZNZ-2, 20.
21. I. Saleh, *A Short History of the Comorians in Zanzibar*, Dar-es-Salaam: The Tanganyika Standard, 1936. This book was written and published for the occasion of Sultan Khalifa b. Harub's Silver Jubilee in December 1936.
22. M. A. Saleh, "L'enjeu des traditions dans la communauté Comorienne de Zanzibar", in: F. Le Guennec-Coppens & D. Parkin (eds.), *Autorité et pouvoir chez les Swahili*, Paris: Karthala, 1998, 221–246, 222.
23. I. Walker, "Identity and Citizenship".
24. See A. K. Bang, *Islamic Sufi Networks*, 51–52, and MKELLE/TARIKH-ZNZ-2, 24.
25. MKELLE/TARIKH-ZNZ-2, 24–25.
26. Notice to Muhammad b. Adam, from the Sanitary Inspector, dated 14 January 1915. Maalim Idris Collection, Mkelle papers.
27. Hamid, *Al-ʿaṣr al-dhahhabī*, 254. See also A. K. Bang, "Zanzibari Islamic Knowledge Transmission Revisited: Loss, Lament, Legacy—and Transformation", *Social Dynamics*, 38:3, 2012, 419–434, for a further discussion of the elegy genre in Zanzibar and in the Islamic tradition.
28. Hamid, *Al-ʿaṣr al-dhahhabī*, 266.
29. W. C. Bissell, "Casting a Long Shadow: Colonial Categories, Cultural Identities, and Cosmopolitan Spaces in Globalizing Africa", *African Identities*, 5:2, 2007, 181–197.
30. For an overview, see W. C. Bissell, *Urban Design*.
31. W. Scholz, *Challenges of Informal Urbanisation: The Case of Zanzibar/Tanzania*, Spring Research Series 50, Dortmund: Dortmund Universität Verlag, 2008.
32. W. C. Bissell, *Urban Design*, 108.
33. W. C. Bissell, *Urban Design*, 247–249.
34. S. Longair, *Cracks in the Dome*, 69–109.
35. Department of Urban and Rural Planning, Zanzibar, *Ng'ambo Atlas: Historic Urban Landscape of Zanzibar Town's "Other Side"*, Edam: LM Publishers, 2018.
36. S. Musa, *Maisha ya al-Imam Sheikh Abdullah Saleh Farsy katika Ulimwengu wa Kiislamu*, Dar-es-Salaam: Lillaahi Islamic Publications Centre, 1986, 5.
37. R. Loimeier, *Between Social Skills*, 377.
38. The background to the inter-Comorian conflict in Zanzibar is discussed in detail in I. Walker, "Identity and Citizenship". The origin of the conflict in Grande Comore and its repercussions in Zanzibar are also discussed in detail in M. A. Saleh, "L'enjeu des traditions". It will also be discussed further in Chapter 5.

39. MKELLE/DIWAN-1, 6.
40. Ahmad Burhan Mkelle, Biographical fragment, Arabic, 5 pages, 2–3. Ahmad Mkelle goes on to say that the poem recited on this occasion unfortunately is among those missing: "were it not for this, I would have written it here". He quotes the first line, as follows: الصلح خير عمنا بعد الشقاق والهناء
41. *Al-Falaq*, 26 February 1938.
42. A. K. Bang, *Sufis and Scholars*.
43. Hamid, *Al-ʿaṣr al-dhahhabī*, 200–201.
44. S. Reese, "The Adventures of Abu Harith: Muslim Travel Writing and Navigating the Modern in Colonial East Africa", in: S. Reese (ed.), *The Transmission of Islamic Learning in East Africa*, Leiden: Brill, 2004, 244–256.
45. ʿUmar b. Ahmad b. Sumayt, *Al-nafḥat al-shadhiyya ilā al-diyār al-Ḥaḍramiyya wa-talbiyyat al-sawt min al-Ḥijāz wa Ḥaḍramawt*, Privately printed, Tarim/Aden, 1955 (reference here is made to the 2nd revised ed., Privately printed, Jiddah, 1988), 125. The poem itself can be found in Hamid, *Al-ʿaṣr al-dhahhabī*, 214–215.
46. Note to Muhammad Burhan Mkelle, ND, Maalim Idris Collection.
47. Interview, with Professor Saleh Idris Muhammad Saleh, Zanzibar, July 2018. Saleh attended Burhan's funeral as a child. The graveyard at Raha Leo is no longer there, as it gave way in the 1960s and 1970s to housing developments introduced by the Revolutionary Council of Zanzibar.
48. The *talqīn al-mayyit* is guidance for the deceased in their encounter with the angels of death. The *talqīn* is usually performed by the funerary leader after the grave has been filled. He approaches the fresh grave, near the head of the newly buried person. He then addresses the dead (or more precisely; the part of the dead person's soul that is accessible after it has left the body) in the grave, on how to respond to the angels that he is soon to encounter. The wording is meant to ensure that the deceased inform the angels that he or she is a Muslim. The fact that the *talqīn al-mayyit* addresses the dead, and the underlying assumption that human intervention can somehow influence God's assessment of the dead, has made this practice a target of reformist criticism. On the debate in Tanzania in the 1990s and 2000s, see F. Becker, "Islamic Reform and Historical Change in the Care of the Dead: Conflicts over Funerary Practice among Tanzanian Muslims", *Africa: Journal of the International African Institute*, 79:3, 2009, 416–434. See also the criticism raised by Muhammad Kasim Mazrui (1912–1982) against funerary practices, in K. Kresse, "'Swahili Enlightenment'? East African Reformist Discourse at the Turning Point: The Example of Sheikh Muhammad Kasim Mazrui", *Journal of Religion in Africa*, 33:3, 2003, 279–309. The *talqīn al-mayyit* is, and has been, a very common part of Islamic funerary practice. For anthropological observations, see, for example, J. Bowen, "Death and the History of Islam in Highland Aceh", *Indonesia*, 38, 1984, 21–38. The *talqīn al-mayyit* was also criticized by Ibn Taymiyya

and by his students. For an example from Mamluk Damascus, see Y. Frenkel, "Islamic Utopia under the Mamluks: The Social and Legal Ideals of Ibn Qayyim al-Gawziyya", *Oriente Moderno*, 90:1, 2010, 67–87. In recent times, the Saudi scholar Ibn Baz condemned the ritual as heresy based on false hadiths, by "people from the Levant". https://binbaz.org.sa/fatwas/16402/حكم-تلقين-الميت-بعد-دفنه (last accessed 22 March 2024).

49. Ahmad Burhan Mkelle, *Mukhtaṣṣār li-taʾrīkh*, 3.
50. @c:The author of the *Ṣalāt al-Mashīshiyya* was the Maghrebi Sufi ʿAbd al-Salam ibn Mashihs (d. 1228). The prayer exists in several translations. It is generally considered one of the most beautiful Sufi contemplations and frequently recited for the sake of its poetic qualities. The translation quoted here is from Deenislam, The Western Sufi Resource Guide: http://www.deenislam.co.uk/dua/mashish.htm (accessed 22 March 2024).

4. THE ZANZIBAR GOVERNMENT CENTRAL SCHOOL AND "MODERN TEACHING METHODS"

1. R. Loimeier, *Between Social Skills*, 34.
2. R. Loimeier, *Between Social Skills*; A. K. Bang, *Sufis and Scholars*; C. Decker, *Mobilizing Zanzibari Women*.
3. R. Loimeier, "Muslim Scholars, Organic Intellectuals, and the Development of Islamic Education in Zanzibar in the Twentieth Century", in: R. Launay (ed.), *Islamic Education in Africa: Writing Boards and Blackboards*, Bloomington: Indiana University Press, 2016, 137–148, 140.
4. A. K. Bang, *Sufis and Scholars*, chapter 9.
5. R. Loimeier, "Muslim Scholars", 143.
6. R. Launay, "Introduction: Writing Boards and Blackboards", in: R. Launay (ed.), *Islamic Education in Africa: Writing Boards and Blackboards*, Bloomington: Indiana University Press, 2016, 1–26, 3.
7. For an overview of nineteenth- and early twentieth-century debates in India and Egypt, see R. Loimeier, *Between Social Skills*, 156–163. For the corresponding debate in Indonesia, see M. Laffan, *Islamic Nationhood in Colonial Indonesia: The Umma Below the Winds*, London: Routledge, 2003, especially chapter 6; and N. Mobini-Kesheh, *The Hadrami Awakening: Community and Identity in the Netherlands East Indies, 1900–1942*, Ithaca, NY: Cornell University Southeast Asia Program Publications, 1999.
8. R. Launay, "Introduction: Writing Boards and Blackboards", 10.
9. For a clear outline of how the epistemic differences play out in Islamic education in West Africa, see R. Launay and Rudolph T. Ware III, "How (Not) to Read the Qur'an? Logics of Islamic Education in Senegal and Côte d'Ivoire", in: R. Launay (ed.), *Islamic Education in Africa*, 255–267.
10. R. Rida, *al-Manar*, 7 December 1904.

11. R. Rida, *al-Manar*, 7 December 1904.
12. R. Rida, *al-Manar*, 7 December 1904.
13. See R. Loimeier, *Between Social Skills*, 271–272, and S. S. Farsi, *Zanzibar: Historical Accounts*, 2nd ed., Privately printed, 1995, 21–23.
14. S. Longair, *Cracks in the Dome*, 63.
15. W. Hendry, "Education", *Samchar*, Silver Jubilee Issue, December 1936. The Silver Jubilee Issue of *Samchar* profiled the progress made during the first twenty-five years of the reign of Sayyid Khalifa b. Harub. The directors of the various departments penned a brief history of health, trade, etc.
16. ZIAR-BA104/44.
17. C. Decker, *Mobilizing Zanzibari Women*; C. Decker, "Reading, Writing, and Respectability: How Schoolgirls Developed Modern Literacies in Colonial Zanzibar", *International Journal of African Historical Studies*, 43:1, 2010, 89–114.
18. C. Decker, *Mobilizing Zanzibari Women*, 30.
19. C. Decker, *Mobilizing Zanzibari Women*, 52.
20. C. Decker, *Mobilizing Zanzibari Women*, 62–63.
21. C. Decker, *Mobilizing Zanzibari Women*, 37–38.
22. *Samchar*, 17 January 1937.
23. *Samchar*, 13 June 1937.
24. J. Glassman, *War of Words*.
25. J. Glassman, *War of Words*, 81.
26. ZIAR-AB/82–268. Non-European Staff and pension. The file gives the following dates for Shaykh Abd al-Bari's service: 1 May 1905–26 June 1930. The reason for retirement is given as "invalided".
27. See R. Loimeier, *Between Social Skills*, *passim*. See also *Supplement to the Zanzibar Gazette*, 10 March 1928, on the retirement of Shaykh Abd al-Bari.
28. *Supplement to the Zanzibar Gazette*, 2 September 1908. The organizer of this event was said to be the *Nadwat Abna al-Watan* (The Sons of the Homeland Club).
29. A. M. al-Barwani, *Conflicts and Harmony in Zanzibar*, Self-published, Dubai, 1997, 51.
30. M. S. Mraja, "The Reform Ideas of Shaykh ʿAbd Allāh Ṣāliḥ al-Fārsī and the Transformation of Marital Practices among the Digo Muslims of Kenya", *Islamic Law and Society*, 17:2, 2010, 245–278. See also Khatib Rajab, "Sheik Abdullah Saleh al-Farsy (February 12, 1912–November 9, 1982): The Great Poet, Scholar and Historian in Zanzibar": https://www.islamtanzania.org/nyaraka/farsy.htm
31. *Supplement to the Zanzibar Gazette*, Arabic section, 3 March 1928.
32. *Supplement to the Zanzibar Gazette*, 10 March 1928, on the retirement of Shaykh Abd al-Bari.
33. Hamid, *Al-ʿaṣr al-dhahhabī*, 222.
34. Hamid, *Al-ʿaṣr al-dhahhabī*, 223.

35. On the life of Abu ʾl-Hasan Jamal al-Layl, see A. K. Bang, *Islamic Sufi Networks*, 63–65.
36. ZIAR-AB82/102. Application for vacant Qadi position in Wete, Pemba, 1953. Abu ʾl-Hasan (then aged sixty-four) was one of the applicants and supplied his CV and letters of recommendation from the Department of Education. The job eventually went to the younger Abdallah Saleh al-Farsy, who resigned quickly after a quarrel over salary.
37. Among others, he composed an elegy for the Ibadi *qadi* Ali b. Muhammad al-Mundhiri upon the latter's death in 1926. This was published in the *Supplement to the Zanzibar Gazette*, Arabic section, 9 January 1926.
38. A. M. al-Barwani, *Conflicts and Harmony*, 50.
39. A. M. al-Barwani, *Conflicts and Harmony*, 64.
40. J. Glassman, *War of Words*, 87. The *Mazungumzo ya Walimu* was the journal published by the teachers in Zanzibar.
41. ZIAR-AB/1–231. Special Report on Education, 1921.
42. ZIAR-BA5/3. Annual Reports, Department of Education, 1925.
43. ZIAR-AB/1–231. Special Report on Education, 1921.
44. ZIAR-BA5/3. Annual Reports, Department of Education, 1925.
45. *Al-Falaq*, 18 February 1939.
46. The numbers in Table 1 refer to the number of each book in the digitized Maalim Idris Collection, EAP1114. They can be found with reference to the number here: https://eap.bl.uk/project/EAP1114
47. This commentary by al-Damanhuri was taught at al-Azhar into the 1930s. See K. El-Rouayheb, "al-Damanhūrī, Aḥmad", in: K. Fleet, G. Krämer, D. Matringe, J. Nawas & D. J. Stewart (eds.), *Encyclopaedia of Islam Three*, Leiden: Brill, 2021.
48. Abu Muhammad Qasim b. ʿAli al-Hariri was a poet from Basra, Iraq (1030–1122).
49. A poem in the *ajrūza* metre.
50. MKELLE/SELF-EDIT, "Autobiographical fragment 1, Hajj".
51. Ahmad Burhan Mkelle, Biographical fragment, Arabic.
52. https://eap.bl.uk/archive-file/EAP1114–1–72
53. https://eap.bl.uk/archive-file/EAP1114–1–38
54. https://eap.bl.uk/archive-file/EAP1114–1–116
55. https://eap.bl.uk/archive-file/EAP1114–1–40 *Murshid al-fityān ilā ʿulūm al-bayān*, Dār iḥyā al-kutub al-ʿarabiyya, Fayṣal ʿĪsā al-Bābī al-Ḥallabī, 2nd ed., ND (comments indicate 1960s). Photographic reproduction of handwritten copy.
56. https://eap.bl.uk/archive-file/EAP1114–1–38 Burhan bin Mohamed Mukella and Saleh b. Ali, *El-Tamrin: Book of Primary Lessons on Grammar*, Zanzibar Government Print, 1918.
57. This introduction is also discussed in A. K. Bang, "Teachers, Scholars and Educationalists: The Impact of Hadrami-ʿAlawi Teachers and Teachings on Islamic

Education in Zanzibar, ca. 1870–1930", *Asian Journal of Social Science*, 35:4/5, 2007, 457–471.

58. The preface is here quoted from the English translation at the back of the 1918 edition. The Arabic-language introduction is not included in the EAP copy, but is attached to other copies and later editions. The wording here is slightly different; while it says that Syrian and Egyptian books are of little use to Zanzibari children, it does not describe them as "grandiose and abbreviated".
59. Jurji Zaydan, "Kuttāb al-ʿarabiyya wa-qurrāʾuhā", *al-Hilal*, October 1897. Here quoted from T. Philipp (ed.), *Jurji Zaidan and the Foundations of Arab Nationalism*, Syracuse, NY: Syracuse University Press, 2010, 204.
60. EAP1114-MIC-064. https://eap.bl.uk/archive-file/EAP1114–1–64, Hifni Bey Nasif, Muhammad Effendi Diab, Mustafa Ṭamum and Muhammad Bey Saleh, *Kitāb al-Durūs al-naḥwiyya li-talāmidh al-madāris al-ibtidāʾiyya*, 4 vols, Cairo: Matbaʿa al-Amiriyya, 1913. The copy in the EAP collection bears a note that it was first owned by Said b. Abd Allah al-Kharusi, but as it was found among Burhan's books it is likely that it passed to him at some stage.
61. H. Kalmbach, *Islamic Knowledge and the Making of Modern Egypt*, Cambridge: Cambridge University Press, 2020, 225.
62. The Dutch consul in Jeddah made this observation in 1921. See M. van Bruinessen, "Kitab Kuning: Books in Arabic Script Used in the Pesantren Milieu", *Bijdragen tot de Taal-, Land- en Volkenkunde*, 146:2/3, 1990, 226–269, 242.
63. H. Kalmbach, *Islamic Knowledge*, 110–115, 150–155 and *passim*.
64. H. Kalmbach, *Islamic Knowledge*, 153.
65. K. Versteegh, "Learning Arabic in the Islamic World", in: G. Ayoub & K. Versteegh (eds.), *The Foundations of Arabic Linguistics*, III, Leiden: Brill, 2018, 245–267, 254.
66. Hamid, *Al-ʿaṣr al-dhahhabī*, 231.
67. MKELLE/DIWAN-1, no page number.
68. M. ʿAbduh, *Risālat al-Tawḥīd/The Theology of Unity*, translated from the Arabic by Ishaq Musaʿad and Kenneth Cragg, London: George Allen & Unwin Ltd, 1966.
69. S. al-Mughayri, *Juhaynat al-Akhbār*, 533.
70. J. Aley, *Enduring Links*, Self-published, Zanzibar, 1992, NP.
71. R. Loimeier, *Between Social Skills*, 346.
72. R. Loimeier, *Between Social Skills*, 380.
73. On the life of Sayyid Omar Abdallah, see M. Bakari, *The Sage of Moroni: The Intellectual Biography of Sayyid Omar Abdallah, a Forgotten Muslim Public Intellectual*, Nairobi: Kenya Literature Bureau, 2019.
74. *Al-Falaq*, 21 January 1939 (Report in English); *al Falaq*, 29 Dhu al-Qiʿda, 1357 (Report in Arabic). The translation from Arabic to English was made by Burhan Mkelle's long-standing collaborator, Juma Aley.
75. *Al-Falaq*, 13 May 1939. The report covers the feast marking the departure of

the Director of Education, W. Hendry. Hendry here thanked the recently retired Burhan, and made a point of mentioning his decorations.

76. MKELLE/DIWAN-1, 2.

5. MODERN JOBS: THE ZANZIBARI CIVIL SERVICE

1. D. Commins, *Islamic Reform: Politics and Social Change in Late Ottoman Syria*, Oxford: Oxford University Press, 1990, 34–48.
2. D. Commins, *Islamic Reform*, 47–48.
3. ZIAR-DI1/2. Staff and Salary, 1913.
4. ZIAR-DI1/3. Staff and Salary, 1914.
5. The district courts in Zanzibar had been in operation since the BuSaidi era. In 1897, Zanzibar was divided into three districts, the courts to be held in Mkokotoni, Mwera and Chwaka. For more on the Zanzibar legal system in the early colonial period see E. Stockreiter, *Islamic Law*, 27–45 and *passim*.
6. The question is rather why Sayyid Mansab b. Abd al-Rahman chose to take on work as a *qadi* of Chwaka in the first place. Neither Farsy nor any other source I have seen give any explanation on this. Nor is it clear if Sayyid Mansab b. Abd al-Rahman actually spent much time living in Chwaka. See A. S. Farsy, *Baadhi ya wanavyoni wa Kishafii wa Mashariki ya Afrika/The Shafiʿi Ulama of East Africa, ca. 1830–1970: A Hagiographic Account*, translated, edited and annotated by R. L. Pouwels, African Primary Texts 2, Madison: University of Wisconsin, 1989, *passim*. On the role of Sayyid Mansab b. Abd al-Rahman in Lamu, see A. K. Bang, *Sufis and Scholars*, 102, and A. K. Bang, *Islamic Sufi Networks*, *passim*. See also A. K. Bang, "The Riyadha Mosque Manuscript Collection".
7. ZIAR-DI1/4. Staff and Salary, 1914.
8. ZIAR-DI1/5. Staff and Salary, 1919.
9. MKELLE/DIWAN-1, 9.
10. ZIAR-AB82/226. War Bonuses Petitions. Letter to the Acting Chief Secretary from the undersigned members of the Subordinate Staff, 31 July 1917.
11. ZIAR-AB82/226. War Bonuses Petitions. Letter to the Acting Chief Secretary from the Teaching Staff of the Central Government School in Zanzibar, 22 August 1917.
12. ZIAR-AB82/226. War Bonuses Petitions. Letter to the Acting Chief Secretary from the Subordinate Staff of the Zanzibar Goverment, 18 July 1918.
13. ZIAR-AB82/226. War Bonuses Petitions. Letter to the Acting Chief Secretary from the Arab Clerks in the Service of His Majesty's Government, 19 June 1919.
14. ZIAR-AB82/268. Non-European staff and their pension. Response from the British Resident in Zanzibar to Downing Street, 6 July 1928.
15. ZIAR-AB82/268. Letter to the Chief Secretary, Zanzibar, from the Non-European Civil Service Association, 25 June 1928.

16. ZIAR-AB82/268. Draft Regulations, July 1928.
17. ZIAR-AB82/268. List of Government Retirees, 1928.
18. ZIAR-AB82/268. *Comments to Draft Ordinance for Regulating Pension*, 5 March 1931.
19. ZIAR-AB82/268. Secretariat Circular 4, 1933, amendment of Secretariat Circular 19 of 1931, *Regulations Governing the Grant of Pensions and Gratuities to Non-European Officials*.
20. ZIAR-AB82/268. Petition dated 10 March 1933.

6. MODERN ASSOCIATIONS: ETHNIC AND FAITH-BASED ASSOCIATIONS IN ZANZIBAR

1. I. Weismann, "The Politics of Popular Religion", 47.
2. *Al-Manar*, Vol. 10, no. 5, 1907. Here quoted from M. Haddad, "The Manarists and Modernism: An Attempt to Fuse Society and Religion", in: S. A. Dudoignon, K. Hisao & K. Yasushi (eds.), *Intellectuals in the Modern Islamic World: Transmission, Transformation, Communication*, London: Routledge, 2006, 55–73, 62.
3. M. C. Yildiz, "Mapping the 'Sports Nadha': Toward a History of Sports in the Modern Middle East", in: D. Reiche & T. Sorek (eds.), *Sport, Politics and Society in the Middle East*, Oxford University Press, 2019.
4. For example, physical fitness tests were introduced at the Egyptian Dar al-Ulum from the start, and the curriculum soon expanded to include physical education. See H. Kalmbach, *Islamic Knowledge*, *passim*.
5. L. Patrizi, "Un manuel d'*adab* et d'*akhlāq* pour les temps modernes: les *Jawāmiʿ al-ādāb fi akhlāq al-anjāb* de Jamāl al-Dīn al-Qāsimī (1866–1914)", in: C. Mayeur-Jaouen (ed.), *Adab and Modernity*, 481–503. It is worth noting that al-Qasimi also advised physical activity for women. See also M. Sirry, "Jamāl al-Dīn al-Qāsimī and the Salafi Approach to Sufism", *Die Welt des Islams*, 51:1, 2011, 75–108.
6. L. Fair, "Kickin' It: Leisure, Politics and Football in Colonial Zanzibar", *Africa: Journal of the International African Institute*, 67:2, 1997, 224–251; L. Fair, *Pastimes and Politics*, 227–264.
7. *Supplement to the Zanzibar Gazette*, 11 February 1928.
8. *Supplement to the Zanzibar Gazette*, 11 February 1928, Annual Meeting, Comorian Sports Club. Ibuni Saleh was president for many years. Said Mbaye was treasurer. The club had a "cricket captain", a "football captain" and a "hockey captain".
9. R. Loimeier, *Between Social Skills*; A. Ghazal, *Islamic Reform and Arab Nationalism*; A. K. Bang, *Islamic Sufi Networks*; N. Mathews, "Imagining Arab Communities: Colonialism, Islamic Reform, and Arab Identity in Mombasa, Kenya, 1897–1933", *Islamic Africa*, 4:2, 2013, 135–163; K. Kresse, *Swahili Muslim Publics and Postcolonial Experience*, Bloomington: Indiana University Press, 2018.

10. S. S. Farsi, *Mzanzibari: Asimilia hadithi yake*, Self-published, Oman, ND [1990s], 36.
11. ZIAR-AB12/22, "The Arab Hadramaut Association". Letter from association leader Muhsin b. Ghalib, dated 4 February 1937.
12. ZIAR-AB12/22.
13. I. Walker, "Ali Mfaume: A Comorian Hub in the Western Indian Ocean", in: B. Schnepel & E. Alpers (eds.), *Connectivity in Motion: Island Hubs in the Indian Ocean World*, Cham: Palgrave Macmillan, 2018, 159–180, 165.
14. I. Walker, "Identity and Citizenship".
15. M. A. Saleh, "L'enjeu des traditions", 234.
16. M. A. Saleh, "L'enjeu des traditions", 235.
17. ZIAR/AD-1832. *Rules of the Comorian Association, Zanzibar. Founded on 11th June 1924*, Zanzibar: Huseini P. Press. Here quoted from the English version of the tri-lingual rulebook. I am grateful to Iain Walker for bringing this document to my attention.
18. M. A. Saleh, "L'enjeu des traditions", 236.
19. ZIAR/HC5–87. Saleh Mahomed Sweidan vs the Comorian Association and Habib Haji, 1950. The court case summarizes the history of the association following a dispute over a house held as an asset by the Comorian Association.
20. Centre des Archives Diplomatique de Nantes, Postes Diplomatique et Consulaires, Zanzibar, 748PO/A/14/33. Letter from the Comorian Association to the French Consul, 13 July 1934. I am grateful to Iain Walker for sharing this document with me.
21. ZIAR/HC5–87.
22. MKELLE/COMORIAN ASSOCIATION.
23. Burhan lists the following as part of this first "spirit of reform": "Ahmad b. Muhammad Mlomri, al-Ḥāj Amīr, ʿAjamī (?) b. ʿAbd Allāh b. Mūsā, Muḥammad b. ʿAbd al-Raḥmān, ʿUthmān Muqta..ḥtamāmū (?), Saʿīd b. Muḥammad al-Khishtī, Ṣāliḥ b. …[unreadable], Ḥamīd b. Muḥammad, ʿAbd al-Raḥmān b. Muḥammad b. ʿAbd al-Raḥmān, ʿAlī b. Muḥammad Ṣaghīr, Muḥammad b. Wazīr al-Shāmī, Muḥammad b. Sālim al-Hinzwānī, ʿĪsā b. Ḥasan, ʿAlī b. Muʾmin, Saʿīd b. Muḥammad al-Mās Lambī [or Lamkī?], Aḥmad b. Mūtī and the author of this text [i.e. Burhan himself]."
24. Farsy, *Baadhi ya wanavyoni wa Kishafii*, 106 and *passim*.
25. S. Musa, *Maisha ya al-Imam Sheikh Abdullah Saleh Farsy*, 26–27.
26. *Al-Falaq*, 25 June 1938.
27. MKELLE/DIWAN-2, 17, *Ombolezo la tisa/The ninth elegy*.
28. MKELLE/TARIKH-ZNZ-2, 26.
29. MKELLE/TARIKH-ZNZ-2, 26.
30. J. Glassman, *War of Words*, 85–86. Muhammad b. Abd al-Rahman published articles in *Mazungumzo* that underlined the Arab heritage of Zanzibar, contrasted to African "barbarism". Glassman discusses how Muhammad b. Abd

al-Rahman's view of Zanzibar history and culture drew upon both colonial discourse and on ideas of the Arab "civilizing" role in East Africa. This highlighting of the Arab-Islamic heritage of Zanzibar was very much in line with the portrayal given in the Zanzibari history books used in schools. The work *Milango ya Historia/The Doors of History*, by L. W. Hollingsworth, Ahmad Sayf al-Kharusi, A. M. al-Hadrami and Salim Hilal al-Barwani was first published in 1925, and again in 1929 and 1931.

31. S. Longair, *Cracks in the Dome*, 139–141.
32. Letter from Burhan Mkelle to Saleh b. Yahya b. Said, election committee of the Comorian Association, dated 11 September 1937. Maalim Idris Collection, photographed 20 July 2018, Zanzibar.
33. I. Weismann, *Taste of Modernity: Sufism, Salafiyya and Arabism in Late Ottoman Syria*, Leiden: Brill, 2001.
34. H. Kalmbach, *Islamic Knowledge*, 115.
35. Hamid, *Al-ʿaṣr al-dhahhabī*, 240.
36. Centre des Archives Diplomatique de Nantes, Postes Diplomatique et Consulaires, Zanzibar, 748PO/A/204. Petition de Comoriens. I am grateful to Iain Walker for bringing this document to my attention.
37. I. Walker, "Identity and Citizenship".
38. J. Aley, *Enduring Links*, no page number.
39. ZIAR-AD23/16. The Comorian School.
40. ZIAR-BA5/3. Annual Report of the Zanzibar Education Department, 1931. These were the figures used by the British colonial authorities. The French inspector who arrived to oversee the new school in 1931, apparently counted 282 pupils, all heads counted. I. Walker, "Identity and Citizenship".
41. I. Walker, "Identity and Citizenship".
42. I. Walker, "Identity and Citizenship".
43. I. Walker, *Islands in a Cosmopolitan Sea: A History of the Comoros*, London: Hurst, 2019, 129.
44. A. Hofheinz, "*Rāqī bi-ikhlāqi*: The Moral Turn: From Sufi Shaykhs to Facebook Groups?", in: C. Mayeur-Jaouen (ed.), *Adab and Modernity*, 620–650, 636.
45. See, for example, *al-Falaq*, 26 February 1938, about the activities of the *Jamʿiyyat al-Ukhuwwa wa-l-Muʿawana* in Tarim, Hadramawt. This *jamʿiyya* was founded in the late 1920s, as one of many new, reformist-minded associations in the period. The *Jamʿiyyat al-Ukhuwwa wa-l-Muʿawana* ran schools, extended credit to farmers and published a journal. It was active well into the 1960s, funded by Hadramis in Southeast Asia. See U. Freitag, *Indian Ocean Migrants and State Formation in Hadhramaut: Reforming the Homeland*, Leiden: Brill, 2003, 442–449, 496–499.
46. *Supplement to the Zanzibar Gazette*, Arabic section, 28 August 1926.
47. B. Lia, *The Society of the Muslim Brothers in Egypt: The Rise of an Islamic Mass Movement, 1928–1942*, Reading, UK: Ithaca Press, 1998, 29.

48. H. Kalmbach, *Islamic Knowledge*, 172.
49. J. Jankowski, "Egyptian Responses to the Palestine Problem in the Interwar Period", *International Journal of Middle East Studies*, 12:1, 1980, 1–38; T. Mayer, "Egypt and the Islamic Conference of Jerusalem in 1931", *Middle Eastern Studies*, 18:3, 1982, 311–322.
50. G. Kampffmeyer, "Egypt and Western Asia", in: H. A. R. Gibb, *Whither Islam? A Survey of Modern Movements in the Moslem World*, London: Victor Gollancz, 1932, 101–170. See also G. Kampffmeyer, "Mission und Islam im arabischen Orient", *Die Welt des Islams*, 16, 1934, 6–22; J. Heyworth-Dunne, *Religious and Political Trends in Modern Egypt*, Self-published, Washington, 1950, 11–14.
51. G. Kampffmeyer, "Egypt and Western Asia", 117.
52. S. M. Rizvi, *Muhibb al-Din al-Khatib: A Portrait of a Salafi-Arabist, 1886–1969*, MA Thesis, Simon Fraser University, 1991, 76.
53. A. M. Toibibou, *Ahmad Qamardine (1895–1974): Un intellectual Comorien et ses réseaux*, PhD Thesis, Université Paris Diderot-Paris VII, 2010, 323–328. See also ʿUmar b. Ahmad b. Sumayt, *Al-nafḥa al-shadhdhiyya*, 110.
54. On the networks that made up the *Jamʿiyyat al-Sunna*, see A. K. Bang, *Islamic Sufi Networks*, 188–190.
55. A. K. Bang & R. Loimeier, "Aḥmad b. ʿAlī Manṣab", in: G. Krämer, D. Matringe J. Nawas & E. Rowson (eds.), *Encyclopaedia of Islam Three*, Leiden: Brill, 2013. See also Farsy, *Baadhi ya wanavyoni wa Kishafi*, 8–37.
56. Farsy, *Baadhi ya wanavyuoni wa Kishafi*, 8.
57. Hamid, *Al-ʿaṣr al-dhahhabī*, 260–261.
58. The library was located in the same building as the Comorian School and the office of the Comorian Association. I. Saleh, *A Short History of the Comorians*, 18.
59. MKELLE/SELF-EDIT, "Jamʿiyya Ahl al-Sunna wa-l-Jamāʿ", NP.
60. MKELLE/SELF-EDIT, "Jamʿiyya Ahl al-Sunna wa-l-Jamāʿ", NP.
61. *Al-Falaq*, 8 January 1938.
62. Neither the *Jumiyyat el-Khayri* nor the *Jumiyyat Ahl al-Sahil* have been described in earlier research and remain uknown. The *Shuban al-Muslimin* refers to the YMMA.
63. For a discussion of Arabness between Oman and Zanzibar, see M. Limbert, "Caste, Ethnicity and the Politics of Arabness in Southern Arabia", *Comparative Studies of South Asia, Africa and the Middle East*, 34:3, 2014, 590–598. The arrival of the so-called "Manga" Arabs during the interwar era accentuated the tendency to formulate Ibadi Arabness in terms of genealogy rather than language or even culture.
64. A. Ghazal, *Islamic Reform*.
65. *Al-Falaq*, 15 January 1938.
66. H. Kalmbach, *Islamic Knowledge*, 170–171. Kalmbach names the association *Jamʿiyyat Makarim al-Akhlaq al-Islamiyya* (The Association for Protection of Is-

lamic Morality) and the periodical *Majallat al-Majali al-ʿAbbasiyya wa-Makarim al-Akhlaq al-Islamiyya* (The Magazine of the Abbasid Refuge for the Protection of Islamic Moral Character).

67. J. Heyworth-Dunne, *Religious and Political Trends in Modern Egypt*, 90–91.
68. Centre des Archives Diplomatique de Nantes, Postes Diplomatique et Consulaires, Zanzibar, 748PO/A/14/33. Letter from the Comorian Association to the French Consul, 13 July 1934. I am grateful to Iain Walker for bringing this document to my attention.
69. MKELLE/DIWAN-1, "On Unity", NP.

7. MODERN ISLAMIC PRACTICES: ZANZIBAR IN THE AGE OF CULTURE WARS

1. C. Decker, *Mobilizing Zanzibari Women*, 58–60.
2. D. Scott, *Conscripts of Modernity*.
3. See H. Lauzière, *The Making of Salafism*, chapter 2, 60–94.
4. *Supplement to the Zanzibar Gazette*, Arabic section, 12 June 1926. The notice is headlined "News from Hijaz" and references the death of several pilgrims as they were attacked by Najdi Wahhabis when musicians accompanying the Egyptian *mahmal* (the black cloth covering the *Kaaba*) tried to enter Mecca. The Wahhabis introduced several regulations for the *hajj* that were considered a break with tradition, including a ban on smoking and on openly invoking the name of the Prophet's family at their graves. See W. Ochsenwald, "Islam and Loyalty in the Saudi Hijaz, 1926–1939", *Die Welt des Islams*, 47:1, 2007, 7–32.
5. *Al-Falaq*, 4 March 1939.
6. Muhammad Abdallah Gurnah (d. 1959) was the uncle of the 2021 Nobel laureate of literature, Abdulrazak Gurnah. The family lived close to Burhan Mkelle's family in Malindi-Jongeani. Abdulrazak Gurnah, personal communication, September 2023.
7. *Al-Manar*, Vol. 28, no. 9, 660, 29 Jumada I 1346/24 November 1927.
8. J. Prestholdt, *Domesticating the World*, 113.
9. S. S. Farsi, *Mzanzibari*, 38.
10. *Supplement to the Zanzibar Gazette*, Arabic section, 18 February 1928.
11. H. Lauzière, "The Construction of Salafiyya: Reconsidering Salafism from the Perspective of Conceptual History", *International Journal of Middle East Studies*, 42:3, 2010, 369–389.
12. C. E. Dawn, "The Formation of Pan-Arab Ideologies in the Interwar Years", *International Journal of Middle East Studies*, 20:1, 1988, 67–91.
13. I. Gershoni, "The Evolution of National Culture in Modern Egypt: Intellectual Formation and Social Diffusion, 1892–1945", *Poetics Today*, 13:2, 1992, 325–350.
14. S. M. Rizvi, *Muhibb al-Din*, iv.
15. M. Hatina (ed.), *Guardians of Faith in the Modern World: ʿUlamaʾ in the Middle East*, Leiden: Brill, 2008.

16. H. Lauzière, "The Construction of Salafiyya", 376. Muhibb al-Din worked for a time as a translator for the British consulate in Yemen—and his close professional association with British colonial authorities is a clear common ground with Burhan Mkelle and his associates.
17. S. M. Rizvi, *Muhibb al-Din*, 7. See also D. Commins, "Wahhabis, Sufis and Salafis in Early Twentieth Century Damascus", in: M. Hatina (ed.), *Guardians of Faith in the Modern World*, 231–240; D. Commins, *The Wahhabi Mission and Saudi Arabia*, London: I. B. Tauris, 2006; D. Commins, *Islamic Reform*; I. Weismann, *Taste of Modernity*.
18. S. M. Rizvi, *Muhibb al-Din*, 52.
19. B. Lia, *The Society of the Muslim Brothers*, 30.
20. S. M. Rizvi, *Muhibb al-Din*, 53. The late 1920s saw the growing sense that Islam was "under attack", a sentiment that became increasingly prominent in Egyptian socio-cultural politics. The most evident expression of this was the "League for Defence of Islam", formed in 1933. This coalition included liberals, the Muslim Brotherhood and the YMMA. The same is evident in publications like *al-Fath* and the *Majallat Shubān al-Muslimīn*. See H. Kalmbach, *Islamic Knowledge*, 181–82.
21. *Al-Falaq*, 10 September 1938.
22. On Syed Ameer Ali, see M. Z. Abbasi, "Islamic Law and Social Change: An Insight into the Making of Anglo-Muhammadan Law", *Journal of Islamic Studies*, 25:3, 2014, 325–349; M. Forward, "Syed Ameer Ali: A Bridge-Builder?", *Islam and Christian-Muslim Relations*, 6:1, 1995, 45–62.
23. *Supplement to the Zanzibar* Gazette, Arabic section, 18 August 1928.
24. S. A. Hussain, "Anglo-Muhammadan Law", in: A. M. Emon & R. Ahmed (eds.), *The Oxford Handbook of Islamic Law*, Oxford: Oxford University Press, 2018, 537–550.
25. For examples from West Africa, see O. O. Kane, *Beyond Timbuktu*; O. M. Kobo, *Unveiling Modernity in Twentieth-Century West African Islamic Reforms*, Leiden: Brill, 2012; and T. Østebø, *Localising Salafism: Religious Change Among Oromo Muslims in Bale, Ethiopia*, Leiden: Brill, 2011. For an example of moral guidance in the Somali context, see S. Reese, "Shaykh Abdullahi al-Qutbi and the Pious Believer's Dilemma: Local Moral Guidance in the Age of Global Islamic Reform", *Journal of Eastern African Studies*, 9:3, 2015, 1–17.
26. In his study on the arrival and impact of Salafism in Hama, Syria, I. Weismann even indicates that what takes place is a "Salafi-Sufi synthesis", emerging in the face of secularism. I. Weismann, "The Politics of Popular Religion", 39–58.
27. K. Kresse, *Swahili Muslim Publics*, 65.
28. For a full biography of Arslan, see W. Cleveland, *Islam Against the West: Shakib Arslan and the Campaign for Islamic Nationalism*, Austin: University of Texas Press, 1985.
29. H. Lauzière, *The Making of Salafism*, 136. Lauzière uses the term "Islamic nationalism" to refer to Arslan's ideological programme, pointing to

his concern for the state of Muslim communities throughout the world. I shall return to the question of "Islamic nationalism" in Chapter 8.

30. K. Kresse, *Swahili Muslim Publics*.
31. Hamid, *Al-ʿaṣr al-dhahhabī*, 216–217.
32. Al-Amin al-Mazrui, *Sahifa*, July 1931. Here quoted from K. Kresse & H. Mwakimako (eds.), *Guidance (Uwongozi) by Sheikh al-Amin Mazrui: Selections from the First Swahili Islamic Newspaper*, trans. K. Kresse & H. Mwakimako, Leiden: Brill, 2017, 127.
33. The letter is reproduced in Hamid, *Al-ʿaṣr al-dhahhabī*, 170–171.
34. Presumably because Shaykh al-Amin authorized the prayer for rain (*Salāt al-Istisqāʾ*) on the basis of hadiths. This is a generally accepted prayer in most Sunni traditions. However, it could also be the opposite, that Shaykh al-Amin rejected the legality of this prayer. In any case, he engaged in interpretation and placed the Sunna at the core, which is what pleased Burhan.
35. Burhan here quotes only the last section of the verse: "… and debate with them in the best manner".
36. Hamid, *Al-ʿaṣr al-dhahhabī*, 171.
37. Sayyid Mustafa Lutfi (1876–1924) was an Egyptian author of novels and short stories, and he also rewrote French plays in Arabic. He is generally portrayed as one of the leading figures of the Pan-Islamist movement in Egypt. He had the distinction of being widely read and regarded in the early 1900s, while being retrospectively understood as both a "hack adapter of Western fiction" and a "sensitive translator". See M. Moosa, *The Origins of Modern Arabic Fiction*, 2nd ed., Boulder, CO: Lynne Rienner, 1997, 111.
38. Hamid, *Al-ʿaṣr al-dhahhabī*, 248–249.
39. Also, the letter was most likely intended for publication in *al-Fath*.
40. MKELLE/SELF-EDIT, "Letter to *al-Fath*", NP.
41. M. Farquhar, *Expanding the Wahhabi Mission: Saudi Arabia, the Islamic University of Medina and the Transnational Religious Economy*, PhD Thesis, London School of Economics, 2013, 118–119.
42. The Saudi Scholastic Institute was a run by the first Directorate of Education which the Saudi rulers set up precisely in Mecca in 1926. Their choice of location demonstrates the emphasis the fledgling state placed on Hijaz as core to their educational ambitions (religious, but also non-religious). However, while the purpose of the new Saudi education was clearly to ingrain Wahhabi norms in the population, they also needed to ingratiate themselves with the Hijazi population as providers of services such as education. Perhaps for this reason, the first directors of the Directorate of Education were foreigners who came from outside the hard-line Najdi Wahhabi *ulama*. M. Farquhar, *Expanding the Wahhabi Mission*, 84–90.
43. H. Lauzière, *The Making of Salafism*, 78–80n.
44. M. Farquhar, *Expanding the Wahhabi Mission*, 91.

45. M. Farquhar, *Expanding the Wahhabi Mission*, 97.
46. M. Farquhar, *Expanding the Wahhabi Mission*, 101–102.
47. B. Lia, *The Society of the Muslim Brothers*, 55–56.
48. G. Nordbruch, "Arab Students in Weimar Germany—Politics and Thought Beyond Borders", *Journal of Contemporary History*, 49:2, 2014, 275–295, 281.
49. A. Hofheinz, "*Rāqī bi-akhlāqī*", 623.
50. C. Mayeur-Jaouen, "Feminine or Masculine *Adab*? Education, Etiquette, and Ethics in Egypt in the 1900s–1920s", in: C. Mayeur-Jaouen (ed.), *Adab and Modernity*, 405–434, 407.
51. Here quoted from K. Kresse, *Swahili Muslim Publics*, 80.
52. Abu ʾl-Hasan Jamal al-Layl, *Diwān al-fatḥ wa-l-imdād*, NP, ND, 37.
53. This is according to the report on the 1928 event in the *Supplement to the Zanzibar Gazette*, 1 September 1928. While narrating the event of the 1928 celebration, the reporter states: "It is interesting to note that this mass performance of the ceremony was instituted in Zanzibar as recently as 1924, previous to which it had been customary, as it is even now in most Mohammedan lands, to hold many more or less private celebrations."
54. Salih Muhammad ʿAli Badawi, *Al-riyāḍ bayna māḍīhi wa-ḥādirihi*, 2nd ed., Lamu/Mombasa, 2018; A. H. M. el-Zein, *The Sacred Meadows: A Structural Analysis of Religious Symbolism in an East African Town*, Evanston, IL: Northwestern University Press, 1974; P. Lienhardt, "The Mosque College of Lamu and its Social Background", *Tanganyika Notes and Records*, 53, 1959, 228–242; BinSumeit Khitamy, "The Role of the Riyadha Mosque College in Enhancing Islamic Identity in Kenya", in: M. Bakari & S. S. Yahya (eds.), *Islam in Kenya*, Nairobi: MEWA, 1995, 269–276; P. Romero, *Lamu: History, Society, and Family in an East African Port City*, Princeton: Markus Wiener, 1997.
55. *Supplement to the Zanzibar Gazette*, 1 September 1928.
56. *Supplement to the Zanzibar Gazette*, Arabic section, 28 August 1926.
57. *Supplement to the Zanzibar Gazette*, 6 May 1939.
58. *Supplement to the Zanzibar Gazette*, Arabic section, 31 August 1929.
59. C. Decker, *Mobilizing Zanzibari Women*, 33–34 and 40–41. Decker points to the *mawlid* and *siku kuu* events as occasions where the respectability (*heshima*) and social importance of girls' education was put on display.
60. The Zanzibar national anthem was adopted in 1911 upon the ascension of Sayyid Khalifa b. Harub. The tune was a march that was already played by marching bands, composed by Donald Francis Tovey. It is not clear when Burhan Mkelle added lyrics to the march; it may have been exactly for the occasion of the *mawlid* event. The song was entitled *Salām al-Malik*, but unfortunately I have not been able to find the lyrics. For the tune of the "Sultan's March", see (or rather listen): http://samap.ukzn.ac.za/zanzibar-national-anthem-national-anthem-zanziba
61. *Al-Falaq*, 30 April 1938. Burhan was this year—as most years—appointed to the recitation committee.

62. *Al-Falaq*, 30 April 1938. The author uses the term *midhiyāʿ*, which is open to interpretation. From the context, it may in fact mean both a radio and a microphone: *nashīhā bi-istiʿmāl al-midhyāʿ*: to disseminate by use of a technical device usually translated as radio. An alternative interpretation here is that he proposes to use a microphone during the event. All in all, the context here favours a suggestion of radio transmission.
63. Muhammad b. Ali al-Barwani, *Riḥla Abū Ḥārith*, Zanzibar: Al-Najah Print, 1333/1915, 17–19. See also Scott Reese's translation of this passage in S. Reese, "The Adventures of Abu Harith", 249.
64. These are references to the *maqamāt*, or tonal modes of recitation.
65. Note that the original here says "*al-ḥarakāt al-gharbiyya*" ("Western movements"), which although thematically tempting to translate in this way is probably a printing error.
66. Muhammad b. Ali al-Barwani, *Riḥla Abū Ḥārith*, Zanzibar: Al-Najah Print, 1333/1915, 17–18.
67. Muhammad b. Ali al-Barwani, *Riḥla Abū Ḥārith*, 18.
68. Abu Muslim al-Rawwahi (1860–1920) was the editor of *al-Najah* (where al-Barwani's *Riḥla* was published) and a well-known public intellectual.
69. Hamid, *Al-ʿaṣr al-dhahhabī*, 188.
70. Hamid, *Al-ʿaṣr al-dhahhabī*, 189.
71. Hamid, *Al-ʿaṣr al-dhahhabī*, 196–197. The poem was printed several times, but unfortunately none of the print editions copied by the Mkelle sons bear any date or name of publication.
72. The *Miʿrāj* is both a set of Quranic verses that in veiled words (or allegorical, depending upon interpretation) narrates the story of the Prophet ascending to heaven from Jerusalem, and a model for later textual renderings of the same event. On the historical Muslim understanding of the *miʿrāj*, or the Prophet's night journey to the heavens, see F. S. Colby, *Narrating Muhammad's Night Journey: Tracing the Development of the Ibn ʿAbbas Ascension Discourse*, Albany: State University of New York Press, 2008, and C. J. Gruber, *The Prophet Muhammad's Ascension (miʿrāj) in Islamic Art and Literature, ca. 1300–1600*, PhD Thesis, University of Pennsylvania, 2005.
73. This full name of the association is given in the Arabic section of the *Supplement*. The English version refers to it as the "Jamiyyat al-Sunni". In the Arabic section, its leader Isa al-Barwani is referred to with the honorific title al-Shaykh al-Mukarram ʿĪsā b. ʿAlī b. Īsā al-Barwānī.
74. *Supplement to the Zanzibar Gazette*, 28 January 1928.
75. This verse is one of the few references to a "night journey" in the Quran itself: "Glorified be the one who caused his servant to journey by night from the sacred place of prayer to the furthest place of prayer, whose precincts we have blessed, in order to show him some of our signs. Indeed, [God] is the one who hears, the one who sees" (Q 17:1).

76. Muhammad b. Umar al-Singani is a shadowy figure, who nonetheless seems to have been a core person in the reformist-oriented community. He was also known as a copyist, and features as the copyist of the one known manuscript copy of Abd al-Allah BaKathir's *Riḥlat al-Ashwāq*. See EAP466–144: https://eap.bl.uk/archive-file/EAP466–1–144#?c=0&m=0&s=0&cv=0&xywh=0%2C-774%2C5184%2C5002%3Chttps://eap.bl.uk/archive-file/EAP466–1–144%23?c=0&m=0&s=0&cv=0&xywh=0,-774,5184,5002%3E
77. For a full investigation, see B. O. Vuckovic, *Heavenly Journeys, Earthly Concerns: The Legacy of the Miʿraj in the Formation of Islam*, London: Routledge, 2004.
78. R. Loimeier, *Between Social Skills*, 193. These were general texts widely used in madrasas in Zanzibar in the first half of the twentieth century. See also J. S. Trimingham, *The Sufi Orders in Islam*, Oxford: Oxford University Press, 1971, 208–209.
79. See https://eap.bl.uk/archive-file/EAP466–1–18 Various devotional texts, *Miʿrāj al-Barzanjī: Kitāb ḥadīth al-miʿrāj* by Jaʿfar b. Zayn al-ʿAbidīn al-Barzanjī (d. 1765). (First text in volume up to folio 82, where the *miʿrāj* volume ends.) The copyist is Muhyi al-Din b. Al-Shayh al-Din (?) b. Abi Bakr al-Hatimi, completed on 17 Dhu al-Hijja, 1298/1882. EAP466–1/67. *Miʿrāj al-Bazanjī*, no copyist, ND.
80. ZIAR-ZA8/41–5, *Qiṣṣa al-isrāʾa wa-l-miʿrāj* by al-Barzanjī (d. 1765), copied in Zanzibar, 1862. See L. Declich, *The Arabic Manuscripts*, 80.
81. C. Ahmed, *Ngoma et mission Islamique (Daʿwa) aux Comores et en Afrique orientale*, Paris: L'Harmattan, 2002, 44–46 and *passim*.
82. R. Loimeier, "Traditions of Reform", 135–162. Loimeier refers to the early reformist efforts in Zanzibar as a "false start", which only gained hold mainly though the work of Shaykh al-Amin al-Mazrui.
83. D. Commins, *Islamic Reform*, 80. Commins states that Jamal al-Din al-Qasimi condoned using police to forcibly dissolve events that were deemed "innovation". His methods aside, al-Qasimi also defended several Sufi practices, and particularly promoted al-Ghazali's *Iḥyāʾ ʿulūm al-dīn* and even aspects of Ibn Arabi's teachings. Arguing for a more diverse understanding of the origins of the Salafiyya movement (i.e. beyond Egypt), M. Sirry has placed al-Qasimi in the very wide camp that condemned excesses but not Sufism as a whole. M. Sirry, "Jamāl al-Dīn al-Qāsimī and the Salafi Approach to Sufism", 75–108.
84. R. Loimeier, "Coming to Terms with 'Popular Culture': The *ʿulamāʾ* and the State in Zanzibar", in: R. Loimeier & R. Seesemann (eds.), *The Global Worlds of the Swahili*, Hamburg: LIT Verlag, 2006, 111–129.
85. The entire campaign can be gleaned from ZIAR-AB30/22: Campaign among the Arabs and Africans of Zanzibar and Pemba against extravagant expenditure on marriage feasts and funerals.
86. M. Janson, "Living Islam through Death: Demarcating Muslim Identity in a Rural Serahuli Community in the Gambia", *Journal of the Royal Anthropological Institute*, 17:1, 2011, 100–115, 101.

87. M. Janson, "Living Islam through Death", 100.
88. During the trials or torture of the grave (*al-ʿadhāb al-qabr*), the deceased will be interrogated by two angels named al-Munkar and al-Nakir. They pose a series of questions to ensure that the dead person has died a Muslim. Incorrect answers will lead to physical torture in the grave, lasting until the day of resurrection.
89. F. Becker, "Islamic Reform and Historical Change in the Care of the Dead".
90. *Al-Manar*, Vol. 31, no. 1, 53, 29 Muharram 1349/27 May 1930.
91. For a contemporary description of the debate in the late 1990s/early 2000s, see A. C. Ahmed, "Rites de mort aux Comores et chez les Swahili: Entre islam savant de culture locale", *Journal des Africanistes*, 72:2, 2002, 187–201.
92. L. J. K. Bonate, "Dispute over Islamic Funeral Rites in Mozambique: *A Demolidora dos Prazeres* by Shaykh Aminuddin Mohamad", *Social Sciences and Missions*, 17, December 2005, 41–59.
93. MKELLE/DIWAN-1, "End the Practice of Wailing!"
94. ZIAR-AB30/22. Note by Deputy DC of Pemba, dated 29 January 1936 (Report on a meeting held 27 January 1936 with the "prominent Arabs of Pemba").
95. ZIAR-AB30/22. Opinion of Tahir al-Amawi. See reproduction of the actual *raʾy* in R. Loimeier, "Coming to Terms". The style of the *raʾy* is interesting in its own right. Unlike the classical Islamic style, it is structured as 1, 2, 3 with subsections a), b), etc., and this is expressed not as "alif-ba-jīm" but "alif-ba-sin", probably as an approximation of ABC. The note itself is clearly not in the hand of Shaykh Tahir, but is quite possibly by an Arabic-literate clerk trained in European-style bureaucratic order. The document is dated 12 March 1936, and only the CE date is given. The document is accompanied by a note from the Ibadi *qadi*, Saʿid b. Nasir al-Ghaythi, in his own hand, saying that he agrees with all Shaykh Tahir says.
96. Several hadith explicitly condemn the "wailing congregation" (the *Niyaha/Nawāḥḥa*) as belonging to the *Jahiliyya*. Anything that resembles this practice is condemned.
97. ZIAR-AB30/22: Attached file. Translation of the "Sual wa jawab" (Questions and answers); *Nur al-Islam*, Vol. IV, page 101.
98. J. Glassman, *War of Words*, 89.

8. *WATANIYYA*? TOWARDS A MODERN ZANZIBARI CULTURE

1. A. Ghazal, *Islamic Reform*, 2.
2. C. Decker & E. McMahon, *The Idea of Development in Africa*, 220.
3. J. Glassman, *War of Words*.
4. A. Ghazal, *Islamic Reform*, 9.
5. M. Limbert, "Caste, Ethnicity, and the Politics of Arabness".
6. N. Bertz, *Diaspora and Nation in the Indian Ocean: Transnational Histories of Race and Urban Space in Tanzania*, Honolulu: University of Hawai'i Press, 2015, 59.

7. T. Mitchell, *Colonising Egypt*, Berkeley: University of California Press, 1991, 119.
8. H. Kalmbach, *Islamic Knowledge*, 4.
9. J. R. Brennan, *Taifa: Making Nation and Race in Urban Tanzania*, Athens, OH: Ohio University Press, 2012, 1.
10. J. R. Brennan, *Taifa*, 121.
11. M. Limbert, "Homeland is where the Soul Resides: Travel Prayer, Passports, and Nation in the Western Indian Ocean" (forthcoming). I am grateful to Mandana Limbert for providing me with a copy of this forthcoming work.
12. L. A. Brand, *Official Stories: Politics and National Narratives in Egypt and Algeria*, Stanford: Stanford University Press, 2014.
13. M. Feener, "Cross-Cultural Contexts of Modern Muslim Intellectualism", *Die Welt des Islams*, 47:3/4, 2007, 264–282, 281.
14. On a comparative "hub" and the concept of "ritual hubbing", see I. Walker, "Ali Mfaume: A Comorian Hub".
15. See A. K. Bang, *Islamic Sufi Networks*.
16. Hamid, *Al-ʿaṣr al-dhahhabī*, 230.
17. A. Mazrui & H. M. K. Mazrui, Introduction, in: K. Kresse & H. Mwakimako (eds.), *Guidance (Uwongozi) by Sheikh al-Amin Mazrui*.
18. N. Mobini-Kesheh, *The Hadrami Awakening*.
19. M. F. Laffan, *Islamic Nationhood and Colonial Indonesia*, 189–210. See also A. I. Abushouk and H. A. Ibrahim, *The Hadhrami Diaspora in Southeast Asia: Identity Maintenance or Assimilation?*, Leiden: Brill, 2009.
20. I. Saleh, *Short History of the Comorians*, 9–15.
21. I. Saleh, *Short History of the Comorians*, 16.
22. I. Saleh, *Short History of the Comorians*, 17.
23. I. Saleh, *Short History of the Comorians*, Preface, NP.
24. Hamid, *Al-ʿaṣr al-dhahhabī*, 205.
25. MKELLE/DIWAN-1, 21.
26. MKELLE/DIWAN-2, no page number.
27. من علامة الإيمان حب الوطن I am grateful to Mohamed Aidaroos Noor of Lamu, PhD student at the University of Bergen, for pointing this line out to me. The phrase is not, in fact, part of hadith, but nonetheless frequently quoted, referring to the idea that the first Islamic *hijra* (migration) was indeed a sacrifice—giving up one's homeland for the sake of religion.
28. The same phrase was quoted in the title of an article by the Mzabi Ibadi scholar Ibrahim Abu Yaqsan (1888–1973), published in 1926 in *al-Minhaj* (which was yet another of Muhibb al-Din al-Khatib's publications). In A. Ghazal's reading, the usage is here one that values patriotism as a path to inter-sectarian unity in the face of colonialism. Language, culture and shared ethical values were, according to Abu Yaqsan, bonds that Muslim Arabs shared regardless of their *madhhab*. A. Ghazal, "The Other Frontiers of Arab Nationalism: Ibadis, Ber-

bers, and the Arabist-Salafi Press in the Interwar Period", *International Journal of Middle East Studies*, 42:1, 2010, 105–122, 111.
29. For a reading of Arslan's Islamic nationalism, see H. Lauzière, *The Making of Salafism*, 136–139.
30. S. Arslan, "Li-mādhā taʾakhkhir al-muslimūn? Wa-li-mādhā taqaddum ghayri-him?", 1930. The article was first published as a series of responses in *al-Manar*.
31. India Office, IOR/R/15/1/236. Here viewed at Qatar Digital Library, http://www.qdl.qa/en/archive/81055/vdc_100000000193.0x0000d1 (last accessed 15 February 2024).
32. L. Massignon, "Africa", in: H. A. R. Gibb, *Whither Islam? A Survey of Movements in the Moslem World*, London: Victor Gollancz, 1932, 75–98, 90
33. India Office, IOR/R/15/1/575. Here viewed at Qatar Digital Library.
34. K. Kresse, *Swahili Muslim Publics*, 95.
35. F. Becker, *Becoming Muslim in Mainland Tanzania, 1890–2000*, Oxford: Oxford University Press, 2008.
36. F. Becker, "Commoners in the Process of Islamization: Reassessing their Role in the Light of Evidence from Southeastern Tanzania", *Journal of Global History*, 3:2, 2008, 227–249.
37. I. Walker, *Islands in a Cosmopolitan Sea*, 131–133.
38. On Said Mohamed Cheikh, see Mahmoud Ibrahime, *Parcours d'un conservateur: Saïd Mohamed Cheikh, 1904–1970: une histoire des Comores au XXe siècle*, Moroni: Komedit, 2008 (texte remanié d'une thèse de doctorat d'Histoire de l'Afrique—Histoire, Archéologie et Histoire de l'Art, soutenue à l'Université Paris 7 en 2004); I. Walker, *Islands*, 132–133.
39. M. A. Saleh, "L'enjeu des traditions".
40. MKELLE/SELF-EDIT, "On Said Mohamed Mansab", NP. The former copy has the wrongly attributed date 1965. The introduction written by Burhan Mkelle says: "Verses which I recited during the proceeding (*qudūm*) of Said al-Doktor Mohamed b. Cheikh Mansab, saluting him and praising his deeds and morals."
41. I. Walker, "What Came First, the Nation or the State? Political Process in the Comoro Islands", *Africa: Journal of the International African Institute*, 77:4, 2007, 582–605.
42. N. Minde, S. Roop & K. Tronvoll, "The Turbulent Political History of Zanzibar and its Impact on Contemporary Conflict and Reconciliation", *African Insight*, 49:1, 2019, 68–82.

9. CONCLUSIONS: THE BEGINNINGS OF A MODERN MUSLIM ZANZIBARI CULTURE

1. K. Larsen, "Multifaceted Identities, Multiple Dwellings: Connectivity and Flexible Household Configurations in Zanzibar Town", in: B. Schnepel & E. A. Alpers, *Connectivity in Motion: Island Hubs in the Indian Ocean World*, London: Palgrave, 2018, 180–206, 185.

SOURCES

Zanzibar Institute for Archives and Records

In researching this book, I have mainly used sources deriving from the Zanzibar Institute for Archives and Records (ZIAR). This houses the main publications from the period, such as the Arabic weekly *al-Falaq* and the colonial publication *The Zanzibar Gazette*. ZIAR also houses other material relevant to the emergence of the Muslim modern, such as rulings, legal opinions, petitions to the government, and—not least—government initiatives to implement variously motivated progress.

Maalim Idris Collection/EAP1114

This collection contains the books and manuscripts collected by the late Maalim Muhammad Idris Muhammad Saleh (d. 2012). The collection of printed works were digitized in the period 2018–20 and can be found online here: https://eap.bl.uk/project/EAP1114

The printed works collection is currently housed in the Comorian Association building in Zanzibar Stone Town. In this book, references are mostly made to the printed works in the possession of Burhan Mkelle.

MPrinT Project textual corpus

The reference in this book with the prefix MPRINT- refers to a text collected under the ongoing MPrinT project at the University of

Bergen. The corpus will be brought online in the course of 2025 with the references as given here. Digital copies and catalogue are in Bergen.

The Poetry of Burhan Mkelle

Burhan Mkelle's poetry ranges from prayers and shorter recitations for use in educational settings, via longer didactic verses on the life of the Prophet, to poems of praise for friends and colleagues in Zanzibar, to elegies upon their deaths. His entire production is in Arabic; he is not known to have composed poetry within the Swahili-language *tendi* tradition.

Burhan Mkelle's *Diwan* exists in (at least) three different versions, each compilation containing a different selection. This makes a complete overview of his production hard to establish. In addition, many of his poems were printed during his lifetime, but the versions in the compilations do not give any reference as to where or when. However, it is safe to assume that his poetry was known in the community both through oral transmission (as recitals and prayers in school and public gatherings) and through print in publications like *al-Falaq*.

The earliest dated poem in the entire corpus is from 1330/1911–12; a poem for the emir of the Italian army in Tripoli, in defence of the Muslims (MKELLE/SELF-EDIT).

The latest dated poem is from 1946, calling for unity among Zanzibaris (MKELLE/DIWAN-2, NP, Photo 37/46).

VERSION 1: BURHANIYYĀT

This collection was compiled by Burhan Mkelle himself at some point late in his life, most likely in the 1940s. In his introduction, he gives the reason for compiling his poetry:

> I say that some of the good brothers and many of the students in the Zanzibar schools asked me to collect my verses [for them] which were frequently recited in religious celebrations, especially the recitations on the birth of the Prophet [Khayr al-Bardiyya], best of prayers upon him and the most sincere greetings. [This was] for each of them to

> have a copy of the collection and have a text to refer to. […] I was guided during the collection to add the poems that I found to be the best [the choice words] of congratulation (*al-madāʿiḥ*), celebration (*iltahānī*), lamentation and reproach. So I set to work in response to the petitioners and to aid the reciters who are eager to recite them and of which I would regret the loss, and appreciate its recitation as they are the daughters of my thoughts and the perfumed fragrances of my breath. So I collected it to be a source to contain [my poems], and my intention came through, although I dare not describe their eloquence or style. [Nor do I dare to speak] on the correctness of style and wording, nor how they compare to the stallions of poetry or the masters of *balaghāʾ* who triumphed in the art of poetry to the highest standard and who gathered the most precious and pleasurable jewels. Will my words, next to theirs, have any value/respect except as a bleak counterfeit next to pearls and precious stones?

The compilation consists of seventy-one handwritten, numbered pages. Most are introduced by a comment by Burhan Mkelle himself, where he notes the occasion where/when the poem was first, or regularly recited. The location of the original is unknown, but a photocopy was in the Maalim Idris Collection.

The entire compilation was printed in the study by Muhammad Ahmad Hamid (*Al-ʿaṣr al-dhahhabī li-Zinjibār*, 2021), pages 186–276. Hamid has added additional information in footnotes.

VERSION 2: UNEDITED COMPILATION OF BURHAN MKELLE'S POETRY—REFERRED TO HERE AS MKELLE/SELF-EDIT

This compilation consists of 177 handwritten, unnumbered pages, which include both poetry and prose text by Burhan Mkelle. The location of the original is unknown, but a photocopy was in the Maalim Idris Collection.

From the first pages, it transpires that Burhan Mkelle himself made this compilation, and most likely before the edition referred to above (Version 1: BURHANIYYĀT). Presumably, Burhan did his editing in several stages. This appears to be the first stage, where he collected his writings, and added comments regarding the occasion or usage of the verses. The collection appears to have been compiled in no particular order, although there is an introduction written by Burhan himself and a tentative table of contents where the poems are divided into categories such as praise (*madḥ*), elegies (*mirāth*), etc. The pages may have been re-bundled at a later stage, most likely by his sons in the process of compiling their 2001 edition (see below). Copy in Bergen.

DIWAN IBN MKELLE—REFERRED TO HERE AS MKELLE/ DIWAN 1 & 2

Diwan Ibn Mkelle is a two-volume compilation of poetry collected, selected, partially translated and commented upon by Burhan Mkelle's two sons Muhammad and Ahmad Mkelle, in collaboration with Maalim Muhammad Idris Muhammad Saleh in 2001.

The original is in the possession of Professor Saleh Idris, inherited from the Maalim Idris Collection. Copy in Bergen.

The two-volume compilation consists of photocopies of handwritten or printed versions of Burhan's poetry, from both volumes listed above (*Burhaniyyāt* and MKELLE/SELF-EDIT). It also has a lengthy biographical introduction where the two sons narrate the life of their father. To each poem is added a handwritten introduction in Swahili, discussing the various situations in which each was recited, often with reference to personal memory. Most also have a rendering of the original Arabic in Swahili prose, starting with the phrase "The poet is here saying that...."

Other unpublished works by or related to Burhan Mkelle

Ahmad Burhan Mkelle, Biographical fragment, Arabic

This fragment was originally in the possession of its author, Burhan's son Ahmad. I am grateful to Dr Ridder Samsom for providing me with a digital copy of this document.

MKELLE/COMORIAN ASSOCIATION. History of the Comorian Association

This is a brief, 2½-page history of the origins of the Comorian Association in Zanzibar, clearly written years after its formation around 1925. It is part of the photocopied papers that were in the possession of Maalim Idris.

MKELLE/SELF-EDIT, "Jamʿiyya Ahl al-Sunna wa-l-Jamāʿ".
MKELLE/SELF-EDIT, "Letter to *al-Fath*".
MKELLE/SELF-EDIT, "Autobiographical fragment 1, Hajj".
MKELLE/SELF-EDIT, "On Said Mohamed Mansab".

MKELLE/DIWAN-1, "On Unity".
MKELLE/DIWAN-1, "End the Practice of Wailing!"

LETTER FROM BURHAN MKELLE to Saleh b. Yahya b. Said, election committee of the Comorian Association, dated 11 September 1937. Maalim Idris Collection, photographed 20 July 2018, Zanzibar.

MKELLE/TARIKH-ZNZ-2

This is the "History of Grande Comore" authored by Burhan Mkelle. For the various editions of this text, see A. K. Bang, *Islamic Sufi Networks in the Western Indian Ocean, c. 1880–1940* (2014), Notes on Sources.

BIBLIOGRAPHY

Abbasi, M. Z., "Islamic Law and Social Change: An Insight into the Making of Anglo-Muhammadan Law", *Journal of Islamic Studies*, 25:3, 2014, 325–349.

ʿAbduh, M., *Risālat al-Tawḥīd/The Theology of Unity*, translated from the Arabic by Ishaq Musaʿad & Kenneth Cragg, London: George Allen & Unwin Ltd, 1966.

Abushouk, A. I. & Ibrahim, H. A. (eds.), *The Hadhrami Diaspora in Southeast Asia: Identity Maintenance or Assimilation?*, Leiden: Brill, 2009.

Ahmed, C., *Ngoma et mission Islamique (Daʿwa) aux Comores et en Afrique orientale*, Paris: L'Harmattan, 2002.

———, "Rites de mort aux Comores et chez les Swahili: Entre islam savant et culture locale", *Journal des Africanistes*, 72:2, 2002, 187–201.

———, "Networks of the Shādhiliyya Yashruṭiyya Sufi Order in East Africa", in: R. Loimeier & R. Seesemann (eds.), *The Global Worlds of the Swahili: Interfaces of Islam, Identity and Space in Nineteenth and Twentieth-Century East Africa*, Hamburg: Lit Verlag, 2006, 317–342.

Aley, J., *Enduring Links*, Self-published, Zanzibar, 1992.

Anderson, B., *Imagined Communities: Reflections on the Origin and Spread of Nationalism*, revised ed., London: Verso, 2006 (1st ed. London: Verso, 1983).

Arnold, N., *Wazee wakijue mambo! / Elders Used to Know Things!: Occult Powers and Revolutionary History in Pemba, Zanzibar*, PhD Thesis, Indiana University, 2003.

Asad, T. "Conscripts of Western Civilization?", in: C. Gailey (ed.), *Dialectical Anthropology: Essays in Honor of Stanley Diamond*, Vol. 1, Gainesville: University Press of Florida, 1992, 333–351.

Ayalon, A., "Arab Booksellers and Bookshops in the Age of Printing, 1850–1940", *British Journal of Middle Eastern Studies*, 37:1, 2010, 73–93.

———, *The Arabic Print Revolution: Cultural Production and Mass Readership*, Cambridge: Cambridge University Press, 2016.

Badawi, S. M. A., *Al-riyāḍ bayna māḍīhi wa-ḥādirihi*, 2nd ed., Lamu, Mombasa, 2018.

Bakari, M., *The Sage of Moroni: The Intellectual Biography of Sayyid Omar Abdallah, a Forgotten Muslim Public Intellectual*, Nairobi: Kenya Literature Bureau, 2019.

Bang, A. K., *Sufis and Scholars of the Sea: Family Networks in East Africa, 1860–1925*, London: Routledge, 2003.

———, "Teachers, Scholars and Educationalists: The Impact of Hadrami-ʿAlawi Teachers and Teachings on Islamic Education in Zanzibar, ca. 1870–1930", *Asian Journal of Social Science*, 35:4/5, 2007, 457–471.

———, "Authority and Piety, Writing and Print: A Preliminary Study of the Circulation of Islamic Texts in Late Nineteenth- and Early Twentieth-Century Zanzibar", *Africa: Journal of the International African Institute*, 81:1, 2011, 89–107.

———, "Zanzibari Islamic Knowledge Transmission Revisited: Loss, Lament, Legacy—and Transformation", *Social Dynamics*, 38:3, 2012, 419–434.

———, *Islamic Sufi Networks in the Western Indian Ocean, c. 1880–1940: Ripples of Reform*, Leiden: Brill, 2014.

———, "The Riyadha Mosque Manuscript Collection in Lamu: A Ḥaḍramī Tradition in Kenya", *Journal of Islamic Manuscripts* (Special issue: A. Regourd (ed.), *Manuscripts of Yemen, Circulation of Ideas and Models*), 5:2/3, 2014, 125–153.

———, "Islamic Incantations in a Colonial Notebook: A Case from Interwar Zanzibar", *Cahiers d'Études Africaines*, LIX (4), 236, 2019, 1025–1046.

———, "Double Sided Print: Silent and Communal Reading During the Rise of Islamic Print in East Africa, 1880–1940", in: K. Barber & S. Newell (eds.), *Print Cultures and African Literature, 1860–1960*, Cambridge: Cambridge University Press (forthcoming).

———, "Esoteric Authority and Sufi Networks of the *ḥajj*: Two Zanzibari *ḥajj* Accounts, 1898–1951" (forthcoming).

Bang, A. K. & Loimeier, R., "Aḥmad b. ʿAlī Manṣab", in: K. Fleet, G. Krämer, D. Matringe, J. Nawas & D. J. Stewart (eds.), *Encyclopaedia of Islam Three*, Leiden: Brill, 2013.

Al-Barwani, Muhammad b. ʿAli, *Riḥla Abū Ḥārith*, Zanzibar: Al-Najah Print, 1333/1915.

Al-Barwani, A. M., *Conflicts and Harmony in Zanzibar*, Self-published, Dubai, 1997.

Becker, F., *Becoming Muslim in Mainland Tanzania, 1890–2000*, Oxford: Oxford University Press, 2008.

———, "Commoners in the Process of Islamization: Reassessing their Role in the Light of Evidence from Southeastern Tanzania", *Journal of Global History*, 3:2, 2008, 227–249.

———, "Islamic Reform and Historical Change in the Care of the Dead: Conflicts over Funerary Practice among Tanzanian Muslims", *Africa: Journal of the International African Institute*, 79:3, 2009, 416–434.

Bennett, N. R., *A History of the Arab State of Zanzibar*, London: Methuen, 1978.

Bertz, N., *Diaspora and Nation in the Indian Ocean: Transnational Histories of Race and Urban Space in Tanzania*, Honolulu: University of Hawai'i Press, 2015.

Bever, E. & Styers, R. (eds.), *Magic in the Modern World: Strategies of Repression and Legitimization*, University Park: Pennsylvania State University Press, 2018.

Bissell, W. C., "Casting a Long Shadow: Colonial Categories, Cultural Identities, and Cosmopolitan Spaces in Globalizing Africa", *African Identities*, 5:2, 2007, 181–197.

———, *Urban Design, Chaos, and Colonial Power in Zanzibar*, Bloomington: Indiana University Press, 2011.

Bolton, C., "'Useful' Knowledge and Moral Education in Zanzibar Between Colonial and Islamic Reform, 1916–1945", *Islamic Africa*, 12:1, 2021, 27–54.

Bonate, L. J. K., "Dispute over Islamic Funeral Rites in Mozambique: *A Demolidora dos Prazeres* by Shaykh Aminuddin Mohamad", *Social Sciences and Missions*, 17, December 2005, 41–59.

Bowen, J., "Death and the History of Islam in Highland Aceh", *Indonesia*, 38, 1984, 21–38.

Brand, L. A., *Official Stories: Politics and National Narratives in Egypt and Algeria*, Stanford: Stanford University Press, 2014.

Brennan, J. R., *Taifa: Making Nation and Race in Urban Tanzania*, Athens, OH: Ohio University Press, 2012.

van Bruinessen, M., "Kitab Kuning: Books in Arabic Script Used in the Pesantren Milieu", *Bijdragen tot de Taal-, Land- en Volkenkunde*, 146:2/3, 1990, 226–269.

van Bruinessen, M. & Day Howell, J. (eds.), *Sufism and the "Modern" in Islam*, London/New York: I. B. Tauris, 2013.

Bussow, J., "Muḥammad ʿAbduh: The Theology of Unity (Egypt, 1898)", in: B. Bentlage, M. Eggert, H. M. Krämer & S. Reichmuth (eds.), *Religious Dynamics under the Impact of Imperialism and Colonialism: A Sourcebook*, Leiden: Brill, 2017, 141–159.

Cleveland, W., *Islam Against the West: Shakib Arslan and the Campaign for Islamic Nationalism*, Austin: University of Texas Press, 1985.

Colby, F. S., *Narrating Muhammad's Night Journey: Tracing the Development of the Ibn ʿAbbas Ascension Discourse*, Albany: State University of New York Press, 2008.

Commins, D., *Islamic Reform: Politics and Social Change in Late Ottoman Syria*, Oxford: Oxford University Press, 1990.

———, *The Wahhabi Mission and Saudi Arabia*, London: I. B. Tauris, 2006.

———, "Wahhabis, Sufis and Salafis in Early Twentieth Century Damascus", in: M. Hatina (ed.), *Guardians of Faith in the Modern World*, 231–240.

Constantine, S., *The Making of British Colonial Development Policy, 1914–1930*, London: Routledge, 1984.

Cooper, F., *From Slaves to Squatters: Plantation Labor and Agriculture in Zanzibar and Coastal Kenya, 1890–1925*, New Haven: Yale University Press, 1980.

Czerniak, E. & Davidson, M., "Placebo: A Historical Perspective", *European Neuropsychopharmacology*, 22:11, 2012, 770–774.

Dawn, C. E., "The Formation of Pan-Arab Ideologies in the Interwar Years", *International Journal of Middle East Studies*, 20:1, 1988, 67–91.

Decker, C., "Reading, Writing, and Respectability: How Schoolgirls Developed Modern Literacies in Colonial Zanzibar", *International Journal of African Historical Studies*, 43:1, 2010, 89–114.

———, *Mobilizing Zanzibari Women: The Struggle for Respectability and Self-Reliance in Colonial East Africa*, New York: Palgrave Macmillan, 2014.

Decker, C. & McMahon, E., *The Idea of Development in Africa: A History*, Cambridge: Cambridge University Press, 2021.

Declich, L., *The Arabic Manuscripts of the Zanzibar National Archives: A Checklist*, Supplemento No. 2 Alla Rivista degli Studi Orientali, Nuova Serie, Vol. LXXVIII, Pisa/Roma (Instituti Editoriali e Poligrafica Internazionali): Academia Editoriale, 2006.

Department of Urban and Rural Planning, Zanzibar, *Ng'ambo Atlas: Historic Urban Landscape of Zanzibar Town's "Other Side"*, Edam: LM Publishers, 2018.

Dudoignon, S. A., Hisao, K. & Yasushi, K. (eds.), *Intellectuals in the Modern Islamic World: Transmission, Transformation, Communication*, London: Routledge, 2006.

Eisenstadt, S., "Multiple Modernities", *Daedalus*, 129:1, 2000, 1–29.

Eisenstadt, S. (ed.), *Multiple Modernities*, New Brunswick, NJ: Transaction, 2005.

El-Rouayheb, K., "al-Damanhūrī, Aḥmad", in: K. Fleet, G. Krämer, D. Matringe, J. Nawas & D. J. Stewart (eds.), *Encyclopaedia of Islam Three*, Leiden: Brill, 2021.

Fair, L., "Kickin' It: Leisure, Politics and Football in Colonial Zanzibar", *Africa: Journal of the International African Institute*, 67:2, 1997, 224–251.

———, *Pastimes and Politics: Culture, Community, and Identity in Post-Abolition Urban Zanzibar, 1890–1945*, Athens, OH: Ohio University Press, 2001.

———, *Reel Pleasures: Cinema Audiences and Entrepreneurs in Twentieth-Century Urban Tanzania*, Athens, OH: Ohio University Press, 2018.

Farquhar, M., *Expanding the Wahhabi Mission: Saudi Arabia, the Islamic University of Medina and the Transnational Religious Economy*, PhD Thesis, London School of Economics, 2013.

Farsi, S. S., *Mzanzibari: Asimilia hadithi yake*, Self-published, Oman, ND [1990s].

———, *Zanzibar: Historical Accounts*, 2nd ed., Privately printed, 1995.

Farsy, A. S., *Baadhi ya wanavyoni wa Kishafii wa Mashariki ya Afrika / The Shafiʿi Ulama of East Africa, ca. 1830–1970: A Hagiographic Account*, translated, edited and annotated by R. L. Pouwels, African Primary Texts 2, Madison: University of Wisconsin, 1989.

Federici, S., *Caliban and the Witch: Women, the Body and Primitive Accumulation*, New York: Autonomedia, 2004.

Feener, M., "Cross-Cultural Contexts of Modern Muslim Intellectualism", *Die Welt des Islams*, 47:3/4, 2007, 264–282, 281.

Forward, M., "Syed Ameer Ali: A Bridge-Builder?", *Islam and Christian-Muslim Relations*, 6:1, 1995, 45–62.

Fourie, E., "A Future for the Theory of Multiple Modernities: Insights from the New Modernization Theory", *Social Science Information*, 51:1, 2012, 52–69.

Freitag, U., *Indian Ocean Migrants and State Formation in Hadhramaut: Reforming the Homeland*, Leiden: Brill, 2003.

Frenkel, Y., "Islamic Utopia under the Mamluks: The Social and Legal Ideals of Ibn Qayyim al-Gawziyya", *Oriente Moderno*, 90:1, 2010, 67–87.

Gardiner, N., "Forbidden Knowledge? Notes on the Production, Transmission, and Reception of the Major Works of Aḥmad al-Būnī", *Journal of Arabic and Islamic Studies*, 12, 2012, 81–142.

———, *Esotericism in Manuscript Culture: Aḥmad al-Būnī and His Readers through the Mamluk Period*, PhD Diss., University of Michigan, 2014.

———, "Stars and Saints: The Esotericist Astrology of the Sufi Occultist Aḥmad al-Būnī", *Journal of Magic, Ritual, and Witchcraft*, 12:1, 2017, 39–65.

———, *Ibn Khaldūn versus the Occultists at Barqūq's Court: The Critique of Lettrism in al-Muqaddimah*, Ulrich Hartmann Memorial Lecture, Vol. 18, Berlin: EB Verlag, 2020.

Gauvain, R., *Salafi Ritual Purity: In the Presence of God*, London: Routledge, 2012.

Gershoni, I., "The Evolution of National Culture in Modern Egypt: Intellectual Formation and Social Diffusion, 1892–1945", *Poetics Today*, 13:2, 1992, 325–350.

Ghazal, A., *Islamic Reform and Arab Nationalism: Expanding the Crescent from the Mediterranean to the Indian Ocean (1880s–1930s)*, London: Routledge, 2010.

———, "The Other Frontiers of Arab Nationalism: Ibadis, Berbers, and the Arabist-Salafi Press in the Interwar Period", *International Journal of Middle East Studies*, 42:1, 2010, 105–122.

Glassman, J., *Feasts and Riot: Revelry, Rebellion and Popular Consciousness on the Swahili Coast, 1856–1888*, London: J. Currey, 1995.

———, "Slower than a Massacre: The Multiple Sources of Racial Thought in Colonial Africa", *The American Historical Review*, 109:3, 2004, 720–754.

———, *War of Words, War of Stones: Racial Thought and Violence in Colonial Zanzibar*, Bloomington: Indiana University Press, 2011.

Green, N., "The Religious and Cultural Roles of Dreams and Visions in Islam", *Journal of the Royal Asiatic Society*, 13:3, 2003, 287–313.

———, *Bombay Islam: The Religious Economy of the West Indian Ocean, 1840–1915*, Cambridge: Cambridge University Press, 2011.

Greenwood, A., "The Colonial Medical Service and the Struggle for Control of the Zanzibar Maternity Association, 1918–47", in: A. Greenwood (ed.), *Beyond the State: The Colonial Medical Service in British Africa*, Manchester: Manchester University Press, 2016, 85–103.

Gruber, C. J., *The Prophet Muhammad's Ascension (miʿrāj) in Islamic Art and Literature, ca. 1300–1600*, PhD Thesis, University of Pennsylvania, 2005.

Haddad, M., "The Manarists and Modernism: An Attempt to Fuse Society and Religion", in: S. A. Dudoignon, K. Hisao & K. Yasushi (eds.), *Intellectuals in the Modern Islamic World*, 55–73.

Haj, S., *Reconfiguring Islamic Tradition: Reform, Rationality, and Modernity*, Stanford: Stanford University Press, 2009.

Halevi, L., *Modern Things on Trial: Islam's Global and Material Reformation in the Age of Rida, 1865–1935*, New York: Columbia University Press, 2019.

Hamid, Muhammad Ahmad, *Al-ʿaṣr al-dhahhabī li-Zinjibār*, Amman: Jordan, 2021.

Hatina, M. (ed.), *Guardians of Faith in the Modern World: ʿUlamaʾ in the Middle East*, Leiden: Brill, 2008.

Havinden, M. A. & Meredith, D., *Colonialism and Development: Britain and its Tropical Colonies, 1850–1960*, London: Routledge, 1993.

Hefner, R. W., "Multiple Modernities: Christianity, Islam, and Hinduism in a Globalizing Age", *Annual Review of Anthropology*, 27, 1998, 83–104.

Heyworth-Dunne, J., *Religious and Political Trends in Modern Egypt*, Self-published, Washington, 1950

Hofheinz, A., "*Rāqī bi-akhlāqī*: The Moral Turn: From Sufi Shaykhs to Facebook Groups?", in: C. Mayeur-Jaouen (ed.), *Adab and Modernity*, 620–650.

Hollingsworth, L. W., *Zanzibar under the Foreign Office, 1890–1913*, London: Macmillan, 1953.

Hussain, S. A., "Anglo-Muhammadan Law", in: A. M. Emon & R. Ahmed (eds.), *The Oxford Handbook of Islamic Law*, Oxford: Oxford University Press, 2018, 537–550.

Ibrahime, Mahmoud, *Parcours d'un conservateur: Saïd Mohamed Cheikh, 1904–1970: une histoire des Comores au XXe siècle*, Moroni: Komedit, 2008 (texte remanié d'une thèse de doctorat d'Histoire de l'Afrique—Histoire, Archéologie et Histoire de l'Art, soutenue à l'Université Paris 7 en 2004).

Ingrams, W. H., *Zanzibar: Its History and its People*, London: Stacey International, 2007 (first published 1931).

Jacob, W. C., *For God or Empire: Sayyid Fadl and the Indian Ocean World*, Stanford: Stanford University Press, 2019.

Jamal al-Layl, Abu ʾl-Hasan, *Diwān al-fatḥ wa-l-imdād*, ND, NP.

Jankowski, J., "Egyptian Responses to the Palestine Problem in the Interwar Period", *International Journal of Middle East Studies*, 12:1, 1980, 1–38.

Janson, M., "Living Islam through Death: Demarcating Muslim Identity in a Rural Serahuli Community in the Gambia", *Journal of the Royal Anthropological Institute*, 17:1, 2011, 100–115.

Kalmbach, H., *Islamic Knowledge and the Making of Modern Egypt*, Cambridge: Cambridge University Press, 2020.

Kampffmeyer, G., "Egypt and Western Asia", in: H. A. R. Gibb, *Whither Islam? A Survey of Modern Movements in the Moslem World*, London: Victor Gollancz, 1932, 101–170.

———, "Mission und Islam im arabischen Orient", *Die Welt des Islams*, 16, 1934, 6–22.

Kane, O. O., *Beyond Timbuktu*, Cambridge, MA: Harvard University Press, 2016.

Kaviraj, S., "Modernity and Politics in India", in: S. Eisenstadt (ed.), *Multiple Modernities*, 137–161.

Keane, W., *Christian Moderns: Freedom and Fetish in the Mission Encounter*, Berkeley: University of California Press, 2007.

———, "Secularism as a Moral Narrative of Modernity", *Transit: Europäische Revue*, 43, 2013, 159–170.

Khitamy, B., "The Role of the Riyadha Mosque College in Enhancing Islamic Identity in Kenya", in: M. Bakari & S. S. Yahya (eds.), *Islam in Kenya*, Nairobi: MEWA, 1995, 269–276.

Kobo, O. M., *Unveiling Modernity in Twentieth-Century West African Islamic Reforms*, Leiden: Brill, 2012.

Kresse, K., "'Swahili Enlightenment'? East African Reformist Discourse at the Turning Point: The Example of Sheikh Muhammad Kasim Mazrui", *Journal of Religion in Africa*, 33:3, 2003, 279–309.

———, *Swahili Muslim Publics and Postcolonial Experience*, Bloomington: Indiana University Press, 2018.

Kresse, K. & Mwakimako, H. (eds.), *Guidance (Uwongozi) by Sheikh al-Amin Mazrui: Selections from the First Swahili Islamic Newspaper*, trans. K. Kresse & H. Mwakimako, Leiden: Brill, 2017.

Kumek, Y., "The Sacred Text in Egypt's Popular Culture: The Qur'ānic Sounds, Meanings and Formation of Sakīna (Sacred Space) in Traditions of Poverty and Fear", in: O. O. Kane (ed.), *Islamic Scholarship in Africa*, London: J. Currey, 2021, 204–232.

Kurzman, C., *Modernist Islam, 1840–1940: A Sourcebook*, Oxford: Oxford University Press, 2002.

Laffan, M., *Islamic Nationhood in Colonial Indonesia: The Umma Below the Winds*, London: Routledge, 2003.

Larsen, K., *Where Humans and Spirits Meet: The Politics of Rituals and Identified Spirits in Zanzibar*, New York: Berghahn Books, 2010.

———, "Multifaceted Identities, Multiple Dwellings: Connectivity and Flexible Household Configurations in Zanzibar Town", in: B. Schnepel & E. A. Alpers, *Connectivity in Motion: Island Hubs in the Indian Ocean World*, London: Palgrave, 2018, 180–206, 185.

———, "By Way of the Qur'an: Appeasing Spirits, Easing Emotions and Everyday Matters in Zanzibar", In: Z. Hirji (ed.), *Approaches to the Qur'an in Sub-Saharan Africa*, Oxford: Oxford University Press, 2019, 317–339.

Launay, R., "Introduction: Writing Boards and Blackboards", in: R. Launay (ed.), *Islamic Education in Africa: Writing Boards and Blackboards*, Bloomington: Indiana University Press, 2016, 1–26.

Launay, R. & Ware III, R. T, "How (Not) to Read the Qur'an? Logics of Islamic Education in Senegal and Côte d'Ivoire", in: R. Launay (ed.), *Islamic Education in Africa: Writing Boards and Blackboards*, Bloomington: Indiana University Press, 2016, 255–267.

Lauzière, H., "The Construction of Salafiyya: Reconsidering Salafism from the Perspective of Conceptual History", *International Journal of Middle East Studies*, 42:3, 2010, 369–389.

———, *The Making of Salafism: Islamic Reform in the Twentieth Century*, New York: Columbia University Press, 2016.

Lia, B., *The Society of the Muslim Brothers in Egypt: The Rise of an Islamic Mass Movement, 1928–1942*, Reading, UK: Ithaca Press, 1998.

Lienhardt, P., "The Mosque College of Lamu and its Social Background", *Tanganyika Notes and Records*, 53, 1959, 228–242.

Limbert, M., "Caste, Ethnicity, and the Politics of Arabness in Southern Arabia", *Comparative Studies of South Asia, Africa and the Middle East*, 34:3, 2014, 590–598.

———, "Homeland is where the Soul Resides: Travel Prayer, Passports, and Nation in the Western Indian Ocean" (forthcoming).

Lindqvist, S., *"Exterminate all the Brutes"*, London: Granta, 1997.

Lofchie, M. F., *Zanzibar: Background to Revolution*, Princeton: Princeton University Press, 1965.

Loimeier, R., "Is there Something like 'Protestant Islam'?", *Die Welt des Islams*, 54:2, 2005, 216–254.

———, "Coming to Terms with 'Popular Culture': The *ʿulamāʾ* and the State in Zanzibar", in: R. Loimeier & R. Seesemann (eds.), *The Global Worlds of the Swahili*, Hamburg: LIT Verlag, 2006, 111–129.

———, *Between Social Skills and Marketable Skills: The Politics of Islamic Education in 20th-Century Zanzibar*, Leiden: Brill, 2009.

———, "Traditions of Reform, Reforms of Tradition: Case Studies from Senegal and Zanzibar/Tanzania, in: Z. Hirji (ed.), *Diversity and Pluralism in Islam: Historical and Contemporary Discourses among Muslims*, London/New York: I. B. Tauris, 2010, 135–162.

———, *Eine Zeitlandschaft in der Globalisierung: Das islamische Sansibar im 19 under 20 Jahrhundert*, Bielefeld: Transcript Verlag, 2012.

———, "What is 'Reform'? Approaches to a Problematic Term in African Muslim Contexts", *Journal for Islamic Studies*, 32, 2012, 7–23.

———, *Islamic Reform in Twentieth-Century Africa*, Edinburgh: Edinburgh University Press, 2016.

———, "Muslim Scholars, Organic Intellectuals, and the Development of Islamic Education in Zanzibar in the Twentieth Century", in: R. Launay (ed.), *Islamic Education in Africa: Writing Boards and Blackboards*, Bloomington: Indiana University Press, 2016, 137–148.

———, "Memories of Revolution: Patterns of Interpretation of the 1964 Revolution in Zanzibar", in: W. C. Bissell & M-A. Fouéré, *Social Memory, Silenced Voices, and Political Struggle: Remembering the Revolution in Zanzibar*, Dar-es-Salaam: Mkuki na Nyota, 2018, 37–78.

Longair, S., *Cracks in the Dome: Fractured Histories of Empire in the Zanzibar Museum, 1897–1964*, London: Routledge, 2015.

Lyne, R. N., *Zanzibar in Contemporary Times*, London: Hurst & Blackett, 1905.

Mackenrodt, L., *Swahili Spirit Possession and Islamic Healing in Contemporary Tanzania: The Jinn Fly on Friday*, Hamburg: Verlag Dr Kovac, 2011.

Marcus-Sells, A., *Sorcery or Science? Contesting Knowledge and Practice in West African Sufi Texts*, University Park: Pennsylvania State University Press, 2022.

Martin, B. G., *Muslim Brotherhoods in Nineteenth-Century Africa*, Cambridge: Cambridge University Press, 1976.

Massignon, L., "Africa", in: H. A. R. Gibb (ed.), *Whither Islam? A Survey of Movements in the Moslem World*, London: Victor Gollancz, 1932.

Mathews, N., "Imagining Arab Communities: Colonialism, Islamic Reform, and Arab Identity in Mombasa, Kenya, 1897–1933", *Islamic Africa*, 4:2, 2013, 135–163.

Mayeur-Jaouen, C., "Feminine or Masculine *Adab*? Education, Etiquette, and Ethics in Egypt in the 1900s–1920s", in: C. Mayeur-Jaouen (ed.), *Adab and Modernity*, 405–434.

———, "'There is Matter for Thought': The Episode of the Night Journey and Heavenly Ascension in the *Sira ḥalabiyya*, at the Beginning of the Seventeenth Century", In: D. Gril, S. Reichmuth & D. Sarmis (eds.), *The Presence of the Prophet in Early and Contemporary Islam*, Vol. 1, Leiden: Brill, 2022, 115–150.

Mayeur-Jaouen, C. (ed.), *Adab and Modernity: A "Civilizing Process"? (Sixteenth–Twenty-First Century)*, Leiden: Brill, 2020.

Mbembe, A., *Out of the Dark Night: Essays on Decolonization*, New York: Columbia University Press, 2021.

McMahon, E., *Slavery and Emancipation in Islamic East Africa: From Honor to Respectability*, Cambridge: Cambridge University Press, 2013.

———, "'Marrying Beneath Herself': Women, Affect, and Power in Colonial Zanzibar", *Africa Today*, 61:4, 2015, 27–40.

Minde, N., Roop, S. & Tronvoll, K., "The Turbulent Political History of Zanzibar and its Impact on Contemporary Conflict and Reconciliation", *African Insight*, 49:1, 2019, 68–82.

Mitchell, T., *Colonising Egypt*, Berkeley: University of California Press, 1991.

Mobini-Kesheh, N., *The Hadrami Awakening: Community and Identity in the Netherlands East Indies, 1900–1942*, Ithaca, NY: Cornell University Southeast Asia Program Publications, 1999.

Moosa, M., *The Origins of Modern Arabic Fiction*, 2nd ed., Boulder, CO: Lynne Rienner, 1997.

Morgan, D. J., *The Official History of Colonial Development*, Vol. 1, *The Origins of British Aid Policy, 1924–1945*, London: Macmillan, 1980.

Mraja, M. S., "The Reform Ideas of Shaykh ʿAbd Allāh Ṣāliḥ al-Fārsī and the Transformation of Marital Practices among the Digo Muslims of Kenya", *Islamic Law and Society*, 17:2, 2010, 245–278.

Al-Mughayri, Saʿid b. ʿAli, *Juhaynat al-Akhbār fī taʾrīkh Zinjibār*, Oman: Ministry of National Heritage and Culture, 2001.

Musa, S., *Maisha ya al-Imam Sheikh Abdullah Saleh Farsy katika Ulimwengu wa Kiislamu*, Dar-es-Salaam: Lillaahi Islamic Publications Centre, 1986.

Nimtz, A. H., *Islam and Politics in East Africa: The Sufi Order in Tanzania*, Minneapolis: University of Minnesota Press, 1980.

Nordbruch, G., "Arab Students in Weimar Germany—Politics and Thought Beyond Borders", *Journal of Contemporary History*, 49:2, 2014, 275–295.

Ochsenwald, W., "Islam and Loyalty in the Saudi Hijaz, 1926–1939", *Die Welt des Islams*, 47:1, 2007, 7–32.

Østebø, T., *Localising Salafism: Religious Change Among Oromo Muslims in Bale*, Ethiopia, Leiden: Brill, 2011.

Patrizi, L., "Un manuel d'*adab* et d'*akhlāq* pour les temps modernes: Les *Jawāmiʿ al-ādāb fi akhlāq al-anjāb* da Jamāl al-Dīn al-Qāsimī (1866–1914)", in: C. Mayeur-Jaouen (ed.), *Adab and Modernity*, 481–503.

Philipp, T. (ed.), *Jurji Zaidan and the Foundations of Arab Nationalism*, Syracuse, NY: Syracuse University Press, 2010.

Piraino, F. & Sedgwick, M. (eds.), *Global Sufism: Boundaries, Structures, and Politics*, London: Hurst, 2019.

Pouwels, R., *Horn and Crescent: Cultural Change and Traditional Islam on the East African Coast, 800–1900*, Cambridge: Cambridge University Press, 1987.

Prestholdt, J., *Domesticating the World: African Consumerism and the Genealogies of Globalization*, Berkeley: University of California Press, 2008.

Reese, S., "The Adventures of Abu Harith: Muslim Travel Writing and Navigating the Modern in Colonial East Africa", in: S. Reese (ed.), *The Transmission of Islamic Learning in East Africa*, Leiden: Brill, 2004, 244–256.

———, "Shaykh Abdullahi al-Qutbi and the Pious Believer's Dilemma: Local Moral Guidance in the Age of Global Islamic Reform", *Journal of Eastern African Studies*, 9:3, 2015, 1–17.

———, "'The Ink of Excellence': Print and the Islamic Written Tradition of East Africa", in: S. Reese (ed.), *Manuscript and Print in the Islamic Tradition*, Studies in Manuscript Cultures 26, Berlin: De Gruyter, 2022, 217–242.

Reinwald, B., "'Tonight at the Empire': Cinema and Urbanity in Zanzibar, 1920s to 1960s", *Afrique & Histoire*, 5:1, 2006, 81–109.

Renard, J. (ed.), *Tales of God's Friends: Islamic Hagiography in Translation*, Berkeley: University California Press, 2009.

Reynolds, D. F. (ed.), *Interpreting the Self: Autobiography in the Arabic Literary Tradition*, Berkeley: University California Press, 2001.

Ringer, M. M., *Islamic Modernism and the Re-Enchantment of the Sacred in the Age of History*, Edinburgh: Edinburgh University Press, 2020.

Riyad, U., *Islamic Reformism and Christianity: A Critical Reading of the Works of Muhammad Rashid Rida and His Associates (1898–1935)*, Leiden: Brill, 2009.

Rizvi, S. M., *Muhibb al-Din al-Khatib: A Portrait of a Salafi-Arabist, 1886–1969*, MA Thesis, Simon Fraser University, 1991.

Robbins, J., "God is Nothing but Talk: Modernity, Language, and Prayer in Papua New Guinea Society", *Amercian Anthropologist*, 103:4, 2001, 901–912, 902.

Robinson, F., "Religious Change and the Self in Muslim South Asia Since 1800", *South Asia: Journal of South Asian Studies*, 22, 1999, 13–27.

Romero, P. W., "'Where Have all the Slaves Gone?' Emancipation and Post-Emancipation in Lamu, Kenya", *Journal of African History*, 27:3, 1986, 497–512.

———, *Lamu: History, Society, and Family in an East African Port City*, Princeton: Markus Wiener, 1997.

Saif, L., "From *Ghāyat al-ḥakīm* to *Shams al-maʿārif*: Ways of Knowing and Paths of Power in Medieval Islam", *Arabica*, 64:3/4, 2017, 297–345.

Saleh, I., *A Short History of the Comorians in Zanzibar*, Dar-es-Salaam: The Tanganyika Standard, 1936.

Saleh, M. A., "L'enjeu des traditions dans la communauté Comorienne de Zanzibar", In: F. Le Guennec-Coppens & D. Parkin (eds.), *Autorité et pouvoir chez les Swahili*, Paris: Karthala, 1998, 221–246.

Scholz, W., *Challenges of Informal Urbanisation: The Case of Zanzibar/Tanzania*, Spring Research Series 50, Dortmund: Dortmund Universität Verlag, 2008.

Schulze, R., "The Birth of Tradition and Modernity in 18th and 19th Century Islamic Culture: The Case of Printing", *Culture and History* (Special issue: J. Skovgaard Pedersen (ed.), *The Introduction of the Printing Press in the Middle East*), 16, 1997, 29–72.

Scott, J., *Conscripts of Modernity: The Tragedy of Colonial Enlightenment*, Durham, NC: Duke University Press, 2004.

El Shakry, O., *The Arabic Freud: Psychoanalysis and Islam in Modern Egypt*, Princeton: Princeton University Press, 2017.

El Shamsy, A., *Rediscovering the Islamic Classics: How Editors and Print Culture Transformed an Intellectual Tradition*, Princeton: Princeton University Press, 2020.

Sheehi, S., "Al-Kawakibi: From Political Journalism to a Political Science of the 'Liberal' Arab Muslim", *Alif: Journal of Comparative Poetics*, 37, 2017, 85–109.

Sheriff, A., *Slaves, Spices and Ivory in Zanzibar*, Oxford: Oxford University Press, 1987.

Sheriff, A. & Ferguson, E. (eds.), *Zanzibar under Colonial Rule*, London: J. Currey, 1991.

Sirry, M., "Jamāl al-Dīn al-Qāsimī and the Salafi Approach to Sufism", *Die Welt des Islams*, 51:1, 2011, 75–108.

Stockreiter, E., *Islamic Law, Gender and Social Change in Post-Abolition Zanzibar*, Cambridge: Cambridge University Press, 2015.

Stolz, D. A., "'By Virtue of your Knowledge': Scientific Materialism and the *fatwās* of Rashīd Riḍā", *Bulletin of SOAS*, 75:2, 2012, 223–247.

Sumayt, ʿUmar b. Ahmad b., *Al-nafḥat al-shadhiyya ilā al-diyār al-Ḥaḍramiyya wa-talbiyyat al-sawt min al-Ḥijāz wa Ḥaḍramawt*, Privately printed, Tarim/Aden, 1955. Reference here is made to the 2nd revised ed., Privately printed, Jiddah, 1988.

Tayob, A., "Decolonizing the Study of Religions: Muslim Intellectuals and the Enlightenment Project of Religious Studies", *Journal for the Study of Religion*, 31:2, 2018, 7–35.

Toibibou, A. M., *Ahmad Qamardine (1895–1974): Un intellectual Comorien et ses réseaux*, PhD Thesis, Université Paris Diderot-Paris VII, 2010.

Trimingham, J. S., *The Sufi Orders in Islam*, Oxford: Oxford University Press, 1971.

Varisco, D., "Illuminating the Lunar Stations (*manāzil al-qamar*) in al-Būnī's *Shams al-maʿārif*, *Arabica*, 64:3/4, 2017, 487–530.

Versteegh, K., "Learning Arabic in the Islamic World", in: G. Ayoub & K. Versteegh (eds.), *The Foundations of Arabic Linguistics*, III, Leiden: Brill, 2018, 245–267.

Vuckovic, B. O., *Heavenly Journeys, Earthly Concerns: The Legacy of the Miʿraj in the Formation of Islam*, London: Routledge, 2004.

Walcott, D., "The Schooner *Flight*" (9. "Maria Concepcion and the Book of Dreams"), in: D. Walcott, *The Star-Apple Kingdom*, New York: Farrar, Straus & Giroux, 1979: https://allpoetry.com/The-Schooner-%27Flight%27

Walker, I., "What Came First, the Nation or the State? Political Process in the Comoro Islands", *Africa: Journal of the International African Institute*, 77:4, 2007, 582–605.

———, "Identity and Citizenship among the Comorians of Zanzibar, 1886–1963", in: A. Sheriff & E. Ho (eds.), *The Indian Ocean: Oceanic Connections and the Creation of New Societies*, London: Hurst, 2014, 239–265.

———, "Ali Mfaume: A Comorian Hub in the Western Indian Ocean", in: B. Schnepel & E. Alpers (eds.), *Connectivity in Motion: Island Hubs in the Indian Ocean World*, Cham: Palgrave Macmillan, 2018, 159–180.

———, *Islands in a Cosmopolitan Sea: A History of the Comoros*, London: Hurst, 2019.

Weismann, I., *Taste of Modernity: Sufism, Salafiyya and Arabism in Late Ottoman Syria*, Leiden: Brill, 2001.

———, "The Politics of Popular Religion: Sufis, Salafis and Muslim Brothers in 20th-Century Hamah", *International Journal of Middle East Studies*, 37:1, 2005, 39–58.

Wicker, E. R., "Colonial Development and Welfare, 1929–1957: The Evolution of a Policy", *Social and Economic Studies*, 7:4, 1958, 170–192.

Wittrock, B., "Modernity: One, None, or Many? European Origins and Modernity as a Global Condition", *Daedalus*, 129:1, 2000, 31–60.

Yildiz, M. C., "Mapping the 'Sports Nadha': Toward a History of Sports in the Modern Middle East", in: D. Reiche & T. Sorek (eds.), *Sport, Politics and Society in the Middle East*, Oxford: Oxford University Press, 2019.

El-Zein, A. H. M., *The Sacred Meadows: A Structural Analysis of Religious Symbolism in an East African Town*, Evanston, IL: Northwestern University Press, 1974.

Zemmin, F., *Modernity in Islamic Tradition: The Concept of "Society" in the Journal* al-Manar *(Cairo, 1898–1940)*, Berlin: De Gruyter, 2018.

INDEX

Abd al-Aziz Al Saud. *See* Ibn Saud
Abd Allah al-Hadrami, 82, 170
Abd Allah BaKathir, 42, 109, 118
Abd Allah Muhammad al-Hadrami, 67–8
Abd al-Rahman b. Muhammad al-Kindi, 67
Abdallah Saleh al-Farsy, 42, 50, 81, 83, 109
Abu 'l-Hasaṇ Jamal al-Layl, 67, 118, 120, 142, 149, 170
Abu Bakr BaKathir, 42, 120
Abu Harith, 52, 146–7, 163, *See* Muhammad b. Ali al-Barwani
adab, 10–12, 13, 15, 59, 62, 142, 158, 159, 161, 180–1
Ahmad al-Buni, 27, 29
Ahmad b. Sumayt, 19, 34, 47, 50, 52, 92, 109, 112, 127, 130–1, 147, 178
Ahmad Mlomri, 109–10, 119, 124, 165, 178
akhlāq, 10–13, 16, 33, 123, 138, 140, 141–2, 159–60, 181
Alawiyya, 14, 120
al-Azhar, 59–60, 66, 74, 156
al-Falaq, 5, 52, 69, 82, 110, 115, 117, 122, 123, 129, 132, 144–6, 161
al-Fatḥal-Aghar, 5, 131–2, 134, 137–8, 141, 179
al-Hilal, 5, 36
Ali Muhsin al-Barwani, 65, 67, 81
All-Muslim Association of Zanzibar, 115–16
al-Manar, 5–6, 23–4, 27, 30, 32, 34, 36, 61, 66, 100, 109, 129, 131, 134, 153
al-Najāḥ, 5
Arab Association, 5, 52, 65, 66, 101, 102–3, 122–3, 144, 179

Babi al-Hallabi Publishers, Cairo, 29
Barza mosque, 109, 117, 119
Beirut, 6, 52, 80
Bombay, 6, 7, 29

Cairo, 5, 6, 29, 52, 75, 77, 109, 116, 131, 178
Coastal Arab Association (Arab Sahel Association), 103
Comorian Association, 100, 103–4, 106–7, 107–9, 109–14, 118–19, 122, 123–5, 143, 164–7, 169, 180
Comorian School, 79, 107,

111–14, 134, 164, 165–6, 169, 170

Dar al-Ulum, 66, 76–8, 111, 140, 162, 178
Dar-es-Salaam, 161–2, 167, 173
Dutch East Indies. *See* Indonesia

Egypt, 5, 11, 19, 23, 36, 52, 60, 63, 65–7, 76–8, 86, 91, 95, 111, 116, 123, 131, 133, 137, 144, 146, 162, 163, 171, 175

Gofu mosque, 117, 119
Government Central School, 39, 49, 57, 61–4, 65–6, 67–9, 77–8, 78–9, 80–1, 83, 95, 111–13, 134–5, 145, 147, 169
Grande Comore, 44, 52, 110, 113, 165, 168, 174
Grande Mariage, 50, 104, 168

Hadramaut Association, 103
Hadramawt, 45, 52–4
Haji Amir, 110
Harold Ingrams, 4, 29, 149
harusi ya aada, *see Grande Mariage*, 50, 105
Hassan al-Banna, 116, 131, 141
heshima, 12–13, 59, 79, 145, 154, 158, 181
Hijaz, 52, 73, 77, 109, 129, 139–40, 149

Ibn Khaldun, 28
Ibn Saud, 138, 140
Ibn Taymiyya, 20, 28, 130, 153
Ibuni Saleh, 44, 102, 168, 171
Ikhwani Safaa, 130–1
Ikoni, 44
India, 4, 7, 18–19, 35, 52, 60, 67, 86, 91–2, 132–3, 161, 167, 172
Indonesia, 12, 19, 60, 140, 166–7
Isa al-Barwani, 132–3

Jamal al-Din al-Afghani, 15, 32
Jamal al-Dīn al-Qāsimī, 101–2, 151
Jamiyat al-Sunna, 117–21, 121, 124, 131–2, 136, 142, 143, 148–50, 169
Juma Aley, 81, 112
Jurji Zaydan, 11, 20, 69, 77, 137, 180

Khalifa b. Harub, 43, 63, 83
khitima, 152, 155, 156

Marnadibu al-Ingazijiyya (Bint Suja Abd Allah), 47–8
mawlid, 35, 40, 42–3, 50, 79, 83, 115, 130, 143, 144–8, 150, 157–8, 162, 169, 177, 180
Mawlid al-Miʿrāj, 148–51
Mkelle b. Adam, 45–7
Mombasa, 41, 53, 132, 133, 135–6, 165, 168, 172
Muhammad Abduh, 28, 30, 34, 80, 109
Muhammad Al-Inbabi, 77
Muhammad b. Abd al-Rahman, 110
Muhammad b. Ali al-Barwani, 52, 146
Muḥammad b. ʿAlī b. ʿAbd al-Bāqi, 26
Muhibb al-Din al-Khatib, 5, 116, 131, 137–8, 171
Muslim Brotherhood, 15, 115, 116, 123, 131, 141, 179
Mwongozi, 81

Nāṣir b. Ja-ʿid al-Kharūṣī, 26
Nasir b. Sulayman al-Lamki, 52, 170

Non-European Civil Service Association, 93–6, 97, 99, 120

Qadiriyya, 14, 16, 42

Rashid Rida, 5, 19, 23–4, 28, 30, 32, 34–5, 61, 80, 100, 127, 129–30, 131, 139–40, 151, 153, 156, 157, 181–2
Raya bt. Hemed b. Rashid al-Barwaniyya, 52
Riyadha, 27, 89, 150, 165

Sahifa, 133, 136, 172
Salafism, 14–16, 85, 175, 183
Saleh b. Abdallah al-Farsy, 50
Samchar, 63, 69
Saudi Scholastic Institute, The, 140
Sayyid Ali b. Hummud, 130
Sayyid Barghash, 4–5, 46, 130
Sayyid Khalifa b. Harub, 43, 88, 133, 170
Sayyid Mansab b. Ali, 109, 118, 165
Sayyid Manṣab b. ʿAbd al-Raḥmān b. Muḥammad al-Husaynī, 89
Sayyid Said bin Sultan, 3
Sayyid Umar Abdallah, 81
Shādhiliyya, 14, 16, 42, 51, 54–5, 105, 120, 165
Shakib Arslan, 131–2, 134, 137, 139–40, 171–2
Shams al-Maʿārif, 29
Shaykh Abd al-Bari (ʿAbd al-Barī al-ʿAjīzī), 65–7, 68, 83, 89, 91, 95, 144
Shaykh al-Amin, 41, 73, 133–7, 139–40, 142, 157, 166, 171, 172–3, 173, 178, 179, 180, 182
Sufism, 14–17, 19, 20, 36, 69, 141, 182
Syed Ameer Ali, 15, 133

Tahir b. Abi Bakr al-Amawi, 92, 132–3, 143–4, 149, 155

Umar b. Sumayt, 41–2, 50, 53, 144, 163, 165
ustaarabu, 12–14

Wahhabi, 34, 129–31, 133, 137, 139–40, 157, 178–9
Wahhabism, 15, 129, 137, 140, 175

Young Muslim Men's Association, The, 116–17, 122

Zanzibar Gazette, The, 4–7, 65, 102, 115, 129, 143–5, 148
Zanzibar National Party, 81
Zanzibar Non-European Civil Service Association, 93–6